2006

Welfare, Society, and the Helping Professions
/An Introduction

Quentin F. Schenk
University of Wisconsin-Milwaukee
with Emmy Lou Schenk

Welfare, Society, and the Helping Professions

/An Introduction

Macmillan Publishing Co., Inc.
New York
Collier Macmillan Publishers
London

Copyright © 1981, Macmillan Publishing Co. Inc.
Printed in the United States of America

Macmillan Publishing Co., Inc.
866 Third Avenue, New York, New York 10022

Collier Macmillan Canada, Ltd.

Library of Congress Cataloging in Publication Data
Schenk, Quentin F
  Welfare, society and the helping professions.

  Includes bibliographies and index
  1. Public welfare—United States. 2. social
service—United States. I. Schenk, Emmy Lou,
joint author. II. Title.
HV91.S29 1981   361'.973   80-19491
ISBN 0-02-406800-4

Printing: 1 2 3 4 5 6 7 8   Year: 1 2 3 4 5 6 7 8

Preface

Welfare, Society, and the Helping Professions is designed as an introductory text for those preparing for work in the human services professions. It is also for persons in other lines of work who are interested as citizens in understanding the contribution that welfare programs make to the national well-being.

This book documents and describes the relationships that exist between welfare programs and the society in which they are found. It deals with the effects of organized welfare activity in regard to society, on the occupational groups that work in welfare programs, and on the members of society who are recipients of welfare services. Furthermore, because the human services professions intend to have an impact on some aspect of society, the book examines the nature of the change that can be achieved through welfare programs.

There are many points of view surrounding these topics. There are differences over theory, differences over techniques, and differences over anticipated outcomes for welfare programs. Because of these differences, there is risk in writing a book that goes beyond a mere catalog or description of programs. The examination of function and consequences of function is almost guaranteed to produce conclusions with which readers will occasionally disagree. This is because there is no one theoretical model that appeals to all, nor is there a theory comprehensive enough to answer all questions of concern.

This can be seen, not as problematic, but as a sign of vitality among the occupations and disciplines involved with the welfare enterprise. It is our hope that this book will provoke discussion about the varying points of view presented, as well as about our own point of view which we also insert from time to time. We hope that such discussion will aid in the clarification of the issues that exist in welfare, and also in furthering agreement concerning the contributions of welfare programs to individuals and society.

This book reflects our perception of the nature of society—that there is interdependence among its various parts, but this interdependence is not precisely systematic. There is some independence among the parts of society, the characteristics of which may vary from time to time. We also hold that a society is inherently committed to stability. The change that takes place under most conditions is accommodative change, that which is necessary to maintain the society as it exists with as little reconstruction as possible. Fundamental change is strongly resisted and comes about only when enough members of a society perceive the destruction of the social order to be imminent unless some drastic steps are taken.

The book is divided into four parts. Part 1 presents definitions of welfare and discusses various factors that influence the delivery of welfare services in the United States. Part 2 describes the characteristics of welfare programs in the United States. Part 3 explains how welfare programs are organized so they can be made available to those who need them, and discusses the wide variety of occupational settings in which social workers provide services to those who come for help. Part 4 presents a number of possibilities for the future that range from the continuation of things as they are to fundamental changes in societal goals and structure. In addition, the glossary includes definitions of terms that human services professionals frequently encounter in welfare programs.

Many colleagues have provided crucial advice and encouragement. Primary among these is Professor John Teter, on whom we tried out a number of ideas, and who generously furnished material essential to the book. We are also grateful to David Hollister, Robert Magill, Robert Neubauer, Dorothy Pearson, and Roosevelt Wright for their critical reviews and to Eve Koehler for her assistance in readying the manuscript. We extend our thanks to our editor, Kenneth J. Scott. Without his concerned persistence the book would have never materialized. And last, but perhaps most important, we thank the many students who listened with patience and understanding while the ideas and form for the book were being developed. Their comments and questions forced us to clarify our thoughts as we worked to set them down.

Contents

part/one

Helping Others in the American Context

part/two

Categories of Programs

part/three

The Work Place

part/four

Trends

Welfare, Society, and the Helping Professions
/An Introduction

part / one

Helping Others in the American Context

chapter/1
Defining Welfare

Each year a large percentage of federal and state budgets is devoted to welfare funding. In spite of this, or perhaps because of it, welfare is one of the most controversial issues of our times. Among the members of the general public there is little agreement about what welfare is, what it should accomplish, and how much should be spent on it—whatever *it* is. If you were to walk down the street and ask each passerby what he or she thinks about welfare, you would hear a variety of opinions. Continue your walk through the corridors of the schools that train human service professionals or the agencies in which welfare programs are put into practice and you would also find debate about the meaning of welfare.

To illustrate the range of opinion we will first present some of the varying definitions of welfare. Then, because it is futile to discuss something until it is clear exactly what is being discussed, we will give the definition of welfare on which this book is based and explain why we define welfare in this particular way.

Some Definitions

Webster's defines welfare as, "state of well-being or doing well, the condition of health, prosperity, and happiness; well-being." The word was used in this sense by the framers of the Constitution when they wrote in the Preamble that one of their purposes was to "promote the general welfare."

However, welfare has taken on a more restrictive meaning in that it is now commonly used to denote the large public and private programs that assist people to obtain well-being. Nonetheless, the meaning of the word welfare is in as much dispute as ever. The focal points of the debate are:

1. Who should receive welfare ?
2. What kind of assistance should be given?

To some, welfare means only the economic assistance given to the poor and needy. According to an official governmental definition,* welfare is "[income] transfers where the benefits are based on the recipient's income. Welfare programs are sometimes referred to as 'means-tested' or 'income-tested' programs. 'Income assistance' program is a category that is frequently used synonymously with 'welfare'."[1]

Many human services professionals prefer a more inclusive use of the term. They usually add the word "social" and thus speak of "social welfare." For instance, the 1971 *Encyclopedia of Social Work* defines social welfare as generally denoting "the full range of organized activities of voluntary and governmental agencies that seek to prevent, alleviate, or contribute to the solution of recognized social problems or to improve the well-being of individuals, groups or communities."[2]

A later edition of the *Encyclopedia* says, "Social welfare is an organized effort to insure a basic standard of decency in relation to the physical and mental well-being of the citizenry."[3] In neither case is economic assistance specifically mentioned.

Some definitions combine economic assistance with social services in their definitions of welfare. Friedlander states that social welfare is "a system of laws, programs, benefits, and services which strengthen or assure provisions for meeting of social needs recognized as basic for the welfare of the population and for the functioning of the social order."[4] Frederico says that economic assistance is included in welfare when he defines social welfare as "improving social functioning and minimizing suffering through a system of socially approved financial and social services at all levels of the social system."[5]†

From these examples, it can be seen that the definitions of welfare fall

* See also Chapter 8, Document 2 for a similar definition of welfare in the president's message to Congress, August 1977.

† Both Friedlander and Frederico make their definitions imprecise by the frequent use of the words they are defining in their definitions.

into three types. One is the strictly economic definition. A second concentrates on the provision of personal services designed to help an individual improve his or her circumstances through modification of behavior. The third combines the first two but emphasizes the provision of personal services. Both the second and third types attempt to enlarge the scope of welfare to include the total population.

At the 1974 International Conference on Social Welfare, the *United States Committee Report* used the term social welfare to denote

> (*1*) the wide range of services designed to attain ways of life acceptable to individuals and the community, sometimes thought of collectively as the "social aspects of development" and including services designed to strengthen the individual confronted with economic, physical, mental, or social disabilities, together with (*2*) those aimed at influencing the remedy of conditions leading to dependency.

The report, written by John Turner, then went on to say that

> The scope of social welfare in the U.S. is not as broad as social work professionals concerned with the question would like it to be. While the preferred definition suggests improvements in social conditions for all, ... in actual practice the scope of social welfare has a narrower more residual orientation. ... The principal targets of social welfare are then, in spite of our [social workers] preferences for a broader view, special groups in the population whose social situation is problematic (i.e.) ... the poor, the handicapped, the dependent, the deprived, the deviant, the disadvantaged, the alienated.[6]

We agree with Turner. For the purposes of this book, welfare is defined, not as it theoretically (or hopefully) might operate, but as it presently actually does operate in the American society: *Welfare is a combination of economic maintenance and social service programs designed to make the poor and underprivileged as self sufficient as possible.*

Welfare and Inequality

There is an unequal distribution of social and economic resources throughout the American society, and at present the stability of this pattern is more in evidence than is change. Yinger discusses both inequality and the patterns of stability in his classic, *A Minority Group in American Society.* He says

> individuals are not only different, but higher and lower, lords and peasants, chiefs and Indians. If this ranking system persists over a period of time, so that there is opportunity for it to be built into institutional patterns, and to influence significantly the [behavior] of individuals, ... we speak of stratification.[7]

The stratification of a society can be measured only relatively for it involves comparison of members of the society with each other. One of the important means of establishment of position in the stratification hierarchy in American society is by the type of work that individuals do, that is, by their occupations. The professional occupations are at the top of the scale and unskilled or manual occupations are at the bottom.[8] The income of individuals is related to the type of work that they do. Professional occupations generally have the highest income; manual or unskilled occupations have the lowest. Therefore, income is stratified in relation to occupational stratification. Those without any occupation, those with no history of work, those who lack employment—these individuals are ranked at the very bottom of the stratification hierarchy.

Bendix and Lipset state that stability and change are the most important issues in stratification.[9] Social stability supports the existing stratification of the society, whereas social change aims toward its modification. These issues are important to welfare programs, for the amount of stability or change in a society affects the goals of welfare programs, the services given, and the qualifications and activities of the persons who staff welfare programs. The programs then that distribute economic and social resources to the persons at the bottom of the stratification hierarchy are called *welfare programs*.

When we speak of welfare, therefore, we are speaking of the programs for economic maintenance or social services designed for those persons at the lower end of the stratification rankings in the society. This includes both those who are unemployed and those who have jobs that pay so little that the individual cannot support himself or herself or his or her dependents. Additionally, welfare programs are concerned with those individuals who would find themselves downwardly mobile to the point where they would have insufficient resources if there were no programs to provide aid and assistance.

We point this out so emphatically because there are many types of income transfers and social services provided by both the public and private sectors that are not generally perceived as welfare programs. If an income transfer is made to a person farther up on the stratification hierarchy, it is called a tax rebate or perhaps a guaranteed low interest loan, or a price support, or disaster relief. Likewise, social services offered to persons who rank higher on the stratification hierarchy are not called welfare programs. When social services are made available to these persons, they have names like Boy Scouts, YMCA, the Muscular Dystrophy Fund, Red Cross, adoption services, displaced homemaker services, and the like.

Staffing Welfare Programs

Human services professionals who staff welfare programs come from many different disciplines. They are physicians, psychologists, nurses, teachers, physical therapists, social workers, and so on. But not all these human service professionals work in welfare programs. Many are employed in programs that are designed more for the "middle class." Many are in private practice. Many combine welfare work with other employment.

It is important to make this distinction so that you will understand that this text is *not* directed toward social workers alone nor is it concerned *exclusively* with social work. It is concerned with *welfare programs* and it is directed toward the many types of human services professionals whose work is in some way connected with welfare. However, because it is expected that many persons interested in social work as a career will be using this text, we are including in Chapter 12 an inventory of social work occupations and settings that will illustrate the many opportunities for employment open to social workers, both within welfare programs and without.

As you read this book, and begin to understand how welfare programs function in the American society, you may find yourself saying, "That's not the way it *should* be!"

We agree.

But then, this is not a romantic book about the way things *should* be. It is a practical book about the way things *are*. It is written to provide you with the knowledge necessary to work effectively with welfare programs as they presently exist. Furthermore, only with this knowledge can you hope to change things to the way they should be in the future.

References

1. Wisconsin Department of Health and Social Services. *An Inventory of Social Insurance Programs and Income Assistance Programs: United States, 1977*. Madison, WI, 1979, p. 31.

2. National Association of Social Workers. *Encyclopedia of Social Work*. Vol. 2. New York: 1971. p. 1446.

3. National Association of Social Workers. *Encyclopedia of Social Work*, Vol. 2. New York: 1977, p. 1503.

4. Friedlander, W. *Introduction to Social Welfare*. 5th ed. Englewood Cliffs, N.J.: Prentice-Hall, 1980, p. 4.

5. Frederico, R. *The Social Welfare Institution, An Introduction*. 2nd ed. Lexington, Mass.: Heath, 1976, pp. 17, 18.

6. *Development and Participation: Operational Implications for Social Welfare*. New York: United States Committee, International Council on Social Welfare, 1974, p. 19.

7. Yinger, M. *A Minority Group in American Society*. New York: McGraw-Hill, 1965, p. 8.

8. Bendix, R., and Lipset, S., eds. *Class, Status, and Power*. Glencoe, Ill.: Free Press, 1953, pp. 454–464.

9. Ibid., pp. 11, 12.

chapter/2

Some Theories of the Nature of Society: How These Theories Influence Welfare Goals

From the earliest times, inequality in the distribution of economic, physical, intellectual, and emotional resources has been a conspicuous feature of all societies. There are, and always have been, persons who enjoy great wealth and persons who are poverty stricken. Some people are born healthy and continue to be so throughout life; others are constantly ill. Some have straight bones, perfect hearing, and 20/20 vision; others are crippled, deaf, or blind. Some have great ability; others are unable to perform the simplest tasks. Some have emotional strength; others suffer the anguish of mental illness.

In regard to these extremes, people have long sought answers to two questions:

1. What are the causes of these inequalities?
2. What should be done to care for those who are afflicted by problems resulting from these inequalities?

The answer to the second question develops from the answer to the first, and, because there is no universally agreed upon answer to the first question, both questions generate controversy. In the United States today there are many large-scale welfare programs designed to care for those who suffer from inequality. Some are sponsored by private organizations, others by the government. Because these programs are designed, operated, and paid for by persons who do not agree on the answers to these two questions, the programs also generate controversy.

There are other manifestations of inequality in distribution of resources where disagreement is less evident. Weather is unequally distributed over time and geographic locale. When people discuss the weather, they are also reflecting their concerns about extremes, about too much of one thing and too little of another, but because the understandings about the causes of weather and the protective measures that can be taken are more universally held, disagreement is minimal.

This is because the weather is generally knowable to everyone in the same way. Most persons in the United States have experienced extremes in temperature so that they agree that 20 degrees below zero is excessively cold and that 110 in the shade is excessively hot. No one doubts that the sun brings warmth and that clouds bring rain. Specific information about the weather is based on sophisticated technologies. Those of the news media who distribute this information are usually highly qualified, often with formal training in meteorology. Protective measures, from large scale programs such as Red Cross Disaster Relief to individual remedies such as going south for the winter, are widely understood, accepted, and utilized. Furthermore, no one holds the individual responsible if his or her house is destroyed by a tornado.

Although everyone in a given locale may not suffer equally from heat, cold, or storms, everyone is affected. Flooding, blizzards, and hurricanes are no respecters of rank or privilege. The president of a large corporation can chat with the newspaper vendor on the corner about a sudden rainstorm and each will know what the other is talking about, because they can share the experience of being cold and wet.

The effects of inequality in the distribution of economic, physical, intellectual, and emotional resources, however, are not so easily shared. Few people experience both wealth and poverty. No one can be intelligent and retarded at the same time. It is impossible to be both handicapped and physically fit or to be both mentally ill and emotionally stable. Those who are not afflicted by these manifestations of inequality can only observe and then try to interpret from their observation how these affect another person. It is always more difficult to understand a situation from indirect experience than it is from direct experience. The many different ways in which these inequalities are interpreted by those who do not share directly in the experience produce disagreement about the condition and the needs of those who suffer as a result of their lack of resources.

Information about the meanings of inequality comes from a wide variety of sources such as the government, the churches, educational institutions, local groups, and political parties. The information is often biased in favor of the interests of those who distribute it. Members of the media who distribute this information usually have little formal training in the social disciplines, such as economics, sociology, or psychology.[1]

Even among social scientists who spend their lifetimes studying human beings and societies, there is not the body of shared assumptions that there is among those who study the physical sciences. This is partly because the technology for measurement of social phenomena lacks the accuracy of the technology for measurement of physical phenomena and partly because the physical sciences are less concerned with value judgments than are the social sciences. There are many conflicting and competing theories about how societies and individuals operate, about how these two relate to each other, and about what this all means for humanity. For instance, some theories assume that the individual is more important than the society, whereas others assume the opposite. Some theories are based on the assumption that individuals and societies work together in an orderly fashion; others assume that individuals are constantly in conflict both with each other and with the society of which they are a part. Some assume that human experience has a point of beginning in time and is progressing to an ultimate end that might be either a perfect world or complete destruction of civilization; other theories assume that all human experience is just a milling around, with the society as a whole heading in no particular direction. Some theorists see great change taking place; others say that, while some of the elements of society may change, the basic relationships among the elements remain the same. Any of these assumptions and resultant theories (as well as others not mentioned) may be used to answer question 1, that is, to explain the causes of inequality.

These assumptions and theories are not merely toys in the hands of theorists. They form the basis of human action. When programs are planned to deal with the problems that come from inequalities of distribution of economic, physical, intellectual, and emotional resources (i.e., when programs are planned in response to question 2), the recommended course of action will conform with the theory that anyone who develops programs holds about the characteristics of society and the relationship of the individual to the society.

For instance, if the planner believes that individuals are themselves responsible when they possess too few resources to satisfy their needs, he or she will expect individuals to do their best to secure more of these resources. The welfare program will be designed to be small and temporary and directed toward changing the individual. If, on the other hand, the planner believes that society is responsible for the problems faced by the individual, the welfare program will be designed to be large, permanent, and directed toward changing the society rather than the individual.

To summarize, there are many welfare programs sponsored by the American society to assist those who suffer from inequality. Since these are planned and staffed by persons who do not hold a single, unified explanation of society and its relationship to the individual, these programs are, like the assumptions and theories on which they are based, competing and conflicting.

The rest of the chapter will outline four theories of society and illustrate the type of welfare program that each theory supports. It is important to understand these varying theories: otherwise it will not be possible to understand why welfare programs are established as they are, why they deal with their clientele as they do, and why they are supported by some members of society and criticized by others.

While not all theories of society will be discussed, the four theories that have been chosen have particular implication for welfare services. Welfare services developed in response to a perception held in common by members of the society who felt that "something was wrong" with a particular social circumstance and that "something should be done about it." When some kind of change was perceived as being needed, a program to "do something" subsequently developed. But the type of program that developed was organized in accordance with the idea of what change was deemed necessary by those in charge of developing the programs. This in turn depended on the explanations those in charge held about the nature of society. Since welfare programs emerged over a period of time, the perceptions of the type of change needed also changed. Differing programs have been and still are based on differing theories.

The four theories chosen for discussion reflect the differing explanations that are used to develop, defend, and criticize welfare services. Taken together, they illustrate how conflicting and competing theories when put to use produce conflicting and competing programs as well as partisan groups of people who are concerned with the use of welfare programs.

The four theories of society to be presented are

1. evolutionary theory
2. functionalism
3. conflict theory
4. cyclical theory

Evolutionary Theory

The fundamental feature of evolutionary theory is change. All forms of life are subject to modification by the ongoing forces of individual and social life. This change has three characteristics:

1. It moves in a determined direction.
2. It moves from simple to complex forms.
3. It involves "trial and error," for as a variety of forms develop, some are not as useful as others. Over time, the least useful forms disappear, and the most useful survive. The popular phrase that describes this process is "survival of the fittest."

Charles Darwin, the naturalist, was the first scholar to develop evolutionary theory. It appeared originally in 1859 in his book, *The Origin of Species.*

Some years later Herbert Spencer and Emile Durkheim translated Darwin's biological theories into theories about society. They described society as changing from simple to complex entities. Instead of society continuing to consist of a series of independent rural villages, they suggested that the direction of development was toward large, interdependent, industrialized societies tied together with institutions that integrated their functions, primarily government. At the same time, they saw individuals as becoming more adaptable, for they no longer lived in isolated villages‹ but rather, were required to participate in the activities of a society that was continuously changing in the direction of increased specialization and complexity.

Other writers built upon these ideas and added features to them. Lewis H. Morgan, for instance, saw the evolution of the social forms of life taking place in predictable stages. He believed that these stages were in a direction from less to more desirable. These stages moved from savagery to barbarism to civilization. Morgan was also one of the first to introduce the idea that social change was in the direction of social betterment. He called this evolution a "necessary sequence of progress." Morgan expounded these ideas in this book, *Ancient Society,* which appeared in 1877.

Evolutionary theory is utilized by contemporary theorists to explain the ongoing processes of change that are built into all forms of social life. For instance, Neil Smelser describes the process of industrialization in evolutionary terms: industrialization supplants traditional techniques with scientific knowledge, subsistence farming with commercial production, human and animal power with power-driven machines, and farm and villages with urban concentrations. Smelser states that these changes permeate the total society, profoundly affecting political, educational, familial, and class arrangements.[4]

Contemporary theorists often view the direction of change still to be in the direction of social betterment. Herbert Sahlins, writing in *Evolution and Culture,* states that "evolution generates progress: higher forms arise from, and surpass, lower."[5] Sahlins says that this progress is from less to higher energy transformation, from lower to higher levels of integration, and from less to greater all around adaptability.

Evolutionary theory has several important implications for welfare services:

1. It provides an explanation for the development of welfare services.
2. It serves as a rationale for the use of welfare services to achieve social reform.
3. It serves as a rationale for critics of welfare services who see the elimination of welfare in itself as a major social reform.

In *Industrial Society and Social Welfare,* Harold Wilensky and Charles LeBeau utilize evolutionary theory to explain the development of welfare services.[6] Welfare programs, they state, tend to evolve from the residual stage to the institutional stage. A residual program is a temporary one. It lasts only until the passing of the crisis that generated it in the first place. Then the program is discontinued. When another crisis occurs, another short-term program will be initiated, and then it, too, will be terminated when the crisis is past. Wilensky and LeBeau state that there is a trend for an industrial society to move from an explanation that poverty and underprivilege are rooted in individual causality to an explanation that poverty and underprivilege are rooted in the workings of society. When the accepted explanation is that poverty is rooted in individual causality, residual welfare programs will be the most prevalent. When the explanation evolves to accept poverty and underprivilege as rooted in workings of society, then institutional programs will supplant residual ones.

Institutional welfare programs are those that society adopts as a permanent part of its structure. Institutional forms of welfare programs integrate the poor and underprivileged into the society to a much greater extent than do residual forms of welfare programs.[7] Wilensky and LeBeau tried not to ascribe positive or negative values to the trends that they described. However, their discussion of the transition from residual to institutional welfare programs for retired workers (presented in the following paragraphs) can be seen as an example of evolutionary progress.

Before 1935 society provided no overall organized way in which to assist those who had become too old to work and had insufficient resources on which to live. During this residual stage of aid to the elderly, local private programs provided sporadic aid in the form of Christmas baskets and occasional gifts of clothing. Local public programs cared for some in old folk's homes or on county farms. Still, many handicapped and elderly persons who had no families to care for them simply starved.

The Great Depression of the 1930s resulted in such widespread suffering that the country responded with many types of relief. One of these was the Old Age Insurance Program, which was part of the Social Security Act that was passed in 1935. For the first time in the history of the United States, the entire society assumed the responsibility of caring for those who were no longer able to work. A commitment was made to provide them with an income based on the number of years they had worked and on the amount of money they had contributed to the Social Security program. Since that beginning in 1935 the Old Age Insurance program has become more and more institutionalized. It now includes almost every occupational category including the self-employed, and the benefits have risen substantially.

In addition to furnishing a rationale for explaining the gradual development of complex welfare programs, evolutionary theory also served to sustain the reformers who observed the prevalence of poverty, ill health, and other hazards that accompanied the industrial revolution. If one believed in the evolution of the society toward a better, more satisfactory state, one could also be hopeful that the present hazards would eventually be eliminated through the built-in processes of social evolution. One early group to formulate this point of view was the Fabian Society in Great Britain, which emerged during the latter part of the nineteenth century. The society was founded by Sidney and Beatrice Webb, and George Bernard Shaw, the famous playwright, was a prominent member. The Fabian Society believed that in a piecemeal fashion, over a period of time, by the workings of the built-in processes of society, the problems that existed would be corrected and that the members of society would eventually obtain from their society what they wanted and what they deserved. This they called the "inevitability of gradualism." They saw government as the social form most important to this process. So they worked to assure that government would accelerate reform by formulating plans for social programs for Great Britain that would make government the primary agent for reform and the gradual elimination of inequality.

In 1964, President Johnson enunciated the same ideas in his "Great Society" speech to Congress. He stated that approximately 15 per cent of all Americans live at the poverty level and that because the American society was sufficiently wealthy, the federal government would embark on a program designed to reform the society and thereby eliminate poverty and the hazards associated with this aspect of inequality.

This theme has been carried forward by the presidents following Johnson. Although their subsequent statements have not been as dramatic as those contained in the Great Society proposals, recent administrations have sought to reform welfare programs to assure every American a basic income to protect him or her from the hazards of extreme deprivation. The proposals made over the years fall in line with the general assumptions of the reformers who believed that the inevitable processes of social evolution would assure, some day, that all needy persons would be cared for by programs supported by society. In fact, as evolutionary processes proceed, it has been said, there will ultimately be no needy persons, because scientific advances will eliminate all mental and physical and social problems. This follows the basic tenet of the "progressive" school of social evolutionary theorists—that is, that change is constantly taking place and that in general the change is for the better.[8]

Contradictory as it may seem, evolutionary theory also forms the basis for the argument that welfare services stand in the way of the betterment of society and therefore should be eliminated. Those who take this stand believe that the built-in processes of society if left to function without interference would eventually operate to eliminate inequality. These persons further believe that those who suffer from the hazards of inequality are not "fit" and therefore if not artificially supported by welfare services would not survive. In other words, they are inferior forms of human life and would eventually disappear through the operation of the evolutionary process of "survival of the fittest." "Survival of the fittest" combined with the "necessary sequence of progress" means to many people that welfare programs are unnecessary. The natural processes of society, harsh as they might be in the short run, should not be interfered with, for the elimination of the unfit will in the long run benefit the more capable members of the human race.

Functionalism

In contrast to evolutionary theory, functional theory focuses on the stability of society rather than on the changing nature of society. This idea was also borrowed from the biologists, who observed the manner in which life forms had interdependent substructures that, while distinct, worked in cooperation with each other to create a unit different from and greater than each single part. They saw society as being like the human body, with many parts, each part working in a consistent relationship with other parts to form the overall unit. Herbert Spencer and Emile Durkheim[9] were the first to develop this view of society, which was refined by later scholars into the explanation of society called functional theory.*

Classical functional theory makes three basic assertions about society:

1. The parts of a society work together in harmony.
2. All the parts of a society as they exist are beneficial to the society and the individuals within it.
3. Society would not work well without any of its existing parts.[10]

These assertions leave little room for change. What exists is useful. What exists is necessary. Therefore by this theory, if social resources are unevenly distributed, it is only because this distribution serves society and its members better than would any other pattern of distribution. In fact, Kingsley Davis, a prominent functional theorist, stated in 1949 that social inequality is a device by which societies ascertain that the most important positions are filled by the most qualified persons. He stated further that the most important positions suffer from a shortage of qualified personnel and thus offer the greatest rewards. Those positions that are less important have an abundance of personnel available to them and offer minimal rewards. Inequality is thus inevitable, because all positions can never be equal in importance, and all people are not equally qualified for the more important positions. This arrangement is beneficial to everyone, because the survival and well-being of every individual depends on the survival and well-being of society.[11]

Even though functionalists emphasized the stable characteristics of society, they could not completely ignore the existence of friction and change among some parts of society. Strikes do occur. Family structures do change. These factors of change led to a modification of the classical assertions:

---

* We mentioned Spencer and Durkheim in the section on evolutionary theory. These writers utilized portions of evolutionary theory to explain how society reached its present state. They then concentrated on the description of society as they observed it operating about them. Most of their writings dealt with society in its present state of affairs. Since they concluded that society was for the most part stable, they analyzed the nature of that stability and ignored the forces in society that might work toward modification of the present state of affairs. For this reason Spencer and Durkheim are also identified with functional theory.

1. The parts of society are not as well integrated as are the parts of biological organisms. There is some independence of function of the parts of society.
2. This independence causes tension to arise among the various parts, threatening the balance of society as a whole.
3. Change then modifies the parts of society that are in tension, which reduces the tension and brings the parts back into balance with each other. The threat to the overall operation of society is thus eliminated.[12]

In accounting for change, this view does not project any drastic modification of the character of society. Change only serves to reduce societal tension and to keep the balance among the parts of society that is necessary to its proper functioning.

Functionalism has been the dominant perspective in American social thought.[13] Functionalist theory, as it focuses on the status quo, lends credence to the continued existence of inequality and the beneficial function of welfare services as they are presently found in American society. Many persons argue from the functionalist perspective when they justify the continued existence of poverty and the maintenance of welfare services much as they are presently organized. It is commonly stated that the poor are poor because they are not qualified for better positions in society and that, because poverty has been one of the continuing characteristics of the American society, its existence must be beneficial to the society as a whole. In general, according to functionalist theory those living in poverty make little protest; they accept their conditon as being the best they can attain in the society and perceive the necessity of poverty for the well-being of society as a whole. However, poverty sometimes produces tension because more highly qualified members of society receive a disproportionate share of the social resources. This threatens the balance of society, so some change must occur to restore the balance and assure the continued functioning of society. Welfare services, from the functionalist perspective, operate to ascertain that the poor receive sufficient resources so that balance is maintained and when the balance is threatened, channel resources to the poor to restore the balance. Welfare services can therefore be considered functional to the well-being of society.

We have discussed how evolutionary theory provides an understanding of the development of the Old Age Insurance provisions of Social Security Act. Functionalist theory is often also used to provide an explanation for the continued existence and expansion of the Social Security Act. The serious economic problems of the 1930s threw society into imbalance as so many older persons lost their life savings and were unable to obtain sufficient employment to support themselves that a serious threat arose to the well-being of society. In fact, the imbalance was so widely felt that one extreme proposal, the Townsend Plan almost became a reality. According to this plan, anyone over the age of 65 would received a guaranteed monthly income of $200, which had to be spent before the recipients could receive any more money. This was perceived by members of other parts of the social system as too extreme a remedy because it would take too much away from the more affluent sectors. A compromise was reached in the Old Age Insurance provisions of the Social Security Act, which provided a modest sum for retired persons according to their accumulated work history. The insurance programs of the Social Security Act helped to maintain the necessary balance among the parts of the social system, for serious imbalances would result if persons who were no longer able to work had no means by which to sustain themselves. The Social Security Act also made provision for those who could not qualify for insurance because of an unsatisfactory work history. Under the Old Age Assistance provision, these persons too old to work could receive support for personal sustenance if they had no resources available to them from any other source.

Other forms of welfare services can also be discussed from the perspective of functionalist theory. For example, from the functionalist point of view, the family as it exists is a requisite to the well-being of society. Welfare services oriented toward the family therefore aim at maintaining a stable family with characteristics that are accepted throughout society. In this type of family both parents are present, the family is economically self-sufficient, the children are in school and not out in the community getting into trouble, and the family participates in societally approved activities. Mothers receiving such services as are provided by the Aid to Families with Dependent Children program are encouraged to marry and discouraged from living with men to whom they are not married. Efforts are made to get the children into "Headstart" programs so that they will do well in school and thus be able to obtain work when they grow up (become qualified for a respected position in society) and therefore not cause problems in the community (not contribute to societal imbalances).

From a functionalist point of view, it can be argued that the Economic Opportunity Act of 1964 was formulated in response to the instability reflected in the civil rights activity of that period. The Economic Opportunity Act initiated some small changes, but overall it had little effect on the existing state of affairs. Perhaps its most important accomplishment was that it identified able persons in the civil rights movement and moved them into more important positions in society. When the civil rights movement was no longer considered to be a significant threat to social stability, the Economic Opportunity Act was quietly dismantled.

Because, from a functionalist point of view, the survival and well-being of the society is paramount, it is necessary for individual members of society to see that it is in their best interests to contribute to this survival and well-being. Functionalists would deny that there is conflict between the interests of society and the interests of the individual, asserting that is what is good for society is good for the individual, and vice versa.[14] From this point of view, it can be argued that services to individuals contribute to the well-being of society, because welfare services aim to ensure that each person is an adequately functioning member of society. If an individual is physically ill and cannot afford medical services, then the society should take responsibility to provide these services for a sick individual cannot contribute to society. If a person is unqualified to hold a position of value in the society, that individual should receive training so that he or she will be able to work for the well-being of the society. If the individual is emotionally dysfunctional, that individual should receive psychiatric, psychological, or social case work services so that he or she will be changed into a functioning, contributing member of society.

Therefore, from the standpoint of the functionalist explanation of society, welfare services are beneficial to society because they operate to guarantee the existence of the parts of society, to maintain the balance of the social system, and to restore the balance, if for some reason it is disturbed.

Conflict Theory

Conflict theory, like functionalism, recognizes the existence of a social system in which there is interdependence among its various parts. Unlike functionalism, however, which emphasizes balanced relationships with the parts of society working together in harmony, conflict theory states that

1. The relationship among the parts of society are competitive rather than cooperative.
2. These competitive relationships produce instability rather than balance.
3. This instability generates conflict among the various parts of society.
4. Through the process of conflict among the various parts of society, change is built into the society.

Karl Marx, the great conflict theorist of the nineteenth century, saw conflict as the primary law of civilization. To Marx, the parts of society were the social classes, each possessing its own special needs. Each class works to meet its own needs rather than to meet the needs of society as a whole. Even though the various classes are constantly at loggerheads Marx felt that this would, in the long run, lead to a better society: "Without conflict, no progress; this is the law which civilization has followed to the present day. ... The history of all societies up to the present is the history of class struggles."[15]

Marx, in his revolutionary doctrine, theorized that the principal conflict was between the capitalist classes and the worker classes. He felt that inequality would eventually be eliminated because the workers would take the means of production out of the hands of the capitalists and redistribute the resources "each to his own need." For Marx, conflict was the process by which the goals of society were assured, and by which the proper direction of the society was maintained. He felt that the result of conflict would be the eventual elimination of inequality and the establishment of the worker's paradise, or utopia.

Most contemporary conflict theorists do not see conflict as a means toward the perfectability of the human society. They see conflict as a given condition of existence, as a necessary process that must occur for rules and policies to be developed. If any direction is evident, it is that those who are strong will continue to exploit the weak and that the weak will fall farther and farther behind in the struggle. Although they do not see conflict as radically altering the social structure, they do see it as the means by which specific issues are settled and specific problems are solved; in other words, accommodations are made.

Contemporary conflict theorists such as Ralf Dahrendorf conceptualize human existence as a struggle against inequality. Those who have more keep trying to hang on to what they have and to use what they have to gain even more. Those who have less try to get more by taking from those who have more. The struggle is between the powerful and the less powerful. However, the less powerful have it within their means to develop enough power to get what they want and thus minimize some of the inequality. In this way, the social order is assured and the existing society continues, because there are relatively few individuals who are so disillusioned that they wish to destroy the whole society. These theorists believe that this process of perceived inequality, followed by conflict and eventually by accommodation, is the major ingredient of human existence. In this sense, conflict is one of the major means for maintaining an uneasy social equilibrium. Thus functionalism and conflict are perhaps less contradictory than they seem at first glance.[16]

Conflict theory is utilized by persons concerned with welfare programs who perceive poverty and underprivilege arising from social conditions rather than from individual characteristics. Saul Alinsky utilized contemporary conflict theory when he organized those who lived and worked near the Chicago stockyards to secure resources within the present structure of society that they did not have and that they thought were rightfully theirs. After his work in Chicago, Alinsky moved to other parts of the nation to teach other groups how to utilize conflict techniques to obtain resources and rights not heretofore accorded them.[17]

Cesar Chavez, Alinsky's star pupil, has spent many years teaching farm workers in the American Southwest to use conflict techniques to secure what they want from their employers. Some success has resulted. For instance, when Chavez began his work, it was illegal for farm workers to organize to achieve their goals, but as a result of their confrontation tactics the State of California in 1975 passed legislation recognizing their right to organize. The struggle is still going on.[18]

Conflict theory can also be utilized to explain the problems of persons who are institutionalized because they are unable to care for themselves. Two psychologists, Michael Glenn and Richard Kunnes, have proposed that most individuals who are served by public mental institutions do not suffer from problems generated by their own characteristics. Instead, they state that services offered in mental institutions help people to

> adjust to the conditions of their oppression, not change these conditions. The affluent are served in private practice; the disadvantaged are policed in community mental health programs. They cool people out and get them focused on their own heads and feelings from whence they never return. And the clients even foot this part of the bill for their continuing oppression. Indeed, they are supposed to be grateful, too.[19]

Glenn and Kunnes offer the following program of action:

> We don't need any new "radical theory" of psychology. What we need is to sweep away the noxious notions of bourgeois psychology. But bourgeois psychology can't simply be replaced by revolutionary thought in the textbooks; it involves a change in the entire structure of our society, and an actual transfer of power from one class to another.
>
> In this sense, the main task is to involve ourselves more and more in the political struggles going on today. We cannot separate "therapy" or "psychology" from the political context. We can't develop "radical therapy" apart from the revolutionary struggle, unless by radical therapy we're talking only about a safe, nonstruggle field of expertise.[20]

Alinsky, Chavez, and Glenn and Kunnes do not foresee that their programs will produce revolutionary change in the total society as did Marx in the grand scope of his conflict theory. Glenn and Kunnes want to change the conditions of those who are served by mental institutions just as Chavez wants to change the conditions of the farm workers in the Southwest. Conflict is a technique used to bring about a realignment of relationships between antagonistic special-interest groups.

Cyclical Theory

Cyclical theory is similar to functionalist theory in that it emphasizes stability in the relationship of the parts of society to each other. Functionalism, however, states that the various parts of society retain their identity through time. Cyclical theory varies on this theme by stating that

1. Elements of society appear, disappear, and reappear.
2. This appearance, disappearance, and reappearance occurs in regular predictable patterns over a period of time.
3. These patterns affirm order rather than change.

The ideas expressed in cyclical theory are among the oldest explanations of society. The ancient scholar in Ecclesiastes wrote, "What has been is what will be, and what has been done is what will be done; and there is nothing new under the sun. Is there a thing of which it is said, 'See, this is new?' It has been already in the ages before us"[21]. One of the stained glass windows in the cathedral at Amiens, France shows a wheel of fortune. On it mankind is depicted as going up and down, round and round, always in a circle. The downward position symbolizes bad times and the upward position symbolizes the good which were thought to follow each other with monotonous regularity.

It is easy to find examples in everyday circumstances that seem to bear out cyclical theory. Winter is followed by summer. Droughts are followed by floods. Wars are followed by periods of peace. Economic booms are followed by depressions. Periods of sexual freedom are followed by periods of sexual repression. History repeats itself, we are told, and everything that exists now existed in times before. If there is any change, it is only because something may manifest itself in a form more suitable to the present.

The following, from Wilbert Moore, is an example of the current use of cyclical theory:

> In terms of behavior, many elements of persistence are more nearly cyclical, the near repetition of sequences of action over various time periods. All enduring groups or social patterns exhibit characteristic rhythms. Even in those rare instances where a small group of persons is in "constant interaction" (or constant for the waking hours), the rhythms required for bodily functions, the ordering of the various collective activities in some sequence, impose a cyclical pattern or recurrence. Over the longer term, their recurrence marks an element of order, and their results precisely prevent more disorderly or changeful manifestations of the normal tensions intrinsic to patterned behavior.[22]

Frances Piven and Richard Cloward in their book, *Regulating the Poor*, describe how welfare services follow recurrent cycles.[23] First, unemployment causes the number of people on relief to increase. This causes concern on the part of the "elites" who develop work programs for the poor in order to get them off relief. When things improve, work relief is restricted. This restriction causes extreme hardship and suffering to the poor and unemployed that continues until another recession occurs, at which time the relief rolls explode. This signals the beginning of the relief cycle all over again. This cycle has been recurring for the past seven centuries, and Piven and Cloward say that, barring any "true reform," this cycle will repeat itself indefinitely:

> The restoration of work through the relief system, in other words, makes possible the eventual return to the most restrictive phase in the cycle of relief-giving. What begins as a great explosion of direct relief ends finally with a sharp contraction of the rolls. As the Depression wore on, direct relief was replaced by work relief, then work relief was abolished, and millions of the poor were rapidly shunted into a labor marker where there was insufficient work. It was not for three decades that the poor were to get relief again, despite spreading unemployment in agriculture and in the

cities. Meanwhile, the few who were allowed to remain on the rolls were once again subjected to the punitive and degrading treatment which has been used to buttress the work ethic since the inception of relief several centuries ago. And why should it have been otherwise? With order restored, there was no force to sustain the concessions made at earlier stages. Relief-giving is never popular, work relief costs billions of dollars, and a placid poor hardly constitutes a political constituency whose interests must be taken seriously. Advocates of relief reform may argue that their reforms will be long-lasting, that the restrictive phase in the cycle will not be reached, but past experience suggests otherwise.[24]

Summary

In this chapter we have given a brief overview of four theories of society. We have illustrated how these theories can be used to understand welfare programs.

These theories are the well-developed statements of academic scholars; yet the reader will have noticed that there is wide variation among statements. All are based on the observation of processes in the environment, but, as an example, the observations of evolutionary theorists led them to perceive change all about them, whereas the observations of functionalists conclude with stablility. Conflict theorists emphasize instability and struggle among the parts of society; cyclical theorists see repetition. The lack of agreement is not surprising, because once someone begins to develop an explanation concerning the nature of any phenomenon, one tends to ignore that which does not fit into the explanation and to be sensitive only to that which does. This generates difficulties when the theories are applied at the program level.

Herein lies one of the problems with welfare services today—an important reason why people talk about the "welfare mess." Programs have been started that conform to the different explanations of society. This means that the programs have different goals and different techniques for achieving those goals. Contradictory programs with conflicting goals often exist side by side.

All four explanations demonstrate that change and stability co-exist in society. However, no theory deals with both, because each concentrates on one almost to the exclusion of the other. There is considerable reason to develop an explanation that will simultaneously take change and stability into account. Efforts along this line can be found in the writings of Lenski[25] and LaPiere[26] but there is still much work to be done.

Until such a general theory is developed, an understanding of evolutionary theory is necessary to understand why welfare programs have developed as they have. To understand how welfare programs are organized today, one needs an appreciation of functionist theory, as many welfare programs operate to maintain the present societal balance, that is, to prevent significant change in the areas with which those welfare services are concerned.

Conflict theory and cyclical theory are also important to the student of welfare programs. When a welfare program is controversial or is not well accepted, conflict theory helps to explain the nature of the controversies. Conflict theory also helps in understanding the arguments that exist among the many groups concerned with welfare programs. Cyclical theory helps one to understand the programs that come and go in response to recurrent patterns in the society.

All four explanations have merit and must be used at one time or another if one is to understand the nature of welfare programs and their function in society. Though of course it is arguable, we believe that functionalist theory is the most useful in explaining the current state of welfare programs. Therefore, in the chapters that follow we will use the following assumptions to guide discussion of welfare programs in the American society:

1. The goals and general organization of the American society are quite stable and have been so since its beginning.
2. Welfare services, the organizations developed to deliver these services, and specific welfare programs have changed over time and are still changing.
3. These structural changes in welfare are not directed toward the modification of the values and institutions of society but, rather, toward their maintenance.
4. At present, the changes observed in welfare programs are changes that tend to reduce instability and maintain order in society.

In subsequent chapters we will deal with the organizational and programmatic implications of these assumptions for welfare programs. However, since most welfare programs are directed toward individuals, it is also important to understand the theories that are used to describe the nature of individuals and their function in the American society. Explanations of society and individuals complement each other and are indispensable to an understanding of the patterns of welfare programs and the manner in which they operate.

Chapter 3 will present brief statements of the most important features of several theories of the individual.

References

1. *Human Behavior* Editorial—"The Sticky Social Issues Beat". Vol 6, No. 11. (November 1977): 64.

2. Spencer, H. *Principles of Sociology.* New York: D. Appleton & Co., 1898, pp. 214-217

3. Durkheim, E. *The Division of Labor in Society.* trans. G. Simpson. Glencoe, Ill: The Free Press, 1947, pp. 10-18.

4. Smelser, N. "The Modernization of Social Relations," in M. Weiner, ed., *Modernization.* New York: Basic Books, 1966, pp. 110, 111.

5. Sahlins, M., & Service, E., ed. *Evolution and Culture.* Ann Arbor: Univ. of Michigan, 1960, pp. 12, 13.

6. Wilensky, H., and LeBeau, C. *Industrial Society and Social Welfare.* New York: Free Press, 1965.

7. *Ibid.*, p. 139.

8. Appelbaum, R. *Theories of Social Change.* Chicago: Rand McNally, 1970, pp. 17–30.

9. *Ibid.*, p. 10.

10. Merton, R. *On Theoretical Society.* New York: Free Press, 1967, pp. 80–86.

11. Davis, K. *Human Society.* New York: Macmillan, 1949; p. 376.

12. Moore, W. *Social Change.* Englewood Cliffs, N.J.: Prentice-Hall, 1963, ch. 4.

13. Poloma, M. *Contemporary Sociological Theory.* New York: Macmillan, 1979, p. 28.

14. *Ibid.*, pp. 26, 27.

15. Marx, K. "Manifesto of the Communist Party" in L. Feuer, ed., *Marx and Engels: Basic Writings on Politics and Philosophy.* Doubleday, 1959, pp. 7, 27.

16. Dahrendorf, R. "Toward a Theory of Social Conflict," *Journal of Conflict Resolution.* (June 1958): pp. 170–183.

17. Alinsky, S. *Reveille for Radicals.* Chicago: Univ. of Chicago, 1964.

18. *Milwaukee Journal*, November 23, 1975. Part 1, p. 20.

19. Glenn, M., and Kunnes, R. *Repression or Revolution?* New York: Harper, 1973, p. 13.

20. *Ibid.*, pp. 180, 181.

21. Eccles. 1:9, 10.

22. Moore, W. *Op. cit.*, pp. 5, 47–49.

23. Pivens, F., and Cloward, R. *Regulating the Poor.* New York: Vintage, 1971, pp. 331–348.

24. *Ibid,* pp. 347, 348

25. Lenski, G. *Power and Privilege.* New York: McGraw-Hill, 1966.

26. LaPiere, R. *Social Change.* New York: McGraw-Hill, 1965.

chapter/3

Some Theories About Individual Behavior: Values And Norms

In Chapter 2, we discussed some of the theories that people use to explain the functioning of society. However, the theories selected for discussion did not offer much information about individual behavior. Thus, because all social behavior is ultimately dependent upon the way in which individuals interact face to face, this chapter will introduce some of the varying theories that offer explanations for the behavior of individuals. It is important, however, to understand that the theories of individual behavior often conflict with each other, as do the theories of society. Therefore, the theories about the individual also give conflicting answers to the two questions raised in Chapter 2:

1. What causes inequality?
2. What should be done to assist those who suffer because of inequality?

First of all, let us discuss how theories are developed. Many are under the impression that the study of individual behavior is the exclusive domain of psychology. While it is true that psychologists do make a speciality of this study, psychology is not the only academic discipline that devotes time and attention to it. Sociologists also study the individual, although they tend first to study society and then to generalize to the individuals who comprise it. Most perceive individuals to be a small reflection of the larger society. They see individuals as formed by society and subject almost exclusively to its controls. Social psychologists study the reciprocal relationship between the individual and society, and they too offer theories about individual behavior. Biologists pay less attention to the mental state of individuals and seek answers to questions about individual behavior through the study of innate or instinctual drives. Medical research is oriented toward the way in which individual behavior is influenced by chemicals or disturbances in bodily functioning.

Theories about individual behavior also arise from outside the academic physical or social disciplines. All individuals (including human services professionals) interpret their own behavior and the behavior of others with whom they interact. They observe themselves and others and try to make sense out of what they see. They try to figure out why one person reacts one way to a certain stimulus whereas another person reacts differently. They try to set standards for proper behavior in a given situation. They look for ways of changing their behavior or that of others. They form expectations about the outcome of given situations based on past behavior observed in an individual with whom they interact or even based on the observed behavior of a person whom they consider similar to the person with whom they are interacting. The interpretations they make often combine "popular" explanations with elements derived from the sophisticated theories contained in the academic disciplines. Then they tend to generalize these interpretations into a theory on which they base their subsequent behavior.

As a human services professional, you may interact on a face-to-face basis with welfare recipients. You may also interact with government officials, members of neighborhood groups, taxpayers, philanthropists and co-workers and supervisors. To do so, you must be sufficiently sure of your own choice of a theory of individual behavior to maintain a consistent approach with those with whom you are interacting. At the same time, it is necessary to recognize that there are other theories and that other people may not always agree with what you believe should be done in a given situation.

This probably sounds confusing. Indeed, many who have been connected with welfare work for a lifetime find it so. Still, the best way to eliminate confusion is to determine the source of the confusion. When one understands that different theories produce different programs or that a certain program can be explained by several theories, it becomes possible also to understand why welfare programs do not present a unified approach to the problems of inequality, why competing programs can exist side by side sometimes even in the same agency, how it is that co-workers often give conflicting advice to their clients, and why there is no agreement on the part of the public as to what outcome should be expected from welfare programs.

This chapter will help you to understand why these varying theories exist, to see how they agree or disagree, where they overlap or leave gaps, and what effect theories have on program development. The theories will not be discussed on the basis of relative merit and the descriptions given should not be considered complete.

It is not possible to discuss in detail all the theories about individual behavior in this book. Therefore we will present the theories according to the way they answer the following questions:

1. What determines the behavior of individuals?
2. How is individual behavior evaluated?

Two important relationships will be analyzed in the discussion: 1) the relationship between the theories and society, and 2) the relationship between the theories and welfare programs.

The Determination of Individual Behavior

Most theories can be placed in one of five classifications according to the assumptions they make about what makes individuals behave as they do:

1. theories of the autonomous individual
2. theories of the programmed individual
3. theories of the mechanical individual
4. theories of the evolutionary individual
5. theories of the integrative individual

The Autonomous Individual

Autonomous means self-governing, without outside control. Theories that stress the idea that the individual is autonomous state that each person is a separate, self-controlled entity. Despite the problems that may have existed for that person in the past, each person is presently responsible for his or her own behavior. Each person chooses to do whatever he or she is doing and is ultimately responsible for whatever rewards or punishment come from these choices. People have used the theory of the autonomous individual to explain the behavior of others for thousands of years and continue to do so today.

The concept of the autonomous individual developed from early religious ideas that each person has the capacity to choose to do either good or evil. For instance, Adam and Eve chose to eat the apple and thus brought about the wrath of God and their own eviction from the Garden of Eden. Until the Reformation, however, it was assumed that the rewards for good behavior would not necessarily be made manifest in this life. With the Reformation, religious thought (particularly that of Calvinism) put even more emphasis on the importance of rigid "self-control." With the rise of secularism, the idea that life after death consists of either eternal punishment or eternal bliss became less and less popular. The rewards for autonomy today are to be experienced in the here and now. Although secularized, the idea that individuals are autonomous, self-controlled entities who can choose the sort of life they wish to lead remains as popular as ever.[1]

A modern version of the autonomous individual is the "self-actualized" person. The autonomous march to the "beat of their own drummers." They make enough money to satisfy their own needs but never allow their needs to be so excessive that they become "wage slaves." They see to it that their jobs are "relevant." They learn how to take off excess pounds by eating sensibly and by "running for their lives." They learn how to avoid stress, how to have "healthy relationships" and "joyous sex lives," how to "say no without feeling guilty," how to "look out for #1," how to become assertive, how to raise perfect children, how to give up smoking or other harmful drugs, how to "avoid the coming bad times," and all the other things that scores of *how to* books tell people they will be able to accomplish if they put their minds to it. The fact that these books are best-sellers attests to the hold that the idea of autonomy has on the popular culture.

These books range from the Horatio Alger novels about poor boys who worked hard selling newspapers and eventually became millionaires to those by Norman Vincent Peale, *The Power of Positive Thinking*[2] and *You Can If You Think You Can*[3], and by Wayne Dyer, *Your Erroneous Zones*[4] and *Pulling Your Own Strings.*[5]

One doesn't have to read a full length book to learn how to take advantage of the autonomy that many tell us is inherent in all individuals. Each month, magazines run articles that stress this theme. For instance, the cover for the September 4, 1979 issue of *Woman's Day* says that inside are articles on "The Surefire Key to Success—Learn What You Want to Do," "All Tensed Up? Try Our 5 Stress Beating Exercises," and "Why Some People Get Fat and What to Do About It."

When individual behavior is explained on the basis of individual autonomy, the poor are seen to be poor because of their own doing (or perhaps lack of doing). They would not have to be poor if they really wanted to be otherwise; if they weren't so "lazy", if they just had "self-control." According to this reasoning, the poor should not receive welfare services, because such services destroy their motivation to do anything for themselves. They are content to rely on the fruits of the labors of others. Sometimes, however, charity (which by this theory is defined as the voluntary sharing of the products of one's own labors to help the less fortunate through a period of hard times) can be endorsed, but this charity should be only temporary because it tends to destroy the "incentive to work." The poor (being autonomous) will seek to remain sufficiently poor to receive aid because they easily learn to enjoy being taken care of by others.

This theme was stated by Malthus in 1798 when he wrote, "dependent poverty ought to be held disgraceful." The poor person "has no claim of right on society for the smallest portion of food beyond which his labour will fairly purchase," and if he and his family were "saved from feeling the natural consequence of his imprudence, he would owe it to the pity of some kind benefactor."[6]

In 1845, in the United States, the New York Association for Improving the Condition of the Poor printed a manual of instruction for its "friendly visitors" that stated that "the evils of improvidence can never be diminished, except by removing the cause by elevating the moral character of the poor and by teaching them to depend on themselves.

Since the idea of individual autonomy is still dominant in the popular culture, it is still utilized to explain the existence of poverty. One encounters it nearly every time one questions the reasons for poverty and inequality. One often hears that "jobs are available but the poor are too spoiled to take them," that "people who are smart enough to become welfare cheaters are also smart enough to support themselves if they only would," that the poor should be "forced to take jobs so that they learn the value of work," and so on.

President Carter's proposal for welfare reform would provide grants for all families whose income is below the poverty line. The grants would be sufficient to bring the family income up to 65 percent of the poverty line.* Thus the families would be only 35 percent poor.[8] Presumably this is enough to keep them from actually starving but not enough to destroy their incentive to find gainful employment. The proposal is a considerable improvement over the policy advocated by Malthus, but it still assumes that individuals are responsible for their poverty, if only for a portion of it.

Irving Kristol's article, "Human Nature and Social Reform," uses the theory of the autonomous individual to criticize welfare services.[9] Kristol states that human beings possess an innate characteristic called motivation. This motivation, if left alone or if supported by educational programs, will enable individuals to be successful and to avoid a life of poverty, crime, or dependency. He goes on to say that welfare programs as they are presently constituted destroy this natural motivation and foster the very characteristics they were ostensibly developed to prevent and that the only reform that should be instituted is elimination of present welfare programs so that the natural motivation of those receiving welfare services can reassert itself and guide them toward a successful, independent, productive life.

The Programmed Individual

In contrast to the autonomous individual, where the issue involves the will to perform in a certain way, the theory of the programmed individual is concerned with the specific behavior in which individuals engage. The theory of the programmed individual states that there are internal mechanisms of control that cause the individual to behave in a determined fashion. These arise either from some innate organic characteristics or from earlier experi-

---

* For the full presentation of this proposal, see Chapter 8, Document 2

ences that developed built in directives. In either case the individual has little control over what his or her behavior will be in any given situation.

Some of the early proponents of this theory such as Bain and McDougall, stated that the programming was inborn or instinctual, that the behavior of individuals emanated from internal characteristics present at birth, and that these tendencies toward behavior were subject to little modification by experience following birth.[10, 11]

These early statements of the theory were modified, particularly by Freud,[12] to include the idea that an individual becomes programmed by his or her early experiences, most of which are provided by one's father and mother. If these early experiences are well managed, then proper progamming results, and the individual proceeds through life meeting each new challenge with success and happiness. If the programming is defective, it is not the fault of the individual but, rather, the fault of the parents or other caretakers. This defective programming results in unsuccessful behavior on the part of the individual. If successful behavior is to appear, the individual must relive in his or her mind the early experiences and during this process establish a reprogramming of the early experiences so that satisfactory behavior can result.

According to Erikson[13], Glaser and Strauss[14], and Levinson[15], the programming results in a series of crises that individuals must traverse in the course of their lives. If they resolve these crises satisfactorily, their lives will be fulfilling and successful; if not they will experience frustration and a sense of failure. The theory of the programmed individual was popularized by G. Sheehy in her book *Passages*,[16] in which she states that it is determined that adults pass through certain identifiable crises that they must resolve if their lives are to be successful and happy.

Early organized approaches to welfare services explained poverty and underprivilege through the theory of the autonomous individual. The subsequent view that internal characteristics of individuals prevented them from modifying their behavior to take advantage of the resources in their surroundings led to the emergence of a new approach in dealing with the poor and underprivileged. The problem of the poor was defined in 1940 by Gordon Hamilton as "The person whose 'congenial drives' [sic] are not provided for in his culture is in a bad way, and if what he wants to do is strongly disapproved by society he may be in a very bad way indeed."[17]

The new techniques for dealing with the problems of the poor are called "treatment," "case work," "group work," or "therapy." These endeavor to assist the poor and underprivileged on an individualized basis. The objective of the one-by-one approach is to find out what internal characteristics or "congenial drives" are prohibiting the individual from "self-determination and self-development."[18] The effort of the worker is then to correct the impact of previous experiences that programmed the individual improperly, to teach the individual skills so that his or her inner propensities could be satisfied in the situation, or to find a situation in which the individual could live that would be better suited to his or her unique capabilities.

The explanation of individual behavior by the theory of the programmed individual is prevalent in the popular culture, especially when it comes to giving reasons why certain persons are poor. For instance, a high proportion of the black American and Hispanic populations are poor and receive welfare services. This observation leads many people to the prejudiced conclusion that there is some inherent defect in the personal makeup of members of these minority groups that prevents them from obtaining permanent employment or living in adequate housing. When one says that a certain member of a minority group is poor because of skin color or ethnic background, that person is applying the theory of the programmed individual in a disciminatory way by saying that skin color or ethnic backgound is an inherent characteristic that determines that individual members of minority groups will continue to behave in ways that will keep them poor.

The Mechanical Individual

The theory of the mechanical individual states that individuals respond predictably to the external forces that impinge upon them. Rather like a weather vane, which faces north when the wind blows from the north, the theory of the mechanical individual states that individuals will behave in response to the cues that they receive from their environment. This theory differs from that of the programmed individual in one important respect: the theory of the programmed individual is primarily concerned with *internal* forces that determine behavior whereas the theory of the mechanical individual is concerned primarily with *external* forces that determine behavior .

John Watson, one of the earliest proponents of the theory of the mechanical individual, developed the terms stimulus and response, stating that a stimulus is a condition that calls out for action, which is the response. A stimulus is provided by the environment, external to the body; the response follows immediately upon the presentation of the stimulus.[19] Shortly thereafter, Pavlov wrote about his famous dog that could give a specific response to a specific stimulus, such as salivation at the sound of a bell or the lifting of a paw upon receiving a small electrical shock.[20] The importance of Pavlov's experiments is that individuals can learn to provide specific responses to specific stimuli. For the purposes of simplification and clarity, we call this the theory of the mechanical individual because the person acts much like a machine, behaving in response to inputs from the external, mainly physical, environment. In an automobile, for instance, if one puts gasoline in the tank, uses the proper procedures to start the engine, engages the gears, and steers the machine properly, it will transport the operator to the destination. However, improper fuel, poor starting procedures, placing the transmission in reverse, and steering left rather than right will prevent the machine from reaching the destination. A specific response requires a specific stimulus.

The most famous contemporary proponent of the theory of the mechanical individual is B. F. Skinner. His research contributed to an approach to the modification of behavior called conditioning therapy. Conditioning therapy stems from the conception that unsatisfactory individual behavior represents persistent unadaptive habits that have been learned. What needs to be done, then, is to undo the habit patterns that cause the undesired behavior and substitute other more satisfactory, stimuli so that satisfactory behavior will result.[21] Sheldon Rose, in *Behavioral Therapy*[22], describes how techniques based on conditioning therapy can be used by human services professionals to change the behavior of parents who receive Aid to Families with Dependent Children (AFDC).

The Evolutionary Individual

In Chapter 2, we described the three essential elements of evolutionary theory: the importance of change, the progression from simple to complex forms of life, and the directionality of change. The theory was then applied to society. When used to explain individual behavior, this approach emphasizes that individuals are constantly changing, that they change in a certain direction, and move from simple to complex behavior.

Most of those who utilize evolutionary theory to explain individual behavior do so in conjunction with the theory of the programmed individual, the programming being an internal disposition to act in a way that develops from a combination of internal characteristics and life experiences. This internal disposition to act can be identified throughout the life span of the individual. There are appropriate behaviors that vary as the individual evolves from infant to child to adolescent to adult to senior citizen. If individuals exhibit behavior judged to be appropriate to the stage of their evolution, they are said to be developing satisfactorily, and it can be anticipated that they will move to the next stage of development without difficulty.

The theories of Erik Erikson might also be placed in this category. He writes of the "eight ages of man" and discusses the "strengths" that must be gained in those consecutive stages of development (evolution): oral sensory, muscular anal, locomotor genital, latency, puberty and adolescence, young adulthood, adulthood, and maturity.[23]

Piaget, the Swiss psychologist, states that there are stages in the development of the ability to think and reason that also evolve in a logical fashion, one after the other.[24] Kohlberg and his associates at Harvard state that an individual's moral development tends to progress through an orderly series of sequential stages. The Kohlberg view is based on six stages of moral thought, with the individual's ability to progress from one to another depending on corresponding progress in the ability to think and reason.[25]

The theory of the evolutionary individual when combined with the theory of the programmed individual is used widely by human services personnel. Home economists such as Goldberg and Deutsch[26] describe how individuals in families progress through a predictable life cycle. When an individual has difficulty progressing from one developmental stage to another, welfare services can facilitate the evolutionary process by assisting individuals to live up to the demands that each phase of life presents for them.

In *Social Group Work, A Helping Process,* Konopka describes the evolution of group experiences for the individual as he or she progresses through the various phases of life. Konopka utilizes the evolutionary scheme of progression of Erikson, and shows how a social worker can use the group setting to assist individuals "at each stage of development to find fulfillment through qualitative group associations or they will be damaged in one way or another."[27]

The Integrative Individual

The theories of the individual presented up to this point have concentrated on a single major determinant of behavior. The theories of the autonomous, programmed, and evolutionary individual focus on the origin of behavior from inside the individual; the theory of the mechanical individual focuses on the external factors which influence that individual's behavior.

Others have looked at these theories and have seen validity in both points of view. Hence those theorists state that a satisfactory explanation of individual behavior must take into account both the internal and the external determinants for behavior. This approach is called the theory of the integrative individual because it sees individual behavior as the result of a constant process of adaptation to inner desires, expectations, and emotions as well as to the desires, expectations, and emotions of other persons, the process taking place in specific settings.

Early twentieth century scholars Charles Cooley and George Herbert Mead noted that individuality developed in humans as a result of their interaction with others, particularly with those whose contact they valued highly.[28] Moreover, individuals tend to define themselves according to how they think they are perceived by important persons about them.[29]

Contemporary writers such as Goffman[30] and Hewitt[31] have taken the ideas of Mead and Cooley and have elaborated on the situational aspects of this interaction between the individual and others about him or her. These writers state that behavior is situated; that is, it takes place in specific time and space settings. A single individual behaves in a variety of situations throughout any given day. According to the integrative point of view, the combination of the place of the interaction and the time in the life of the individual when the experience takes place must be taken into account to obtain the best explanation of behavior.

Those who explain behavior in terms of the integrative individual point out that the inner, interpersonal, and situational aspects of behavior require a relative rather than an absolute approach to the explanation of individual behavior.[32] This approach holds that it is not possible to describe any single individual as either "this" or "that": the description, rather, depends on the situation in which the individual is behaving, on the persons with whom the individual is interacting and on the way in which the individual defines himself or herself as a result of previous experiences. So, the behavior of the individual can be understood only in light of the constant integration that the individual performs in attempting to behave in a fashion that strikes a balance between internal demands, demands from others, and demands placed on the individual resulting from the space and time in which behavior takes place.

This theory is still in the process of being refined and has not as yet had much impact on human services personnel. Recently, however, the idea of the integrative approach is beginning to be recognized by writers in the human services field such as Pincus and Minahan

> a [theoretical] model should avoid conceptualizing social work practice in such dichotomous terms as person/environment, clinical practice/social action, and microsystems/macrosystems. We believe the strength of the profession lies in recognizing and working with the connections between these elements.[33]

The Evaluation of Human Behavior

Up to now, we have been discussing theories that attempt to explain why individuals behave as they do. What we have not discussed is why some behaviors might be preferred over others. This decision is made by the use of values and norms. An understanding of values and norms is important because human services professionals are expected to go a step beyond the scholars who theorize about the society or the behavior of individuals. They are expected to "do something" to change the behavior and the circumstances of their clients. Before this can be done, the human services worker must make a judgment in regard to which aspects of the client's behavior or circumstances are satisfactory and which are problematic.

To illustrate, human services workers in the course of their duties constantly make evaluations and decide on courses of action in such areas as

1. Whether an individual who comes to a public assistance agency needs financial help and, if so, how much.
2. Whether the individual who seeks aid needs psychological counseling.
3. In the case of a child referred to an agency, whether conditions in the home warrant removing the child from the home, to a foster home, group home, protective services, or the like.
4. If an individual has committed a crime, whether to recommend probation, incarceration, or parole.
5. Whether educational assistance might help an individual learn job related skills, homemaking, parenting, and so on.
6. Whether activities should be provided for individuals who might otherwise create disruption in their neighborhoods.
7. Whether conditions of housing, sanitation, safety, and public services in a section of the city are satisfactory, particularly in relation to the effect that these conditions may have on the residents of the area.

8. Whether an individual suffering from an illness is also facing psychological or financial problems and if so, the assistance necessary to help the individual resume independent life in the community.
9. Whether services should be provided for an elderly person and, if so, the kinds of services necessary.

It is not possible for evaluations to be made unless there are some yardsticks by which the worker makes comparisons. If, for instance, an individual says that he or she does not have enough money for food, clothing, or medical care, how does the worker make the judgment that this is indeed the case. The worker will ask certain questions. How much money is needed? Is the individual employed? If not, why is the individual unemployed? Are there others that are affected by the individual's lack of resources?

The fact that these questions are apparent to most of us suggests that there might be reasons why these questions are raised instead of others.* One reason is that certain values exist in our society that are pertinent to the operation of welfare services. These values may be defined as the goals toward which individual behavior is directed. For instance, in the American society there is the *value* of taking care of those with insufficient resources. There is the *value* of promoting health rather than illness. There is the *value* of work and thus there is the *value* of being responsible for providing one's own material resources. Because these *values* exist in our society, the questions raised here and their answers provide the yardsticks used by human service workers to decide what should be done.

The behaviors that individuals utilize to accomplish these *values* are governed by complicated sets of rules that permit certain kinds of behaviors and prohibit others. These rules are often called *norms*. We will discuss some of the *norms* that have relevance for welfare services.

Absolute Norms

Some of the rules that govern individual behavior have existed in our society, often without much change for a considerable period of time. These rules are to be observed by all members of the society to which they pertain without exception. These are called absolute norms.

One of the most familiar series of absolute norms are the Ten Commandments contained in the Old Testament of the *Bible*. Some present-day examples of absolute norms are

1. Everyone must wear clothes.
2. All children between the ages of six and sixteen must attend school.

---

* For instance, questions such as has the individual ever been to Denmark? Or, at what age did one learn to cut his or her toenails? These questions probably would not occur to us as important in this situation and, indeed, they are not.

3. People must place food in their mouths with their hands or by using a knife, fork, or spoon. People do not lap up their food from a bowl on the floor.
4. Parents must care for their children.
5. At least one person in the family must work to provide the family necessities.
6. An individual should be on welfare only temporarily.

Absolute norms are so pervasive in society that most individuals see it as their responsibility to adhere to them. The norms are taught at an early age and they become a part of the individual's consistent method of behavior. Without voluntary adherence to absolute norms, no amount of enforcement by public agencies would be effective in assuring obedience.

Absolute norms are frequently expressed through formal rules and regulations, the enforcement of which is the province of the public agency concerned–the police, the school, or the welfare department. All persons to whom absolute norms apply are expected to abide by them.

Relative Norms

In contrast to norms that are perceived as permanent and universally applicable, some rules of behavior exist in relation to the circumstances in which the individual finds himself or herself. What is normal *depends.* Certain behavior is valued, but the specifics of that behavior depend on the circumstances (the time and the place in which that behavior takes place).

This year "keeping up with the Jones" may require the purchase of a station wagon. Next year the requirement might be a small car or a four-wheel-drive vehicle. Young people who would not dream of smoking pot in their parents' home often do so with their peers. A person might pray in church on Sunday that the poor be relieved of the burden of their poverty and on Monday raise the rent on the dilapidated houses that he or she owns in the center of the city. There is no perceived incongruity between the two actions taken, for what the person does *depends* on the situation in which the individual finds himself or herself. When the rules for behavior vary from situation to situation they are called relative norms. There are other examples. One wears different clothes to school or to work than one wears to a formal party. One applauds an entertainer in a theater setting but does not applaud when a soloist sings well in church. The difference between relative norms and absolute norms and among relative norms themselves often are responsible for argument, discussion, and controversy.

Take, for instance, the value that our society places on life, the absolute norm being that killing is always wrong in all situations. The relative norm that is derived from this states that some killing is all right if it is done to protect another's life. Thus, under some circumstances, the uniformed police officer is not punished for killing a criminal or the marine for killing an enemy of the country. The Supreme Court ruling that abortion is legal until after the third month of pregnancy is an example of an attempt to make a legal application of a relative norm. It shows how a norm can move from absolute to relative and back again.

Norms once perceived as absolute can give way to relative norms over a period of time. A "woman's place is in the home" was accepted as an absolute norm not too long ago. As a result, women were generally excluded from work outside the home except for menial, low-paying jobs. This view has changed radically in the last fifty years, so that now nearly 50 percent of adult women in the United States are gainfully employed outside the home. Therefore, whether or not a mother seeks employment will *depend* on how old the children are, the availability of baby-sitters, the financial needs of the family, her personal desires, her job skills, her husband's attitude toward her employment, and so on. Many women work until their first child is born, take time off while the child is young, and go back to work when they decide the time is right for doing so. The absolute norm that a woman's place is in the home has given way to the relative norm that a woman can now be gainfully employed under certain circumstances.

Child labor is another example of the change in norms. As recently as 70 years ago, young children worked 12 and 14 hours a day under appalling conditions in factories and mines. They were often given jobs that were considered too unpleasant for the grownups. Most people, if they thought about it at all, believed this to be a good thing. The working children brought money home to their families, and the work kept them out of trouble.[34]

Over the years, however, it was perceived that this kind of treatment was not good for growing children; moreover, technological developments eliminated many of the jobs held by children as requirements for technical skills increased. Child labor laws were passed so that today, if a parent were to force his or her child to work at these backbreaking tasks[35] the parents would be considered child abusers and would probably be prohibited from such behavior by a law enforcement agency. A child must now have a work permit to be employed, and the working conditions are usually rigidly spelled out and monitored.

On the other hand, most newspapers are still being delivered by young people, and migrant workers' children frequently labor in the fields with their parents. Work permits for jobs can be obtained for many reasons. The absolute norm regarding the value of work that prevailed against "the sloth of children, their idleness by which they are corrupted"[36] has given way to the relative norm that children probably shouldn't work but are often permitted to do so, *depending* on the situation.

Normative Pluralism

A distinguishing characteristic of the American society is that it is made up of many differing groups with differing standards that they apply to themselves and to the world about them. Groups have differing standards by class[37], by place of residence[38], by region of the country in which they live[39], by ethnic group[40], and by religious affiliation.[41] Each of these utilizes absolute and relative norms close enough to those existing in the overall American society for these groups to remain members of it, but there is enough variation among the groups in their unique definition of absolute and relative norms that the resulting behavior can vary considerably. This condition is known as "normative pluralism."

An example is the widely held value that a commitment should be made by persons who desire to live together. The absolute norm for this value dictates that a man and woman must be legally married, particularly if they wish to raise a family. The right to make the laws governing marriage and divorce is by the U.S. Constitution reserved to the states; thus the laws enacted to regulate the behavior of individuals around marriage vary considerably from state to state. Some states demand a waiting period or a blood test before issuing a license. Some do not. Divorces can be obtained for a variety of reasons depending on the state of residence. In some, it is possible to remarry almost immediately. In others, a long waiting period is still required. Some outlaw cohabitation. Others interpret cohabitation in almost the same terms as a legalized marriage.

Religious interpretations vary even more, ranging from seeing divorce as impossible, because a marriage is considered to be an indissolvable sacrament, to seeing divorce as a matter of individual conscience over which formal church regulations have no control.

Ethnic and class membership of marrying couples dictates the manner of courtship and the type of celebration that follows the marriage ceremony. Of course, the ceremony itself varies enormously.

There are many other examples of normative pluralism. For instance, one might interpret smiling to be a universal expression of pleasure. But the frequency and manner of smiling varies from region to region in the United States. B. and E. Feder state

> a person's smile makes him or her noticed away from home. The Americans who smile the most live in the Southeast, those who smile the least live along the Great Lakes. Southerners in Buffalo, New York will stand out for their extraordinary propensity to smile. A young woman may smile with impunity at strangers on Atlanta's Peachtree Street, but to do so in New York's Times Square would invite unwelcome advances or an arrest for soliciting.[42]

In the same article Dr. Benjamin Spock is quoted as noting that

> one of the sharpest differences between today's middle aged people and young adults is the tendency of the older group to smile automatically— at cab drivers, at salespersons or at individuals to whom they are being introduced. Younger adults tend not to smile under similar circumstances.

The example of smiling may seem somewhat inconsequential, but it is not. Human services workers are frequently called upon to make evaluations of the behavior of their clients. Thus, a worker from New England might conclude that the frequent smiles of a client from the South indicates a lack of seriousness or even instability, whereas a worker from the South might classify a client from the North as sullen or depressed because he or she rarely smiles.

Normative pluralism can be observed even in a single community. The overall American society attaches great value to work. This value is so close to an absolute norm that it is almost unheard of for anyone to advocate idleness. Nonetheless, the interpretation of this norm as it applies to welfare programs comes closer to normative pluralism than it does to an absolute norm. One group in a community might advocate that welfare programs be abolished because they feel that such programs discourage work. Another might feel that programs should be set up so that they force persons to work for the assistance they receive. Still another group might advocate a program in which the assistance given is tied to the standard of living and has no relationship to whether or not a member of a family works because they feel that such a program furnishes the most encouragement for people to work.

Human services workers are called upon to recognize the regional, ethnic, and religious differences that exist to understand the manner in which differences arise regarding the application of norms to welfare services. They should also understand these differences to avoid misjudging the behavior of the recipients of welfare services.

The existence of the variety of norms often creates a dilemma for human services workers because the agencies for which they work are governed by laws and regulations (absolute norms) that are supposed to be enforced whenever they are applicable, without exception. These absolute norms often run counter to the norms of the worker who may believe that other rules should apply rather than the official ones of the agency. The recipient of services on the other hand may believe that the agency and the worker should permit behavior different either from that expected by the agency or from the worker.

Despite the normative pluralism that exists in the United States, the absolute norm that couples must be married if they are to indulge in sexual activity is still enforced by welfare agencies. Although the days may have passed when human services workers were sent out to spy on persons obtaining public assistance, it is possible for a woman who receives financial assistance through the Aid to Families with Dependent Children program to have her benefits taken away if it becomes known that she is cohabiting with a man outside the bounds of marriage.

Summary

In this chapter we have discussed five classifications of theories about individual behavior according to the assumptions that each makes about the causation of behavior. We also discussed the derivation and use of norms in judging or evaluating behavior.

The first three explanations for individual behavior concentrate on the internal characteristics of individuals. The fourth concentrates on the external forces to which individuals respond. The fifth utilizes both the internal characteristics of an individual and the situational aspects in which the individual finds himself or herself to explain behavior. This last approach (the integrative approach) is not yet widely used by human services professionals.

Human services workers are obliged to make judgments about the behavior of the recipients of welfare services. These judgments are made in accordance with rules, often called norms. Absolute norms, which are rules of fairly long standing, are expected to be observed by everyone to whom they apply. Relative norms are used more selectively depending on the situation to which the behavior is related. Both absolute and relative norms exist side by side in the American society. Furthermore, both absolute and relative norms can vary depending on the ethnic or residential characteristics of the group or the geographical area of the country. This complicates the task of the human services worker as he or she applies the rules to recipients of welfare services.

Theories of individual behavior explain how behavior develops and suggest the techniques to change it. Values and norms are utilized to make judgments about what should be changed in individual behavior. Theories and norms for behavior derive from the social structure, and are comparable with the directionality of the society.

All these theories and norms are at one time or another used by human services workers to accomplish the objective of welfare programs. We stated in Chapter 2 that welfare programs are functional; that is, they operate to maintain order and stability in society. Since this is the case, services to individuals (the major concentration of services in welfare programs) generally contribute to the order and stability of society as well because the theories and norms generally utilized in welfare programs are those that emphasize individual responsibility rather than societal responsibility for a person's behavior. Furthermore, most programs use theories and norms that emphasize the necessity for the individual to adapt his or her behavior to the requirements of society. They almost never emphasize the idea that society should be modified to accommodate the individual.

This brief discussion of the explanations of society and of individual behavior show how they complement each other in the operation of welfare services in the American society. This background is necessary if one is to understand the organizational and programmatic characteristics of American welfare services.

Chapters 4 and 5 will present a history of the development of welfare programs, which will add the context of time to your understanding of the contemporary structure of welfare programs and services.

References

1. Weber, M. *The Protestant Ethic and the Spirit of Capitalism*. New York: Scribner, 1958, pp. 99–128.
2. Peale, N. V. *The Power of Positive Thinking*. Englewood Cliffs, N.J.: Prentice-Hall, 1954.
3. Peale, N. V. *You Can If You Think You Can*. Englewood Cliffs, N.J.: Prentice-Hall, 1974.
4. Dyer, W. *Your Erroneous Zones*. New York: Crowell, 1976.
5. Dyer, W. *Pulling Your Own Strings*. New York: Crowell, 1978.
6. Malthus, T. *Essays on the Principles of Population*. London: J. Johnson, 1798, p. 341.
7. Coll, B. *Perspectives in Public Welfare*. Washington, D.C.: Dept. of Health, Education, and Welfare, 1971, p. 22.
8. *Milwaukee Journal*, September 14, 1979, Part 1, p. 6.
9. Kristol, I. "Human Nature and Social Reform," *The Wall Street Journal*, October 18, 1978, p. 11.
10. Bain, A. *On the Study of Character*. London: Longmans, Green & Co., 1862.
11. McDougall, W. *An Introduction to Social Psychology*. Boston: J. W. Luce, 1915.
12. Freud, S. *Three Contributions to the Theory of Sex*. New York: Dutton, 1962.
13. Erickson, E. *Childhood and Society*. New York: Norton, 1963, pp. 261–263.
14. Glaser, B., and Strauss, A. *Status Passages*. Chicago: Aldine, 1971.
15. Levinson, D. *The Seasons of a Man's Life*. New York: Knopf, 1978.
16. Sheehy, G. *Passages: Predictable Crises of Adult Life*. New York: Dutton, 1976.
17. Hamilton, G. *Theory and Practice of Social Case Work*. New York: Columbia, 1940, pp. 26–30.
18. *Ibid.*, p. 30.
19. Watson, J. B. *Psychology from the Standpoint of the Behaviorist*. Philadelphia: Lippincott, 1919.
20. Pavlov, I. *Conditioned Reflexes*. New York: Dover, 1960.
21. Wolpe, J., et al. eds. *The Conditioning Therapies*. New York: Holt, 1964.
22. Rose, S. *Group Therapy: A Behavioral Approach*. Englewood Cliffs, N.J.: Prentice-Hall, 1978, pp. 167, 173–181.
23. Erickson, E. *Op. cit.*, pp. 261–263.
24. Elkind, D. *Children and Adolescents: Interpretive Essays on Jean Piaget*. New York: Oxford, 1970.
25. Kohlberg, L., and Gilligan, C. "The Adolescent as Philosopher," *Daedalus* (Fall 1971): 1051–1086.
26. Goldberg, S. and Deutsch. F. *Life Span Individual and Family Development*. Monterey, Calif.: Brooks-Cole, 1977.
27. Konopka, G. *Social Group Work: A Helping Process*. Englewood Cliffs, N.J.: Prentice-Hall, 1963, p. 48.
28. Cooley, C. *Human Nature and the Social Order*. New York: Scribner, 1922.
29. Mead, G. H. *Mind, Self, and Society*. Chicago: Univ. of Chicago, 1934.
30. Goffman, E. *The Presentation of Self in Everyday Life*. New York: Anchor, 1959.
31. Hewitt, J. *Self and Society*. Boston: Allyn, 1979.

32. Kagan, J. *The Growth of the Child.* New York: Norton, 1978.

33. Pincus, A., and Minahan, A. *Social Work Practice: Model and Method.* Itasca, Ill.: Peacock, 1973, p. xii.

34. Bettmann, O. *The Good Old Days—They Were Terrible.* New York: Random House, 1974, ch. 9.

35. *Ibid.,* pp. 76, 79.

36. *Ibid.,* p. 78.

37. Warner, L., et al. *Social Class in America.* New York: Harper, 1960, pp. 12–15.

38. Banfield, E. *The Unheavenly City Revisited.* Boston: Little, Brown, 1974, p. 53.

39. Douglass, J. *Defining America's Social Problems.* Englewood Cliffs, N.J.: Prentice-Hall, 1974, p. 20.

40. Whiting, B., ed. *Six Cultures, Studies of Child Rearing.* New York: Wiley, 1963.

41. Nowak, M. *The Rise of the Unmeltable Ethnics.* New York: Macmillan, 1973, ch. 7.

42. Feder, B. and E. "Smiles," *Human Behavior* Vol. 7, No. 12 (December 1978): pp. 42–45.

chapter/4

The Emergence
of Formal
Welfare Programs

Social structure can be defined as the organizing principles of a society and the social forms that spring from these principles.[1] In the previous chapters we discussed a number of organizing principles of the social structure of American society that influence the social form of welfare programs. We now turn to another organizing principle—industralization—and discuss its effect on the social form of welfare programs.

An important characteristic of current welfare programs, one that distinguishes them from the earlier ways developed to care for the needy, is that present-day welfare programs are *formally* organized; that is, special units of society exist whose sole function it is to care for the needy. These units have been explicitly created according to laws; they operate according to stated purposes; they carry out their functions according to specific operating rules and procedures; and they utilize trained personnel to deliver the services.

This was not always the case. For most of recorded history such care as the needy received came from units of society that had many other functions to perform, such as the family, the local community, or the church. This care often depended on personal relationships between donors and recipients. As long as the responsibility for the care of the needy could be carried out on the basis of direct knowledge of who had to be cared for, care for the needy could be *informal*: that is, care did not require special units of society that had to abide by a code that governed performance and outcomes.

Industrialization wrought profound changes in the fabric of society, because, with industrialization, the local community gradually ceased to be economically self-sufficient. It therefore could no longer know or provide for the needy that might be in its midst.

Industrialization led to substitution of nonliving sources of energy for living sources, increase in the consumption of energy and raw materials, increase in production of finished goods for human use, development of technologies to accomplish these tasks, increase in the means to acquire these goods, and development of methods to distribute these goods where they are needed.[2,3] Technological development, a fundamental component of industrialization, consists of the devices, knowledges, and skills by which humans control and utilize physical and biological phenomena, including their own bodies.[4]

Industrialization was marked by a sharp rise in production of goods which could no longer be consumed by the local community. This led to the creation of transportation systems to distribute the goods to distant markets. This development also destroyed the old occupational structure and changed the character of the means of livelihood of members of the local community. Furthermore, as goods were transported into and out of the community, money became an increasingly important form of exchange. The growing necessity of using money created serious problems for individuals who now depended on steady employment and found great difficulty if, for any reason, they could not work.

Industrialization was accompanied by an increase in the size of the population,[5] and it concentrated workers in one setting, all doing specialized tasks. These persons were dependent on their single source of employment for their survival, and, when something happened to the factory, the center of production, large numbers of persons lost their means of support.

Increasingly sophisticated technology necessitated specialization. This furthered the development of technology, which in turn required more specialization. This development changed the amount and character of knowledge. That is, as knowledge increased, it became impossible for one person to know all there was to know so people concentrated on learning what they could about certain things that concerned them. Specialized knowledge led to specialized occupations, each providing a portion of the necessary goods furnished to the society. Specialization of occupations carried over into the provision for the needy, where the people who performed such services received salaries as did other workers in the society.

Specialization also furthered the development of large organizations to coordinate the efforts of the specialists. Étzioni summarizes this trend as follows:

Modern civilization depends largely on organizations as the most rational and most efficient form of social grouping known. By coordination of a large number of human actions, the organization creates a powerful social tool. It combines its personnel with its resources, weaving together leaders, experts, workers, machines, and raw materials. At the same time it continually evaluates how well it is performing and tries to adjust itself accordingly in order to achieve its goals . . . this allows organizations to serve the various needs of society and its citizens more efficiently than smaller and more natural groupings, such as families, friendship groups, and communities.[6]

In this chapter, we will discuss some of the changes that accompanied industrialization and relate these changes to the emergence of formal welfare services. Topics to be discussed are

1. changes in economic organization
2. centralization of power
3. objectivity
4. specialized knowledge
5. relativism
6. impersonalization
7. issues in emergence

Changes in Economic Organization

The way in which a society goes about producing goods and services is called its *economic organization*. Enormous changes have been wrought in the American economic organization by the industrial revolution. These changes gave rise to large welfare organizations.

During the eighteenth century, England pioneered in the substitution of water and steam for human and animal power. Americans were at first unable to duplicate the English inventions that had made the large textile mills in England possible. The problem was solved partly by industrial espionage. Factory plans were stolen and brought to the United States where they formed the basis of development of the great New England textile industry.

People also turned their creative energies to the improvement of agricultural production. As the factories expanded and hired more and more people and as transportation improved, farms began to produce greater surplus either of food for factory workers or raw materials like cotton. In fact, while industrialization is often perceived only as the development of the manufacturing capability of a society, just as basic to the development of industry is the ability of the society to produce sufficient food to support its workers in industry, most of whom moved from the land to the cities as industrialization proceeded.

In 1800, the year of the second census, the total U.S. population stood at 5,297,000, with 6 per cent living in urban areas. By 1900, massive immigration had increased the population to 76,000,000, with 40 per cent defined as living in urban areas.[7] In 1970, the census showed the number of people to be 204,000,000, of which 72 per cent of the whites and 81 per cent of the nonwhites lived in urban areas. Only 4 per cent of the civilian labor force was engaged in agriculture. In 170 years, there was almost a complete turnaround: the percentage of persons engaged in agriculture in 1800 was nearly equivalent to the percentage *not* engaged in agriculture by 1970.[8]

Ethnographic museums show the changes that have taken place. Some of these museums illustrate life at a specific period in early America as though time were frozen. Williamsburg and Old Sturbridge are well-known examples of this type of museum. Both show the houses, the barns, the shops, the equipment used for cooking, cleaning, lighting, heating, manufacture of various items used, and so on. Even as one admires the "charm" of early America, one is also struck by the discomfort suffered by the colonists and by the vast amount of hand labor necessary to get even the simplest of chores accomplished.

In another type of ethnographic museum now being built, several stages of development are shown. Illustrating how conditions changed over time, they thus form vivid links connecting the earlier periods to the present. In these museums, barns, houses, and equipment have been moved from their original locations and rebuilt in a parklike setting usually chosen because it is more accessible to a population center. The buildings are often grouped together by ethnic origin. An example is Old World Wisconsin near Milwaukee. When completed, it will have a Finnish section, a German section, an Irish section, and so on.

Museums of this sort do not attempt to make the restoration cute or quaint, and it is sometimes a shock to visitors who are conditioned by romanticized Hollywood and television versions of the "good old days" to see how early pioneers actually lived.

A typical log cabin was about the size of a single-car garage. A ladder might lead to sleeping quarters in the loft. Such a cabin often housed fifteen or more persons. During times of need, as many as forty persons might have lived together in a structure this size. These crowded conditions almost defy comprehension today. At the same time, these conditions reflect the informal welfare activities that existed at the time. As immigrants arrived they settled close to friends and relatives they had known in the Old World. When times were harsh, resources were pooled, and what was available was shared by all on the basis of need. If a family's house burned down in the winter, the whole family might move in with neighbors until spring made rebuilding possible. They produced their own food and clothing and only rarely found it important to buy at a store. They shared food and equipment with each other.

This kind of ethnographic museum also shows how, as industrialization proceeded and surpluses were accumulated, affluence developed and changed the pioneers' way of life. Close to a tiny log cabin one finds the farmhouse that replaced the log cabin. The newer house and the outbuildings are much larger than the original cabin, but fewer people would have lived in it. A third period shows a larger, more comfortable, farmhouse with labor-saving equipment and conveniences such as a cistern pump to provide water to the kitchen. Such luxury was undreamed of by the first pioneers.

Present-day farms can be observed for comparison. Air-conditioned, stereo-equipped tractors move over a landscape dominated by enormous barns. Irrigation pipes extend like spider webs. Overhead fly the crop-dusters. Present-day farms are large, mechanized, commercial establishments that make a high use of energy and have an equally high output of goods, most of which the farmer cannot consume. The produce of a modern farm must be sold to be of any use to the farmer who needs the money he gets in exchange to buy new equipment, clothing, the many conveniences that modern farm families enjoy, and what really emphasizes the change—most of the *food* eaten by the farmer and his family.

Among the many inventions that made these changes both necessary and possible were the cotton gin invented by Eli Whitney in 1792, the reaper by Cyrus McCormick in 1831, and the tractor by John Froelich in 1892. The labor of many people was replaced by technological improvements. As more and more machines were invented and brought into use, more and more acreage could be placed into production. Fewer people were needed to work the land, but jobs were available in the factories and mills in the cities. Thus as a decreasing number of farmers became more able to produce a surplus, there was also an increasing demand for the surplus produced.

Farmers today produce milk, beef, vegetables, cotton, and tobacco for people they will never see, never know, even as factory workers produce consumer items and machines for unknown users. Farmers do not know the people who are thrown out of work when a factory closes down, even as factory workers do not know what problems are encountered by farmers if they are forced off the land by economic or climatic conditions.

People can distribute goods and resources on the basis of need only to those for whom they know and care and only when they know what their needs are. When more is produced than is needed by the people one knows and when, at the same time, the production is desired by unknown persons, a whole new set of governing economic relationships develops. The introduction of these new governing relationships is one of the most important reasons for the introduction of formal welfare programs.

Centralization of Power

When a society reaches the stage at which it is able to produce surpluses that are useless to the producer unless sold in the marketplace, the struggle against scarcity takes on new dimensions, because the producers must exchange their surplus for other goods or commodities that they need or want.*

---

* When we speak of goods we mean more than material goods such as automobiles or food. Goods can also be social goods such as important jobs, inclusion in exclusive clubs, or psychological goods, such as popularity, respect, and deference from others.

When people need or want certain goods, they will tend to do whatever it takes to obtain these goods. They will tend to subject themselves to the conditions set by the owners of the goods to effect a successful conclusion to the exchange. Thus, those who control the surplus production of a much needed or wanted commodity have power, and, more important, those who control the distribution of a commodity have even greater power because they can withhold the product from the market to create greater demand and, thus, higher prices. Power comes from the ability to furnish (not merely to produce) goods that are desired by some other members of society.[9] As industrialization proceeded, it was quickly learned that, if the producer and the distributor of sought-after goods had power, even more power could be held by those who at the same time controlled both the production and the distribution of the desired goods. For this reason, auto manufacturers try to acquire iron mines, steel mills, rubber plantations, oil wells, and dealer agencies. Film makers try to acquire film studios, theater chains, and television networks. Food chains sometimes own large farms, feed lots, processing centers such as canning plants, and the supermarkets themselves. These large corporations often try to control the newspapers and television outlets to influence the buying habits of the public. Power becomes tremendously concentrated when a very few people control not merely the surplus that has been produced but also the economic activities of the mass of other people who are unable to gain this control over the production and distribution of goods.

The U.S. government made attempts to curb this centralization of money and power. The Sherman Antitrust Act of 1890 was enacted to regulate the consolidation of power, and other types of regulatory legislation followed. The federal income tax amendment to the Constitution was passed in 1909. Government control over continued concentration of economic power has become complicated and controversial. It has been only partially successful. Even with all the programs for controlling the excessive centralization of power over production and distribution of goods, the distribution of wealth in the United States is approximately the same as it was at the time of the American Revolution.[11, 12]

In their book *Regulating the Poor*, Piven and Cloward[13] state that only when those who controlled the production and distribution of the wealth of our society realized that they were in danger of losing their power because of mass discontent with the concentration of wealth did they institute large, centrally controlled organizations to dispense relief to the poor. These developments, described by Piven and Cloward, show that even as power is a major factor in concentrating the means of production and distribution, power is also a major factor in forcing a redistribution of the surplus of production to the poor, who otherwise would receive very little of the surplus. When, according to Piven and Cloward, the poor threatened the stability of the society, some adjustments in distribution were made. This adjustment prompted the development of large, formal organizations to dispense welfare services, because it was only through them that the programs of mass relief could be managed.[14]

Objectivity

In the industrial society, it is not sufficient to know only how to dispose of one's surplus production in the local markets. One must also know the characteristics and wants of those markets dispersed over a wide geographical area. Furthermore, a producer must acquire knowledge of a variety of new technologies as they appear in order to maintain a competitive position. It is impossible to test every new machine personally or to visit every distant market to see for one's self. The subjective knowledge gained from direct experience must be augmented by objective knowledge gained from indirect or vicarious experience.

Objectivity is characterized by emphasis upon viewing ideas, phenomena, events, and so on as external and apart from one's self.[15] To be objective is to be detached, impersonal, and unprejudiced. Objectivity is the stated aim of the scientific method of gaining knowledge.

When enough objective knowledge is amassed, it is possible to make generalizations that presumably apply to a larger sample of whatever is being studied. It is also possible to separate these large samples into smaller segments that share similar characteristics, that is, to categorize the groups to which the information applies.

One can see this process in operation in today's methods of marketing. In preindustrial times, when a cobbler made shoes for a specific individual, he could know, for instance, that Squire Martin's left foot was larger than his right foot. He would therefore make a pair of shoes that took this size differential into account. A modern shoe manufacturer is not concerned with Squire Martin's problem. Instead, he wants to find out how to make the fewest numbers of sizes of shoes and still fit the most people. He needs to obtain the objective knowledge that will enable him to generalize about the expected market. From these generalizations he will make shoes for categories of individuals, infants, teenagers, working people, business executives, the elderly, and so on.

The same process (recognition of the need for objective knowledge, the formation of generalizations, and the development of rules and categories) also took place in the provision of services to the needy. Before industrialization the members of a community knew the circumstances of the needy in a direct way. The poor were not very mobile, and the more well-to-do were able to manage the problems of the poor in the community.

As industrialization proceeded, large concentrations of poor people developed in the urban centers. It became necessary to develop programs to deal with many persons. Those who worked with the needy had no prior knowledge or relationship with the individual persons they wished to help.

Various eleemosynary groups began putting together objective studies in an attempt to understand the meanings and causes of poverty. Early schools of social work,[16] as well as other professional schools and social disciplines, also accumulated objective knowledge about the poor.

These objective studies made it possible to develop generalizations about the poor. As programs were set up, they made use of these generalizations to develop categories of recipients and rules about who should be served by the programs and the ways they should be served. This body of objective knowledge was utilized in the establishment of the large formal organizations that emerged following the Great Depression of the 1930s.

Over the years, both public and private welfare services have become more and more objective; that is, the services they offer are based more and more on studies, generalizations, categories, and rules.

Specialized Knowledge

A major ingredient for continued strength of an industrial society seems to be a continually evolving technology. Thus, technological development is highly prized, and a major effort is directed toward assuring that it takes place.[17]

In the early days of technological development, it was possible for individuals to know everything that had to be known to produce a certain item. The Wright brothers knew all the technology necessary to build and fly the first airplane, but it would have been impossible for the two brothers to know all that must be known to build a modern commercial airliner. That task requires the time and talent of thousands of persons.

As the body of technical knowledge expands, its application must be broken down into segments. Individuals become expert in each segment, and in this way knowledge becomes specialized rather than generalized. Modern institutions of higher education develop and distribute highly specialized knowledge in hundreds of fields ranging from art and accounting through engineering and classical Hebrew to zoology.

As the members of society come to know more and more about less and less, it becomes increasingly difficult to put the knowledge together so that complex tasks can be performed. The existence of specialized knowledge makes for challenging and complicated problems around the integration of effort.

How can the work of the electrician, the hydraulicist, the aerodynamicist, the sheet metal worker, the upholsterer, the painter, the riveter, the nutritionist, the instrument specialist, the truck driver, the janitor, the astronaut, and all the many others be coordinated so that they do what needs to be done, at the proper time and in the proper way, so that Americans can watch a man set foot on the moon on a television screen? Only a large organization such as the National Aeronautics and Space Administration could coordinate such a project.

In the field of welfare, there has also been an increase in specialized knowledge, which requires the coordinated effort of specialists possessing this knowledge if services are to be effective. The physician, teacher, social worker, police officer, judge, and counselor must work together if a neglected child is to receive services at the proper time and in his or her best interests. Only a large organization can bring together the many specialists who might deal with such a child and integrate their efforts in the child's behalf. A major factor in the development of large welfare organizations is the necessity to integrate the application of specialized knowledge and skills.

Relativism

As the body of objective knowledge expands and as individuals become specialists rather than generalists, definitions of problems change. Instead of defining a problem in absolute terms, it is more likely that the problem will be stated in relative terms.

In times past, poverty was defined in absolute terms. Persons who were in danger of starving to death or who had no clothing or shelter were poor. It was equally certain that if able bodied adults were poor they had some sort of moral defect. They were poor because they were lazy, improvident, drunken, or otherwise sinful.[18] Therefore, one knew what to do. In general, the poor were punished, made to work, or placed in institutions. A person who fell into debt was put into prison.

Although some still see poverty in these absolute terms, the majority of society does not. The definition of poverty that is accepted by the government, by human services professionals, and by the poor themselves is that the poor are those persons who have an income below a certain level known officially as the poverty line. This means that the poor are poor not because they are in imminent peril of freezing or starvation (although some may be) but because they have less income than do other members of society. In this way, poverty comes to have a relative definition; it is determined by one's relation to others in the society.

According to Banfield, "The poor today are not 'objectively' any more deprived relative to the nonpoor than they were a decade ago. Few will doubt, however, that they *feel* more deprived—that they perceive the gap to be wider and that, this being the case, it *is* wider in the sense that matters most."[19] The feeling of deprivation relative to the possessions of others means that, no matter what might be done, no permanent solution is possible. On the other hand, the overall society feels an obligation to care for the poor. The poor themselves feel that they should not be permitted to remain in a deprived state and make demands for a certain level of services.[20] This means that services to the poor under a relative definition of poverty will be a permanent feature of the society.

It was estimated in 1976 that 25 million persons lived in households with incomes below the official poverty line.[21] It is not possible for individuals or small groups to deliver services on a continuing basis to such a large group of the defined poor. Only large organizations can deliver these services. The emergence of the relative definition of poverty was then a major impetus to the development of large, formal welfare organizations.

Impersonalization

Today's industrial farmers use very little of what they produce. They sell to distributors and thus do not know the people who do use what they produce or the purpose for which their produce is used. The food they have grown may go to feed the starving or it may go to feed the grossly overweight.

Even as the self-sufficient farmer who produced most of his own food and clothing on site has given way to the mechanized farming industry, so has the cobbler become the large shoe manufacturing firm. The baker, the weaver, the iron monger, and all the preindustrial artisans have been supplanted by factory-produced goods wherein neither the workers nor the owners are able to know or care who uses the products or how they are used.

When the primary producers lost control over the uses of their product, they also lost control over any satisfaction other than the monetary reward that they might have had previously from knowing how what they produced was used. As industrialization spread, with its consequent limitation of satisfaction of production to the monetary reward, the manner in which people gave assistance to the needy also changed.

In earlier times the farmer might have decided to give food to needy persons nearby; the baker might agree to bake bread for a local widow and her children; the cobbler might provide a pair of shoes. The donors knew of the needs of the persons or groups to whom they were contributing.

The donors gave voluntarily; that is, the choice of whether or not to give was the choice of the individual donor. And the giving of the fruits of one's labor made the donor feel good. He or she was held in high esteem by other members of the community and also received recognition from those who received the largess, directly if the assistance were given locally or indirectly if the assistance were sent to another place, as was sometimes done under the auspices of various church groups.

As the donors became separated from the recipients, the donors were also no longer able to participate to any extent in defining what constituted need. The process of defining who was needy and what was needed was gradually turned over to persons who collected and distributed resources on a full-time basis, matching resources with need in terms of the definition of need, in terms of the timing of the assistance, and in terms of the geographical availability of resources. Giving became more and more impersonal.

Today, giving is done either involuntarily, through taxation, or quasi-voluntarily, through organized giving campaigns such as the United Way. While some benevolent and religious campaigns still exist, most support for the poor comes from taxation. This provides minimal satisfaction for the donors. The individuals and small groups who originally took upon them-selves the task of defining and caring for the needy have been supplanted by large organizations who hire specialists on a full-time basis. These organiza-tions distribute the resources (most of which is money collected involuntarily through taxation) to the categories of recipients who are defined as needy.

Issues in Emergence

In the raucous days of early industrialization, the conditions of those who lost out in the struggle for wealth were deplorable.[22] Problems of economic insecurity were seen only as local phenomena. Poverty had no recognition as a national concern.[23]

The nineteenth-century altruists, members of small groups trying to overcome the effects of large organizations who then were developing a national scope, struggled against great odds. It was during the latter part of the nineteenth-century that the giant industrial corporations such as U.S. Steel, New York Central, General Electric, and others were born. In their role as midgets trying to control giants the altruists had sufficiently difficult odds to face, but in addition, they also had ethical and normative battles to wage.

In America the altruistic ethic of concern for others has always been accompanied by the equally strongly held work ethic. Esteem tends to be equated with a sufficiency of worldly goods. The more material goods an individual has, the more that individual tends to be held in high esteem, awe, or fear. Those without material goods are held in pity, contempt, and disgust. The popular attitude in the nineteenth century was (and to a large extent still is) that one's material standing is the product of one's own efforts. The ethic states that if one is hard working, frugal, honest, and respectful of one's betters, one will also be self-sufficient. The fact that there were so many desperately poor people who were often working as hard as they possibly could did little to dispel the popular notion that one's economic situation was the result of one's own doing. The altruists were unable to change the overall state of affairs, but they were successful to some degree in focusing attention on the plight of the poor. In response, there was a growing recognition that something had to be done. Over a period of time, funds were gradually made available to the private efforts that tried to deal with the problems of the poor. At the beginning of the twentieth century, there began to emerge an occupational group known as social workers who were dedicated to the amelioration of the conditions of the poor. Most dealt only with individual needs and did not take on the additional task of trying to correct conditions that gave rise to poverty in the first place.

A few reformers during the latter part of the nineteenth century did feel that the situation of the poor was related to the organization of the society. They tried various methods to correct social conditions on the theory that, in this way, the wealth would be redistributed and poverty would be eliminated.

The efforts to create social movements to counteract the power of the large economic organizations were blunted by the arrival of Dr. Sigmund Freud who took the first of his many journeys to the United States in 1909. Freud had invented a new vocabulary that restated the old ethic that one's troubles are individual, not societal. According to Freud, individuals bring problems upon themselves unconsciously, but, if the individual can be set right, his or her troubles, economic and otherwise, will disappear. By extension, the society will be healthy when and if the individuals in it are made healthy. Lubove states that, as a result of Freud's influence, social workers moved away from any efforts at social reform. Instead they concentrated on "treating" individuals so that they could by their own efforts rise above the conditions that held them captive. No significant national effort emerged to control poverty by redistributing the wealth that was concentrated in the hands of those who controlled the large organizations.[24]

The Great Depression of the 1930s caused a change in the way in which the general population felt about poverty. As the economic decline spread over the country, many people found to their astonishment that poverty was indeed societal in origin; after years of hard work, frugality, honesty, and respectability, people who thought they were part of the middle class found that they were out of work. Savings disappeared, and people who thought it would be impossible for them to be needy found themselves selling apples on the street corners, forced into breadlines, even begging for food. The problems were immense, and no local group had the resources to make even a dent in alleviating the suffering.

Overnight, poverty had become more than trouble for some isolated individuals or groups. It became a national concern, a national issue.

In Chapter 2, we stated that the American society is functionally oriented; that is, it is oriented toward the maintenance of a socioeconomic condition in which change is held to a minimum. In the 1930s this stability was seriously threatened. The rich and powerful, who for the most part survived the market crash in 1929 and who still controlled the large business organizations, began to be concerned, for they could see that, if something was not done, the economic foundations of the country might crumble.[25] After all, the Russian Revolution had taken place less than twenty years before. The riots and the marches on Washington that took place in the early 1930s made the leaders fear that a revolution might be shaping up in the United States. This was not as irrational a fear as one might think today, for by 1932, when President Roosevelt was elected, unemployment had risen to 25 per cent of the total work force.[26]

Something had to be done, and the Roosevelt administration felt that the only place in which sufficient resources could be mustered to attack the problem was at the level of the federal government.

But what could be done?

Because resources had to be developed on a national scale to deal with a national problem, the only way in which to accomplish the task was to build large organizations to deliver welfare services just as large organizations had successfully facilitated the industrialization of the country.

The Civilian Conservation Corps (a youth aid program), the Works Progress Administration (a public works program), the Agricultural Adjustment Administration, the Federal Home Administration, and others were modeled after large industrial organizations. All were initially controlled out of a central headquarters in Washington, D.C. Later on, the states began to complain about the usurpation of their powers, and some of the organizations were decentralized through the development of state divisions. Others, however, such as the Social Security Administration, continued exclusively as a federal program.

These large welfare organizations were charged with restoring lost buying power. Those who could work were given jobs through public works programs; those who could not were given relief. Money was made available for loans and mortgages. After some anxious periods, the program showed that it would work at least sufficiently to maintain an uneasy stability. It was not necessary to face the issue of a fundamental redistribution of the nation's wealth.

Up to this time, welfare programs were generally residual, rather than institutional, but the Great Depression was so widespread a catastrophe that few wanted to take a chance that it might occur again. Some of the major welfare programs were therefore set up on a continuing, or institutional, basis. The Social Security program is an example.[27]

Summary

The appearance of permanent, large welfare organizations was one of the major political economic developments in the history of the United States. For the first time it was officially recognized that the economy on its own could not be trusted to take into account the best interests of all the individuals served by that economy. This development has not been without controversy, for it is interpreted in differing and often conflicting ways. The social reformers saw in this development the possibility that the government might at long last use its considerable resources to eliminate inequality, but the rich and powerful and many of the middle class saw the large, permanent welfare programs as necessary evils that should be cut back and even eliminated as soon as it was feasible.

Chapter 5 will focus on the chronology of persons and events in the emergence of welfare programs.

References

1. de Lone, R. *Small Futures*. New York: Harcourt, 1979, p. 10.
2. Lenski, G. *Power and Privilege*. New York: McGraw-Hill, 1966, ch. 10.
3. La Piere, R. *Social Change*. New York: McGraw-Hill, 1965, ch. 7.

4. *Ibid.*, p. 253.

5. Lenski, G. *Op. cit.*, pp. 301, 303.

6. Etzioni, A. *Modern Organizations.* Englewood Cliffs, N.J.: Prentice-Hall, 1964, p. 1.

7. U.S. Dept. of Commerce, Bureau of the Census. *Historical Statistics of the United States, 1789–1945.* Washington, D.C.: G.P.O., 1949.

8. U.S. Dept. of Commerce, Bureau of the Census. *Statistical Abstrcts of the United States, 1973.* Washington, D.C.: G.P.O., 1973.

9. Galbraith, J. *The New Industrial State.* New York: Mentor, 1967, pp. 58–64.

10. Hirsch, F. *Social Limits to Growth.* Cambridge, Mass.: Harvard U. P., 1976, p. 27.

11. Parker, R. *The Myth of the Middle Class.* New York: Liveright, 1972, p. 54.

12. Will R., and Vatter, H., eds. *Poverty in Affluence.* New York: Harcourt, 1965, pp. 23–47.

13. Piven, F., and Cloward, R. *Regulating the Poor.* New York: Vintage, 1971, ch. 2 and 3.

14. *Ibid.*, pp. 45–111.

15. Douglass, J. *Defining America's Social Problems.* Englewood Cliffs, N.J.: Prentice-Hall, 1974, ch. 2.

16. Axinn, J., and Levin, H. *Social Welfare: A History of the American Response to Need.* New York: Dodd, 1975, pp. 42, 88.

17. Hirsch, F. *Op. cit.*, pp. 27, 28.

18. Mandel, B., ed. *Welfare in America.* Englewood Cliffs, N.J.: Prentice-Hall, 1975, p. 6.

19. Banfield, E. *The Unheavenly City Revisited.* Boston: Little, Brown, 1974, p. 141.

20. *Ibid.*, p. 257.

21. De Lone, R. *Op. cit.*, p. 7.

22. Bettmann, O. *The Good Old Days—They Were Terrible.* New York: Random House, 1974, p. ix.

23. Axinn, J., and Levin, H. *Op.cit.*, pp. 33–50.

24. Lubove, R. *The Professional Altruist.* Cambridge, Mass.: Harvard U. P., 1965, ch. 4.

25. Domhoff, G. *Who Rules America?* Englewood Cliffs, N.J.: Prentice-Hall, 1967, ch. 2.

26. Axinn, J., and Levin, H. *Op. cit.*, p. 162.

27. Wilensky, H., and LeBeau, C. *Industrial Society and Social Welfare.* New York: Free Press, 1965, ch. 6.

chapter/5

Poor Law to Social Security: A Chronological History

This chapter provides a chronological history of social welfare programs in the United States beginning with their background in the Old World. To get from past to present, an orderly listing of the dates is important (e.g., the date of the first private orphanage or the first state operated prison), but it is more important to look behind each set of numbers at the change in perceptions that make each date important, to try to see the individuals or groups of individuals who, by their battles to promote something in which they believed, gave rise to the change.

People make history.

Like a Western, the story of welfare has its good guys and bad guys, its heroines and heroes, and its villains. There are people to cheer: Dorothea Dix and Jane Addams. There are people to hiss: Thomas Malthus and Franklin Pierce. But above all, the history of welfare is the story of people such as Charles Loring Brace and Josephine Shaw Lowell who were convinced that they were doing the right thing, but with whom it is easy to find fault, at least from a modern viewpoint.

The history of welfare is one of action and reaction, because as people identified a problem and attempted to find a solution, they also found that the solutions didn't always work out as they thought they would. Sometimes this was because conditions changed. Sometimes worthwhile solutions fell prey to those members of society who were only too happy to exploit the needy. Sometimes experience showed that the solutions were unworkable

It is also important to keep in mind that, while changes have taken place and are still taking place, these changes are rarely complete. Ideas linger in people's minds; the practices of the past hang on even though they sometimes take new names or renewed forms. For instance, although poor people are no longer forced to enter workhouses in America, there are still many who hold to the philosophy that led to the workhouses' creation. And there are others who would argue that today's prisons are a modern form of an ancient evil.

After saying this, it must be admitted that two dates do stand out from all the rest and should be remembered. These are 1601 and 1935. The first, 1601, was the year of the enactment by the British Parliament of 43 Elizabeth, known as the English Poor Laws. The second 1935, was the date of passage by the U.S. Congress of the Social Security Act.

These two pieces of legislation have some similarities. Both were passed during a period of hard times and were designed to prevent civil disorder. Both were efforts by a central government to make provision for the relief of suffering. Both conceded that certain helpless and needy people deserve assistance. Both were made possible by earlier legislation that provided necessary precedents, and both set patterns for the years that followed. Both separated the poor into categories, almost identical categories as a matter of fact. Both reflected perceptions about poverty common to the time of their passage. However, this last similarity also provides the basis for the great difference between the two pieces of legislation, for during the intervening centuries perceptions about poverty changed.

The English Poor Laws place the blame for poverty squarely on the individual, whereas the Social Security Act reflected a growing recognition that social conditions can cause poverty and that therefore society must assume some responsibility for the poor.

We will look first at the English Poor Laws, then at developments that demonstrated the gradual change in perceptions, and finally at the Social Security Act.

43 Elizabeth—The English Poor Laws

In the 1500s, England's expanding woolen industry, with its strong demand for raw material, made the raising of sheep highly profitable, at the expense of the tenant farmers who worked the land for produce under the feudal society. Farm after farm was enclosed (fenced off) for pasture, forcing large numbers of people to leave homesites to which for centuries they had been bound. Caught in the middle of forces beyond their control, these farmers migrated toward places where industrial development offered them the possibility of jobs. Since the new industries were unable to provide work for all who needed it, and since residency requirements made settlement in a new location difficult if not impossible, many were forced to wander about the countryside doing what they could to find food, shelter, and clothing. These wanderers eventually banded together in their pursuit of life's necessities, and as their numbers swelled, their potential for causing civil disorder increasingly worried the ruling class.[1]

According to Sidney and Beatrice Webb,

> The changing organization of the countryside . . . must have been felt most severely in times of scarcity . . . [and] the years 1594 to 1598 were cold and rainy and resulted in a near famine. . . . Extreme poverty . . . was so apparent . . . as to become the principal subject of legislation in the Parliament that met in 1597.[2]

This Parliament formulated a number of laws to deal with the situation including "a measure for the relief of the indigent" that was amended and re-enacted in 1601 as 43 Elizabeth. The law actually contained very little that was new except the provision that a parish that was unable to support its own poor could levy taxes in certain other parishes to obtain the needed funds. What the new law did do was redraft "various halting and confused statutes of past years into one [law] that was drastic and direct, explicit in its commands and practically enforceable."[3] This last rewriting of the English Poor Law was to stand (in England) with but minor revisions for 250 years.[4]

43 Elizabeth utilized the three categories of poor people that had been defined by a committee established during the reign of Henry VIII. The law gave orders to the authorities on how to deal with each category. In the language of the Elizabethans, the three were:

1. the poor by impotency
   a. fatherless children
   b. aged, lame, blind
   c. those with long-term diseases such as leprosy or dropsy
2. the poor by casualty
   a. the wounded soldier
   b. the decayed householder
   c. those visited by grievous disease
3. the thriftless poor (able bodied)
   a. the rioter that consumeth all.
   b. the vagabond that will abide in no place
   c. the idle person, as the strumpet and others[5]

Children were to be apprenticed, that is, bound out to anyone who would take them. The impotent poor—the helpless, handicapped, elderly, and ill— were to be taken care of either in their own homes (outdoor relief) or in almhouses, hospitals, or other types of "houses of correction" (indoor relief). The able bodied were to be forced to work or face severe punishment.

An important principle established by the law was "the principle of local responsibility" in that church wardens from each parish in combination with persons appointed annually by justices of the peace were to serve "both as overseers of the poor and as collectors of the revenue" that was necessary "to carry the act into effect."[6]

Among its many repressive features, the measure made parents who had the means liable for the support of their children and their grandchildren. Likewise, children were legally responsible for the support of needy parents and grandparents. Even more repressive was the harsh treatment outlined for the able-bodied poor. They could be whipped, branded, put in the pillory, committed to jail and even put to death.

Although the English Poor Laws set up a system to care for the needy, they reflected the thinking of the day in that it made a division between those who were poor because of the acts of God and those who were poor because of the inherent problems of the society in which they lived. The first were to be aided, the second to be punished. Even with the first, however, excessive sympathy was not required. Since they had been singled out by God to bear problems, they bore a slight flavor of sinfulness, and in any event it wasn't necessary to do *too* much for them, because if they bore their burdens with fortitude, they would be amply rewarded in the next world. As for the able-bodied poor, the Elizabethans could not tolerate the idea that their society could cause poverty, so they came down very heavily on those who were able to work and had no employment.

The Poor in Seventeenth Century America

The early colonists were for the most part English. Along with other customs, they brought with them the perceptions that had shaped the English Poor Laws. Thus, 43 Elizabeth set the pattern for relief of the needy in the New World just as it did in the Old.

In the early years, the American colonies were not troubled by wandering bands of the unemployed, but there were many poor people just the same. The mortality rate was high. Parents died leaving destitute children. Widows were often unable to provide for their own support. There were the mentally and physically handicapped, the ill, and, as time passed, the aged.

Although private charity handled many of the problems, public relief was in evidence from the beginning. In reality, it was often difficult to distinguish between the two. The settlements were small and isolated. By mutual agreement the local officials were permitted to decide who needed aid, what kind of aid should be given, and how much each colonist should chip in to provide this aid. Because each settlement took care of "its own," each settlement kept the option to say who might or might not become one of its own. Newcomers were often required to post bonds. The sale of land was controlled by local officials. To make sure that community resources would not be strained, nonresidents who looked as if they might become public charges were "warned out." Sometimes this was done politely, but newcomers who did not take the hint risked being put in the stocks. Often as not the residents got together and threw rocks at the newcomers to encourage them to move on.

By the second half of the seventeenth century, the settlements had grown to such a degree that local communities could no longer be relied upon to handle the problems of the poor. In 1647, the first colonial poor law was enacted by the legislature of Rhode Island. Using 43 Elizabeth as reference, it announced that "each town shall provide for the relief of the poor, to maintain the impotent, and to employ the able, and shall appoint an overseer for the same purpose."[7]

Other colonies enacted similar measures. The first almshouse for the provision of indoor relief was established in Renssalaerswyck, New York in 1657. In 1658 and 1660, almshouses were set up in Plymouth colony and in Boston.[8]

The first organized private charity came about through the recognition that otherwise good people often needed assistance, especially when they first arrived in the community. The Scot's Charitable Society was founded in Boston in 1657 to aid members of its own national group. Over the years, other similar national charities were formed, many of which are still in existence.

By the end of the 1600s, the patterns had been set. The trend toward indoor relief (institutions) was already visible, as was the trend toward centralization of the provision for public relief. Organized private charities had begun. The policy that certain poor people were deserving of care while others were not had been firmly spelled out. Residency requirements were to remain a legal part of public relief until struck down as unconstitutional by a Supreme Court decision in 1969.

1700 to 1800—The Eighteenth Century

For the most part the patterns of the 1600s continued in the 1700s, although changing conditions led to some modification. The eighteenth century saw the initiation of specialization in the forms of indoor relief that would swell to an incredible assortment of institutions in the nineteenth century. During the 1700s private charities assumed more importance than they had in the 1600s, and the responsibility for public relief was passed from the local communities to the larger, more centralized units of government. In most cases this control was taken over by the newly formed state governments, but federal participation in some kinds of poor relief was evident even before the revolution was fully over. According to Trattner, "at this time, social welfare was a partnership. Private philanthropy complemented public aid."[9]

The population of America increased during this century from an estimated 275,000 in 1700 to 5,308,483 in 1800. The population was primarily engaged in agriculture. Even at the end of the century, only 6 per cent was considered to live in urban settings.[10]

As the population grew, indoor relief grew too. Workhouses and almshouses became the rule. These were originally set up as houses of correction designed to provide food and shelter to the needy and thus "correct their situation," but they gradually became places where a "correction" was made in the individual, not in his or her situation. The food was barely sufficient for subsistence (and sometimes not even that), and the work was the most boring, unpleasant drudgery that could be devised. This conformed with the prevailing attitude that the poverty of an able-bodied man was of his own fault and that dependency of such people (and their wives and children) on public relief should be discouraged in every way possible. The ill, handicapped, and elderly often got little better care than did the able-bodied poor.

Between 1720 and 1735, a religious revival called the Great Awakening took place. A corresponding secular revival of sorts was the so-called Enlightenment. This stemmed partially from scientific advances and partially from the philosophy of John Locke who believed that human beings were born without prior imprinting from God and were instead molded by their environment. This combination of religious and secular thought encouraged both individuals and groups to perform many charitable services for the needy.[11]

Examples of private charities were the Society for Encouraging Industry and Employing the Poor, which was founded in Boston, and the Society for Innoculating the Poor Gratis (free medical care to the poor), which was organized by a group of Philadelphia physicians in 1774.

The ambivalent attitudes of this period that produced both humanitarian concern and the harsh treatment of work relief was summed up by Benjamin Franklin, when he wrote to a friend in 1753,

> To relieve the misfortunes of our fellow creatures is concurring with the Diety; it is God like; but, if we provide encouragement for laziness, and supports for folly, may we not be fighting against the order of God and nature, which perhaps has appointed want and misery as proper punishments for, and cautions against, as well as necessary consequences of idleness and extravagance?[12]

That children were objects of concern is demonstrated by the fact that institutions for their care were the earliest of the specialized facilities. The first orphanage, a home for children whose parents had been slain in an Indian raid was set up by the Ursuline Sisters in New Orleans in 1729.[13] In 1740, the Bethesda House for Boys was established near Savannah. Both institutions were privately funded. Apprenticing of children, however, remained the most usual way of providing care. This was done not only with orphans but also with children who were adjudged to be unruly or those whose parents were too poor to support a family. The first publicly supported institution for children, the Charleston (South Carolina) Orphan Home, was not set up until 1790.

It should be kept in mind that then as now poverty was *not* confined to urban areas. An American innovation designed to handle rural poverty was the adaptation of the workhouse, which came to be called the poor farm. The first of these was established near Philadelphia in 1711. The Pennsylvania legislature passed a bill in 1798 that authorized counties to buy farms, set up buildings upon them, and send the poor to work the land. By the end of the nineteenth century almost every county in the United States was to have its own poor farm.[14]

Care for the mentally ill changed somewhat in the 1700s. At the beginning of the century, there was little understanding of mental illness. People who were strange in any way were considered to be afflicted by devils. If they committed some criminal act, they were punished. Those who were cared for by their families were usually locked in barred rooms; those who had no families to care for them either wandered about or were indiscriminately dumped in the workhouses with the poor. The retarded and those with such diseases as cerebral palsy were not distinguished in any way from those who were emotionally disturbed. The first institution for "lunatics" as they were called at the time was not established until 1773, in Williamsburg, Virginia.[15]

Benjamin Rush, who was to become known as the father of American psychiatry, began his work during the last part of the eighteenth century. Inspired by a visit to France where he examined the humane treatment of the insane advocated by Phillipe Pinel, Rush introduced Pinel's methods to Pennsylvania Hospital. He was also on the faculty of the University of Pennsylvania and taught the new methods to his students. He may be credited with initiating many reforms, because he insisted that mental patients were capable of human reactions and therefore should not be left hungry and naked in cold, windowless wards. He removed the iron rings used to chain patients to the walls, separated the sexes, separated the violent from the more orderly patients, assigned patients to simple tasks, saw to it that their living quarters were comfortable, and in general introduced principles that stressed the possibility of cure rather than mere custodial care. In 1812, toward the end of his career, he published the first American textbook on psychiatry, *Medical Inquiries and Observations Upon the Diseases of the Mind.* He was, of course, far ahead of his time. Care of the mentally ill remained pathetically inadequate in spite of his efforts. For the most part "lunatics" remained chained in the basements of the workhouses or jails.[16]

Other events that broke ground were also taking place. In 1776 the Continental Congress adopted a report recommending state pensions for invalid and disabled veterans and for other "unsettled poor." In 1798, the Marine Hospitals Service was initiated to provide medical care for American seamen.[17] This was the first federal program in public health. Taken together, developments such as these show the beginning of federal participation in care for the poor.

By the end of the eighteenth century, although provisions for the poor were by no means good, things were not yet bad enough to provoke widespread concern. The population was still sufficiently uniform in ethnic background and in standard of living so that for the most part direct knowledge of the condition of the poor sufficed. The system inaugurated under the English Poor Law functioned well enough to handle the problems, well enough at least by the standards of the day. In the next century, changing conditions were to strain the system beyond its capabilities. Humanitarianism combined with scientific inquiry would produce new answers.

Before we move to the nineteenth century, however, it is necessary to make another side trip to England, because, even though the American Revolution had separated the governments of the two countries, they still remained close culturally. In England, as in the newly formed United States, both industrialism and scientific inquiry were now permanent features of society.

Of the English theorists who affected the progress of welfare in America, two of the more important were Adam Smith and Thomas Malthus. In 1776, Smith published his great economic treatise, *Wealth of Nations*. In his search for the "invisible hand" that ruled the marketplace, Smith came to the conclusion that the market was itself "self-regulating." He therefore advocated *laissez-faire*—a policy of nonintervention by government in the market processes. He also wrote that the accumulation of capital, that is, the amassing of great wealth by individuals, was a good thing for in the long run this would lead to greater production and an improved society.[18]

Thomas Malthus did not agree with Smith in predicting that society if left alone would progress inevitably toward a better world for all. In 1798 Malthus published *An Essay on the Principle of Population As It Affects the Future Improvement of Society*, which predicted that the mouths of the poor would never be filled, as the "human lot was forever condemned to a losing struggle between ravenous and multiplying mouths, and the eternally insufficient stock of Nature's cupboard."[19] In the Malthusian dilemma, because of the "passion of love," the growth of population tends to outstrip the growth of the food supply; therefore war, disease, and poverty (above all poverty) are not only inevitable, they are necessary to decrease the surplus population. "The view," Malthus wrote, "has a melancholy hue."[20]

Smith and Malthus provided the newly rich industrialists in both countries with the justification needed (they did not need much) to ignore their own contribution to the existence of poverty.

Nonetheless, toward the end of the eighteenth century something was taking place that was completely in opposition to the views of Smith and Malthus. In 1796 the Speenhamland Act was passed. This Act was a primitive effort to provide a guaranteed income in that outdoor relief could be given to the "useful poor who were willing to work" but whose wages were insufficient to support themselves and their families at a subsistence level. By a complicated system based on the price of bread and the size of families, it provided an income floor. The concept failed primarily because of greedy employers who were quick to note that they could save a great deal of money by paying less than subsistence wages and allowing the local governments to make up the difference. Thus instead of improving the conditions of the poor, the Act drove wages down and at the same time increased the cost of poor relief. The so-called "bread scale" soon became very unpopular and was repealed.[21]

The unhappy consequences of the Act killed subsequent efforts to develop a guaranteed income.[22] Only recently has the idea of a guaranteed annual income been reconsidered. However, neither President Nixon's Family Assistance Plan nor President Carter's similar proposal contained in his message to Congress (see Document 2 in Chapter 8) has come even close to passage.

1800 to 1900—the Nineteenth Century

The nineteenth century was a time of tremendous change. America's population rose from a little more than 5,000,000 to nearly 76,000,000. Territorial expansion took place. Inventions of all sorts came into being. Manufacturing increased. The transportation network spread across the land. The cities grew, and by the end of the century about 40 per cent of the population was considered urban rather than rural.[23]

During this period, a few individuals accumulated vast fortunes and the middle class expanded, but, as more and more new arrivals crowded into the city slums—people whose language, dress, customs, and religion seemed strange to those who had come before—the problems of the poor remained unsolved. In many ways things were *relatively* worse for the poor in 1900 than in 1800. Life was easier, safer, more pleasant for those who could afford to take advantage of progress; the lot of the poor suffered by comparison.

Still, scientific inquiry had resulted in the inventions that had made industrialization possible. It was therefore assumed that a scientific examination of the society would provide answers to its problems too.

Even at the beginning of the nineteenth century there were those who believed that this was possible and necessary. The Reverend Thomas Chalmers, a Scottish minister active in the Society for Bettering the Condition of the Poor (in London), is often cited by historians as the originator of modern scientific poor relief and of case work as well.[24] Chalmers emphasized the need for studies of the poor to replace the general assumptions about them as a class. In 1805, in a report to the Society, he stated,

> Let us ... make the inquiry into all that concerns the poor and the promotion of their happiness a science. Let us investigate *practically* and upon *system*, the nature and consequences, and let us unite in extension and improvement of those things which experience hath ascertained to be beneficial to the poor.[25]

Good as this sounds, it must be admitted that Chalmers was opposed to public poor relief for "like his contemporaries [he] considered personal failure as the main cause of poverty and overlooked the economic and social factors outside the power of the individual."[26]

Also despite the belief in scientific inquiry that flowered during the nineteenth century, Mencher says,

> Abstract study of the poor . . . engaged much less effort than did attempts at practical social reform. Humanitarianism was not so much a planned approach as an intense emotional reaction to the cruelty and degradation of the past. There was an extension of the social conscience to those who had been viewed as uncivilized and almost animal like and who were now recognized as humanly sensitive to oppression and suffering.[27]

In the United States the new spirit of humanitarianism resulted at first in the growth of the number and types of institutions to provide indoor relief, plus the formation of countless committees whose purpose it was to "do good to the poor." By the end of the century humanitarianism resulted in the beginning steps in the professionalization of the helping professions, including social work.

From 1800 to 1850, almshouses and poor farms proliferated. Far from being humane, most were only vile catchalls for victims of every sort of misery, misconduct. All were herded together and badly mistreated. At first, it was thought that it would be better for children to be removed to the almshouses with or without their parents than it was for them to be bound out to families who might mistreat them. However, concerned humanitarians soon began to demand reform because, as it turned out, children were even more mistreated in the almshouses. So the idea of separate institutions for children that had been inaugurated in the previous century took over. These orphan asylums housed anywhere from fifty to two thousand children under a single roof. The children's lives were governed by rigid schedules. The children were more often than not abused in many ways by indifferent caretakers. Nonetheless by 1890, more than six hundred orphanages were in operation.[28]

The first state prison was established during the previous century, in 1790, by the Quakers in Philadelphia. Actually this was not only the first state prison but the first real prison too. Local jails were never intended to be any more than places in which convicted felons were held briefly until they were tried and punished by such tender means as flogging, mutilation, hard labor in galleys or mines, or hanging. The first prisons were thus attempts on the part of the humanitarians (particularly the Quakers) to ameliorate the barbaric penal code inherited from England. It was thought that confinement for a period of time would help the individual to see the error of his or her ways and to become a better citizen. In accordance with this view, the new prisons were called penitentiaries. The concept of imprisonment rather than brutal corporal punishment spread and was refined during the nineteenth century. Prisons became larger and inmates were separated into categories by sex, age, and degree of intractability. In 1824 in New York, children were first separated from more hardened criminals in a special public institution for juvenile delinquents called the House of Refuge. The first prison for women was established in Sherborn, Massachusetts in 1879. The first reform school for young offenders was built in Elmira, New York in 1876.[29]

Typical of the many voluntary groups set up for humane purposes were the New York, Baltimore and Philadelphia Societies for the Prevention of Pauperism established in 1818 to help the victims of the War of 1812. Over time these societies became broader in their outlook. The New York Association for Improving the Condition of the Poor was organized in 1843. This was a forerunner of the many charity organization societies. Public charities also had groups interested in their improvement. The first Conference of Boards of Public Charities, precursor to the National Conference on Social Welfare, was held in 1874 and was attended by representatives of the State Boards of Charities in Massachusetts, Connecticut, New York, and Wisconsin.[30]

Throughout this period there was much argument over whether private charities, which provided advice and help designed to elevate the worthy poor from their problems, or public charities, which provided financial assistance and institutionalized care, were more useful. Until about 1850 it was generally considered that outdoor relief demoralized the poor and took away their incentive to work. However, the almshouses had become financially burdensome. Studies showed that outdoor relief might be more economical. For this reason, outdoor relief began its gradual climb toward the dominant form of assistance for the poor.

Except for the short-lived Freedman's Bureau, set up to aid former slaves after the Civil War, the federal government shied away from relief efforts, even though there were attempts by public-spirited citizens to encourage its participation. The story of Dorothea Dix provides a good example of the many battles fought by the humanitarians of this period.

Born in 1802, Miss Dix developed tuberculosis at an early age. She also had frequent bouts with malaria. Despite her physical weakness, she spent her life inspecting the jails, prisons, and workhouses where the insane were confined and in publicizing the shocking conditions that she uncovered. Miss Dix endured the hardship of travel by stagecoach and wagon over more than sixty thousand miles to examine conditions in twenty-seven states.

When she began her work, Miss Dix was principally concerned with arousing the public to correct the many abuses, but gradually she became convinced that, in well-managed institutions, it might be possible to reverse the course of mental illness. She urged the establishment of state institutions, and, during the period when federal land grants were being made, she persuaded Congress to pass a bill appropriating 10 million acres of land for the establishment of hospitals for the insane and 2.5 million acres for institutions for the deaf.

President Franklin Pierce is sometimes cited as a president who had little effect on the course of history, but this is far from the case. In 1854 he vetoed the bill saying among other things that "I cannot find any authority in the

Constitution for making the Federal Government the great almoner of public charity throughout the United States." His veto held, and as a result the federal government gave almost no assistance to state programs of poor relief until the 1930s. Although she failed to change Pierce's mind, Miss Dix did succeed in her efforts to change public attitudes. She was personally responsible for the establishment of thirty-two public and private institutions for the care of the insane.

Although more recently other reformers have come to believe that large-scale institutionalization is not such a good answer to the problem after all, Miss Dix's work should be judged on the basis of the change in attitudes rather than on the system that she helped to set up. According to the *Encyclopedia of Social Work*, "perhaps her greatest accomplishment was to prepare the ground for the mental health movement." She died in 1887.[31]

Another reformer who worked diligently, if not always in an enlightened manner by present standards, was Charles Loring Brace. Born in 1826, he was the founder and for forty years the executive director of the Children's Aid Society of New York. After discovering that countless thousands of homeless children roamed the streets of New York, his organization established children's shelters, industrial schools, free reading rooms, and the like. He worked hard and long to obtain legislation designed to regulate child labor and to promote universal public elementary education.

Brace is usually more frequently remembered, however, for his controversial scheme to transport vagrant children from the "demoralizing" cities to the "more virtuous" rural areas. The so-called orphan trains ran for twenty-five years, and it is estimated that more than fifty thousand children were thus placed in private homes, mostly with farmers in the Midwest. The program came under considerable criticism for there was little investigation of the prospective foster parents, and it is probable that many of the children were exploited as cheap labor. However, later studies showed that the program had been amazingly successful, particularly for the younger children. The Children's Aid Society under Brace's leadership was an important sponsor of many programs that are now considered indispensable to child welfare such as free schools, dental clinics, and classes for the handicapped. Brace helped to formulate future opinion on the value of foster care.[32]

The flow of immigrants to the United States increased during the latter part of the 19th century, and the existing programs became strained beyond their capability. Despite the many studies that had been made and the accumulation of statistics that existed, prevailing public opinion was still that the poor had only themselves to blame. In contributing "survival of the fittest" to the vocabulary, Darwin had intended the phrase to apply only to lower forms of life, but this theory was now transmuted by the social Darwinists to support their contention that aid to the poor only kept alive the less fit who were probably better off dead anyway.[33]

That this philosophy could be interpreted to mean that public assistance would have a bad effect both on the person who received aid and also on society is evidenced by Josephine Shaw Lowell's statement on the economic and moral effects of public outdoor relief. In a paper delivered to the National Conference of Charities and Corrections in 1890, she stated that "the only justification for expenditure of public money is that it is necessary for the public good. That certain persons need certain things is no reason for supplying them with those things from the public funds."

Mrs. Lowell attempted to prove her point by adding a parable in which the "valley of industry" was contrasted to the "valley of idleness." She told how, when concerned citizens who lived on the "hill of prosperity" provided free water to the residents of the valley of idleness, the result was only that they increased in numbers and thus needed more help. Furthermore, the folks who lived in the valley of industry got fed up with doing all the work and moved into idleness themselves.[34]

Lest one judge Mrs. Lowell too harshly, she was a life-long leader in the movement to reorganize both public and private charities in accordance with the principles of "scientific philanthropy." She campaigned for women's suffrage, for improvement in institutions of all types, and for the then new idea of settlement houses. Her dedication inspired many men and women to devote their lives to improving the condition of the poor. Her belief that the able-bodied poor would be encouraged to live in idleness if they were to receive public assistance was shared by many involved in private charity work at the time. Indeed, if the parable summarized here were only slightly revised and delivered at an antiwelfare meeting today, it would probably be hailed as an original and provocative summation of what many still consider to be a serious problem.

Although there were plenty to agree with Mrs. Lowell that the poor must never be "spoiled" by public assistance, the reason she made the speech was to offer a rebuttal against those who did not agree. At the same conference, Mr. Franklin B. Sanborn also delivered a report in which he advocated more and better outdoor relief under public auspices. Mr. Sanborn was perhaps more familiar with the subject than was Mrs. Lowell, having been for many years an inspector of public assistance programs such as almshouses and penal institutions in the state of Massachusetts.[35]

The battle between public and private programs went on—and it is still not completely over.

We mentioned earlier that humanitarianism was a contributing factor toward the professionalization of services. The system of friendly visitors set up by the charity organization societies to investigate the individual cases of poverty was originally staffed by volunteers. However, it soon proved difficult to find enough people who had both the desire to do this work and a sufficient private income to permit them to do it. Paid personnel gradually took over the investigative chores. Then, as it became obvious that these employees needed some sort of training, educational programs were initiated. These training programs eventually led to the establishment of schools of social work shortly after the turn of the century.

One cannot close the discussion of the nineteenth century without mentioning the beginnings of the settlement house movement. Here again

England set the pattern. The first settlement house was established in London by a clergyman, Samuel Barnett, in 1884. The idea that persons from the more prosperous classes should actually go to live (i.e., to settle) among the people they hoped to serve was eagerly adopted in the United States. Some of the most famous were Hull House headed by Jane Addams, the University Settlement headed by Stanton Coit, and the Henry Street Settlement headed by Lillian Wald. Settlements utilized both paid and volunteer personnel and thus contributed toward professionalization. In fact, work in settlement houses was one of the early careers in social work. In Jane Addams's opinion, this offered the additional advantage of providing women with a good way to escape sexist repression.

In Chapter 4 we discussed the social and economic changes that resulted in the emergence of the large welfare organizations. In the nineteenth century these changes were becoming increasingly apparent. Growth of population and territorial expansion had combined with industrialization to make great changes in the economic organization of the country. The newer economic organization provided both the necessity for more care for the poor and the means to provide care. Most aid to the poor during the nineteenth century was given to those in the first two categories that the committe of Henry VIII had established—the children and those who were unable to care for themselves (the aged and the physically and mentally handicapped)—although as a result of industrialization another category emerged—that of the "worthy poor." The worthy poor were those who were working as hard as they could but were still unable to support themselves and their families.

The centralization of economic power that took place during the nineteenth century was made possible by improvements in communications (e.g., such inventions as the telegraph, the telephone, and the camera) and improvements in printing as well as from the building of roads, railroads, and steamship lines. The centralization of power is evidenced by (1) the Civil War, which established the supremacy of the federal government over the states; (2) the formation of the great industrial complexes controlling materials, labor, factories, and markets and often headed by a single individual; and (3) the move from community-based poor relief to state boards of public charities, charity organization societies, and national conferences representing both groups.

At the beginning of the nineteenth century it was still possible to have direct knowledge about the poor. Concerned individuals were usually close to those in need of aid, both in physical proximity and in background. As immigration increased and cities grew, the poor came more and more to be a group apart to be investigated by scientific inquiry. Fields of study such as psychology and sociology were developed.

By the end of the nineteenth century, it was both necessary and possible to be objective about the poor. Professional groups were developing with special interests in public or private charity, with specialized information about their own field of concern. While in theory the objective studies should combine with specialized knowledge to provide the means to see each poor person as an individual, the opposite could be the result. Specialized knowledge and an objective approach can combine to make it possible to speak of the concerns of crippled children, for instance, or prisoners, or the insane as though all crippled children or all prisoners or insane persons had identical characteristics or needs—in short, to emphasize categorization and thus impersonalization. In fact, as organizations to care for the poor grew and became more centralized, the need for categorization grew, with resulting increase in impersonalization of care.

At both the beginning and the end of the nineteenth century, poverty was defined largely in absolute terms, but the increasing comforts of the middle class due to technological improvements such as indoor plumbing, central heating, and electric lights made the situation of the poor seem even more dismal by comparison. Relative definitions of poverty were beginning to emerge.

1900 to 1935

In the early decades of the twentieth century, the United States became the richest nation on earth. Prosperity had developed from technological progress, and there was little doubt in people's mind that any and all remaining problems for the country could and would soon be solved.

Such attitudes were encouraged because this was not only a period of growth and development but also one of reform. Immigration peaked between 1900 and 1910, with nearly 9,000,000 new arrivals, most of whom were forced to crowd into the already dismal tenements of the urban centers. Reforms were spurred by the writings of the "muckrackers." Journalists such as Lincoln Steffens described living condition in the slums and assigned much of the blame to grasping landlords and poor city management. In *A Mind That Found Itself*, published in 1908, Clifford Beers exposed the inadequacies of mental hospitals. Robert Hunter's classic work, *Poverty*, published in 1904, stated that one out of every eight Americans was poor. Federal, state, and local governments responded by passing laws designed to eliminate many of the abuses. However, graft made it easy to bypass many of the reform measures.

Three amendments to the Constitution typify the era. The Sixteenth Amendment, which took effect in 1913, provided for a federal income tax and reflected the increasing power of the central government. Its passage also reflected a general fear that too few persons were getting too large a share of the wealth. The income tax did not result in a major redistribution of income, but it has probably helped to prevent the proportional distribution from getting any more unequal than it already was. There is no doubt that the financial resources that the income tax afforded the federal government made possible the eventual federal expenditures for welfare programs.

Throughout the nineteenth century it was believed that alcohol was one of the principal causes of poverty. The temperance movement was an attempt by the forces of moral righteousness to improve society by removing a major source of temptation. In 1920 temperance advocates achieved a victory of sorts in the passage of the Eighteenth Amendment to the Constitution. Prohibition lasted until the Amendment was repealed in 1933. It had eliminated neither poverty nor drinking.

A more significant reform during this period was achieved by the passage in 1920 of the Nineteenth Amendment, which guaranteed the right of women to vote. One of the rallying points around the call for women's suffrage was that, if women could participate in government, they would set to work to eliminate all forms of social injustice including poverty.

While the federal government remained for the most part uninvolved in welfare, some events pointed toward future developments. In 1909 the first White House Conference on Children was sponsored under President Theodore Roosevelt. In 1912 the Children's Bureau was established in the Department of Labor. In 1920 the first Vocational Rehabilitation Act was passed by Congress. In 1921 Congress passed the Maternity and Infancy Act, which led to the establishment of child welfare services in many states.

During the first decades of the twentieth century both public and private welfare programs were made available mainly to whites. However, a change was in the making, lamentably slow, but in evidence. The National Association for the Advancement of Colored People (NAACP) was founded in 1909 and the Urban League in 1910.

In the first three decades of the twentieth century social work was established as a profession. By 1929 there were 25 accredited schools of social work in the United States and Canada with 1,306 full-time students enrolled in master's degree programs.[36] The first professional organization, the American Association of Social Workers, was established in 1918. This was the forerunner of the National Association of Social Workers.

In the 1920s there was a depression in agriculture, the Teapot Dome Scandal occurred, the stock market produced some quavers, and large segments of the population remained poverty-stricken. Nonetheless, the popular belief held that things were getting better and better. Herbert Hoover reflected the optimism of the period when he stated in 1928 that "the final triumph over poverty would soon take place."[37]

All the optimism was destroyed by the sudden termination of prosperity following the stock market crash in 1929. By 1933, 25 per cent of the labor force was unemployed.[38] People were forced from their homes, hungry and cold. The Great Depression proved once and for all that the responsibility for poverty could lie outside the individual, rather than within. The result was the initiation of federal public welfare programs of which the Social Security Act of 1935 was the most important. From it flows most of the large-scale programs that dominate the present scene.

The ideas contained in the Act were not especially new. After all, most of the provisions were for aid to the aged, the handicapped, and children, the same categories of the poor that were spelled out under Henry VIII. Even the idea of social insurance itself had been around for awhile. Twenty-two years earlier, in 1913, I.M. Rubinow advocated, in his book *Social Insurance*, a comprehensive social insurance system to protect against industrial accidents, sickness, old age, invalidism, death and unemployment.

Whereas under the English Poor Laws the central government ordered the local communities to provide aid but gave them no financial help, under the Social Security Act the federal government made grants to the states so that they could make relief programs available. The Poor Laws encouraged the building of almshouses; the Social Security Act required that the grants be made in cash to people living in their own homes. By so doing, it initiated the gradual process that was to eliminate almshouses. Even though the Act was passed during the midst of the greatest depression the world has ever experienced, industrialization had created a far greater surplus than that which existed in 1601. The federal government was able to initiate permanent public programs of social insurance that were designed to *prevent* certain categories of people from falling into poverty. To the Elizabethans, the idea that any government should attempt to subvert God's will by preventing poverty would have seemed downright sinful. The Elizabethans would also have found incomprehensible the requirement of a "fair hearing" for applicants for relief who believed themselves unfairly treated.

The last two points demonstrate that some change in perceptions had taken place. By inaugurating programs of prevention and by implying that recipients have a "right to assistance," the Social Security Act of 1935 *for the first time* officially recognized that poverty can be caused by societal factors.

This is not to suggest that the problems of the poor were all neatly solved by one piece of legislation or that the arguments over the causation of poverty were settled. Although resources, knowledge, and organizations exist to accomplish the task, change comes slowly because values, attitudes, perceptions of work, and commonly accepted explanations of the causes of poverty are similar to those of Elizabethan times.

The following recent newspaper article illustrates the strength of historical attitudes in relation to contemporary issues in provision for the poor:

A Sample of Thoughts on Poverty from the Halls of Congress

Before the House Agriculture Committee decided last week to drop a requirement that recipients put up cash for food stamps, it had to deal with a pretty girl in a T-shirt, buttons and some homespun philosophy on poverty.

Rep. Steven D. Symms (R-Idaho) wanted to keep the rule that the 5.4 million households receiving food stamps must pay part of the coupons' face value.

If poor families would not have to "invest" in stamps, Symms said, they would take the cash and use it "to buy circus tickets."

Rep. Harold L. Volkmer (D-Mo.) expressed surprise and asked, "The gentleman feels that poor kids should never go to the circus?"

Chart Unveiled

Not if their nutrition will be neglected, said Symms, who feels the poor will spend less money on food with what he referred to during the debate as Elimination of Purchase Requirements (EPR).

He then asked his colleagues to "look at pretty Diane and her chart." The young woman, an employe of Rep. William C. Wampler (R-Va.) had taken off her sweater to reveal a T-shirt emblazoned with a pink "KPR" (Keep Purchase Requirement).

She was standing by a chart drawn by Republican staff members showing their predictions that food spending and farm income would decline if the rule was dropped. Representatives of antihunger groups, wearing blue on yellow EPR buttons, groaned.

Rep. John Krebs (D-Calif.) broke in, saying Symms' assumption was that if extra money were available to the poor, "They would go out and spend it on the circus or on liquor. I have a little more faith in people."

Rep. Richard Kelly (R-Fla.), a former circuit judge, thought hunger pangs would determine the behavior of the poor.

Not the Answer

"Would you not think that when they got hungry that they would be better budgeters and the nation would be stronger for it?" he asked.

Rep. Berkley Bedell (D-Iowa) answered that persons at low income levels "may not be the best budgeters."

"We tend to think that other people have the same intellectual capacity and ability that we do, sitting on this committee," Bedell said. "I do not think you educate people by making them hungry."

Kelly argued that intellectual differences between poor and middle income persons were not that great.

Motivation a Factor

"It is not a question of how poor people are, as to how dumb they are," Kelly said. "If they're hungry, they can budget their money to get food just as the (laboratory) rat can push a button to get the gate to come open."

Missouri's Volkmer said that in the past winter, many families had to choose between paying heating bills and buying groceries. He asked Kelly: "The poor are poor because they want to be poor—is that what you're saying?"

"No, they would just rather do the things that get them poor," replied Kelly, noting that some goals—like becoming a congressman—took special effort.

"They did not have the motivation to do the things that we did to get where we are," Kelly said. Poor people have the same ability but "they just did not utilize it," he added.

Rep. Jerry Huckaby (D-La.) said Kelly lacked compassion for the poor.

Symms responded: "I resent having the judge's motives impugned. We do not owe everybody bread and circuses. That is what happened to every republic in history."[39]

Summary

Chapters 4 and 5 describe how the development of large welfare organizations has paralleled the industrialization of the American society. As industrialization evolved to its present state, the development meant more than an increase in the number of machines in use. Industrialization is also marked by the centralization of power, the change from subjective to objective knowledge, the need for specialized knowledge, and the growth of relativism and impersonalization. As welfare organizations have evolved, they too have included these same features. The change has been from simple to more complex organizational forms. There were long periods of trial and error before the organizations took shape as we know them today, and the structure of the organizations is still changing.

The goal of welfare organizations has never been to alter the fundamental socioeconomic character of the American society but, rather, to assure its continuance with as few modifications in that character as possible. So, it can be said that welfare organizations are evolutionary in structure, but functional in purpose.

This is not to say that welfare organizations have not been effective. They have been so successful in eliminating the absolute poverty common a century ago that today there are few cases of complete starvation or of lack of the housing or clothing necessary for survival. This is a major accomplishment, one for which the American society can be justly proud.

However, the change from absolute to relative definitions of poverty obscures this accomplishment; that is, in relative terms, poverty is still a major social problem. The solution to relative definitions of poverty requires a major redistribution of the wealth of the society, and this the welfare organizations were not created to do. Welfare organizations have been successful in raising the floor of resources for the poor, but they have been remarkably unsuccessful in closing the gap between the rich and the poor. Welfare organizations are not likely ever to eliminate poverty *as it is now defined.*

Even with the conservative goals that welfare organizations have pursued to date, they still generate controversy. The large organizations respond to national interests, and these can be very different from state or local interests. When a collision of interests takes place, public agencies are sometimes forced to alter their policies and programs. Sometimes it is the local interests who are forced to stand aside or to compromise.

The intersection of interests of the various levels of the organizational makeup of the American society and the implication of this for welfare programs is the subject of Chapter 6.

References

1. Axinn, J., and Levin, H. *Social Welfare: A History of the American Response to Need.* New York: Dodd, 1975, p. 10.

2. Webb, Sidney, and Beatrice. *English Local Government: English Poor Law History. Part I. The Old Poor Law.* London: Longmans, 1927, p. 63.

3. Ibid., p. 65.

4. Trattner, W. *From Poor Law to Welfare State.* New York: Free Press, 1974, p. 10.

5. Webb, S. and B. Op. cit., p. 49.

6. Trattner, W. Op. cit., p. 11.

7. *Records of the Colony of Rhode Island and Providence Plantations in New England.* Vol. 1. *1636-1663.* Providence, R.I.: A. Crawford Green, 1856, pp. 184–185

8. Axinn, J., and Levin, H. Op. cit., p. 13.

9. Trattner, W. Op. cit., p. 34.

10. U.S. Dept. of Commerce. Bureau of the Census. *Historical Statistics of the United States 1789-1945.* Washington, D.C.: G.P.O., 1949, p. 25.

11. Trattner, W. Op. cit., pp. 35–37.

12. Smith, H. S., ed. *The Writings of Benjamin Franklin.* Vol. 3. *1750-1759.* New York: Macmillan, 1907, pp. 134, 135.

13. Trattner, W. Op. cit., p. 100.

14. Heffner, W. C. *History of Poor Relief Legislation in Pennsylvania, 1682–1913.* Cleanoa, Pa: Holzapfel Publishing Co. 1913, p. 90.

15. Friedlander, W. *Introduction to Social Welfare*, 4th ed. Englewood Cliffs, N.J.: Prentice-Hall, 1974, p. 69.

16. *Encyclopedia of Social Work, 1977.* Washington, D.C.: National Association of Social Workers, p. 1497.

17. Friedlander, W. Op. cit., p. 98.

18. Heilbroner, R. L. *The Worldly Philosophers.* New York: Simon & Schuster, 1972, pp. 40–72.

19. Ibid., p. 76

20. Ibid., p. 88.

21. Webb, S. and B. Op. cit., pp. 178–181.

22. Mencher, S. *Poor Law to Poverty Program.* Pittsburgh, Pa.: Univ. of Pittsburgh, 1967, p. 225.

23. U.S. Dept. of Commerce. Op. cit., p. 25.

24. Klein, P. *From Philanthropy to Social Welfare.* San Francisco: Jossey Bass, 1968, pp. 282, 283.

25. Mencher, S. Op. cit., p. 79.

26. Friedlander, W. Op. cit., p. 22.

27. Mencher, S. Op. cit., p. 79.

28. Trattner, W. Op. cit., pp. 99-101

29. Barnes, E., and Teeters, N. *New Horizons in Criminology.* New York: Prentice-Hall, 1946, pp. 467–503.

30. *Encyclopedia of Social Work.* Op. cit., p. 1497.

31. Ibid., p. 289.

32. Ibid., p. 87.

33. Komisar, L. *Down and Out in the U.S.A.* New York: Franklin Watts, 1974, pp. 27, 28.

34. Axinn, J., and Levin, H. Op. cit., p. 113.

35. Ibid., p. 93.

36. *Encyclopedia of Social Work.* Op. cit., p. 1237.

37. Hoover, H. *The New Day.* Palo Alto, Calif.: Stanford, 1928, p. 16.

38. *Encyclopedia of Social Work.* Op. cit., p. 1669.

39. *Milwaukee Journal.* "A Sample of Thoughts on Poverty from the Halls of Congress," June 20, 1977, Pt. 1, p. 20.

chapter/6

Convergence of Societal and Individual Interests: Implications for Welfare Programs

There is a reciprocal relationship between any society and the individuals that comprise it. This is because the society expects to receive the cooperation of its members, and individuals look to society for the means to fulfill their expectations, whatever these might be. When societal and individual goals are too divergent, adjustment must be made. Otherwise, the incongruence that develops will cause some form of disruption of the social order.[1]

This chapter is concerned with the ways in which the convergence of societal and individual goals are reached and maintained, particularly in regard to welfare programs. To minimize confusion, we restate that we are discussing welfare programs as they *presently operate* in the American society. These are programs that provide economic maintenance and social services to the poor and underprivileged so that they may be as self-sustaining as possible. Please keep these two points from Chapter 2 in mind as you read this chapter.

Convergence, as we will deal with it, occurs at the local community level, where social policy is put into action, rather than at the national level, where social policy is made. This is because human services professionals must secure the cooperation of the members of the local community, both those who receive services and those who support them, in order to operate successful welfare programs.

In contrast to the formal organizations that further societal goals, the small face-to-face groups in which individuals live out their lives further the personal goals of their individual members. These groupings are important in regulating individual behavior. If formal organizations are to have an impact, they must be able to influence the operation of these local groupings. Therefore, this chapter is also concerned with the interaction of formal organizations with face-to-face community groupings.

Local Groups and Individual Interests

Human activity is located in space and in time.[2] Human beings live out their lives in specific settings, dealing with a limited number of other human beings and with a limited number of specific groups of other human beings. Because each individual is interested in more than merely prolonging his or her existence, each builds a series of expectations or desired outcomes for the situations in which he or she participates.

Because humans are required to cooperate with others to ensure their own individual survival, it is impossible for each individual to obtain complete satisfaction for all his or her expectations. When one's expectations clash with those of others, differences arise, making it necessary to develop some sort of modification of the separate desires of each individual so that the expectations of all the parties can be met. Individuals cannot continue to work together or to cooperate unless they share in common expectations or can modify their expectations on occasion so that other individuals' expectations can also be accommodated.

Each group in which an individual participates requires certain behavior on the part of its members. This results in the establishment of patterns of individual behavior that will be acceptable to other group members. Thus the patterns of behavior of the individual become predictable. This predictability is necessary to ensure that the expectations of the participating members of the group will be met. For individuals to survive and be reasonably satisfied with their lives, it is necessary for them to be members of local face-to-face groups that meet the expectations of the individuals who comprise these groups.[3] Unlike formal organizations, face-to-face groups are concerned with the satisfaction and survival of the individual members of their groups. To accomplish this, each group must exert considerable control upon its members so that no individual can make demands that threaten the basic interests of the other members.

People carry out most of their activities in four different types of groups in the local community:

1. work groups
2. residential groups
3. peer groups
4. leisure groups[4]

Almost all individuals participate in one or more of these groups, and some participate in all these types of groups. All who participate in these groups do so in their own unique way, but at the same time the individuals must behave in ways that do not violate the rules of the groups to which they belong. Individuals who do not conform will not continue their membership for long. Instead, they will probably look for other groups that will accept their behavior and accommodate their desires. Individuals who are outside a group but desire to become members must demonstrate that they have the attributes that will make them desirable members of the groups that they hope to join.[5]

These four groups frequently overlap in composition and in characteristics, but even so most can be categorized as being primarily one or another of the four types. These groups may be totally informal, in which case they can be discerned only by observing the relationships among the members; in other cases they may be formally organized. However, we are not talking here about large formal organizations such as Rotary, American Federation of Labor, the American Legion, the Daughters of the American Revolution, or the National Organization of Women, except as these might be manifested at the local level where individual interests are accommodated. For instance, the Sierra Club is a national organization with an overall interest in the environment. A local member might be uninterested in whether or not Alaska is maintained as a wilderness, more interested in the preservation of a local wetland, but most interested in the planning of next year's canoe trips. He or she will be in a group with local Sierra Club members who have a like interest in canoeing. It is the operation of this type of small group that may exist within a formal organization that we are discussing, as well as those face-to-face groups that have no formal organization whatever.

Work groups are associations that are formed when people come together because of the activities required to earn their livelihood. These might be very informal, as in a car pool or a group that meets every morning before work to have breakfast together in a local restaurant or meets in a bar on Friday night to celebrate the end of the week. Others are more formal; for instance, a local chapter of a union, a local business group, or a local professional organization such as the funeral directors' association.

Residential groups are associations formed by persons who live close to each other, whether in apartment buildings or in single-family residences. These might be very informal, as with those neighborhood groups who get together to organize a rummage sale or have a block party. A residential group may be formed among parents who have common concerns about the local school. Other neighborhood associations operate to maintain ethnic purity or to get the local government to provide better snow removal, stop signs at an intersection, or rat control. Tenants' groups might be concerned with conditions relating to their apartment buildings or their rent structure, or the preservation of exclusivity.

Peer groups are those in which members share given characteristics; such as, age, sex, or class position. Any of the groups just described may have peer characteristics, but there are groups who use peer characteristics as the major organizational criterion. Examples are adolescent groups and gangs, debutant groups such as the Junior League, other groups where age is a criterion for membership such as Junior Women's Clubs, the JayCees, senior citizens' groups, and so on.

Leisure groups are those in which participation is related to recreational pursuits. These may cover a wide range of activities from active sports clubs to groups that come together because of their interest in gourmet cooking, card games, discussions, or a particular craft. These groups might be promoted by a larger formal organization of which the participant is a member, or they may simply spring up when several individuals who have met through other groups in which they are members discover that they have a mutual interest.

Note that we have not included the family as a type of informal community group. This is because a family is composed of individuals with kinship ties. As such, the family does not necessarily represent the sentiments of portions of the community in the same way as do the groups we have listed. In fact, members of a family might hold membership in many different groups. Members of a family define their positions in the community by virtue of their membership in informal community groups, not solely by virtue of membership in a family.

We have also not mentioned "special-interest" groups. On the one hand, all face-to-face groups are special-interest groups because they are formed to meet the needs of individual members. On the other hand, the term "special-interest" group has come to mean people who have banded together to influence the political process or to put pressure on the government. All groups have the potential for becoming this type of "special-interest" group, but that is not their primary function.[6]

One of the most important objectives of human services personnel in dealing with their clients is to obtain membership for them in one or more of these informal community groups, particularly the work groups. The family, moreover, is one of the primary targets of welfare services. Much of the welfare services effort toward the family is to prepare its members to become accepted in one or more of the informal community groups we have described.

Governing Relationships Among Informal Groups

Formal organizations operate on the basis of rules, regulations, and codified laws. Local informal groups also develop rules that regulate the way in which they coordinate their activities with other groups in the community. These rules of operation are not codified or written down as are those of formal organizations, but they nevertheless can be identified. Students of local communities classify these rules of operation under two headings: representative law and compromise law.

Representative law is a term used to denote agreement among the various groups in a community as to what constitutes desirable forms of behavior.[7] Representative law expresses the sentiments, values, standards of conduct, and other rules that are jointly held by the various informal groupings in the community. It is usually not codified or explicit. It may be contrary to codified laws in the community. Representative law denotes the "commonsense" rules that exist in the local community by which members of informal groupings govern their behavior.

For example, even though it may be against the law for a dog to run loose in a neighborhood, a police officer will probably talk to the owner rather than cite him or her formally. This kind of action is usually far more acceptable to the local residents than a police officer's taking the owner of a wandering dog into custody, no matter what the law might read.

Compromise law arises out of the disagreements that come from the existence of a large variety of interests that are found among local community groups.[8] Compromise law results from the differences in goals and rules for behavior among groups. If any one of the groups is able to make its own interests dominant, then the interests of the other groups suffer. Goals and rules are established, therefore, to prevent any one group in the local community from completely dominating the others. Compromise law may seem to favor the interests of one local group over another or to keep the various groups in static relationships with each other, but it also forces each of the groups to respect the basic rights of the others.

For example, a group of adolescents in a residential area of a community might have standards of behavior different from those of their parents. Perhaps they want to play their stereo sets loudly, do some drinking and shouting, and drive their cars about the neighborhood at high speed. Some of the residents will object to all of this behavior; others may object to some of the behavior but not to other parts of it, and some may not object to any of the behavior. There is a compromise worked out in most situations. It may be that the young people will be permitted to play their stereos and drink together in one of the backyards in the neighborhood but not to drive their cars about the area as they might want to do. Should they try, they would be subject to the sanctions of their parents or neighbors. Someone may even bring in the police to enforce the compromise law. On the other hand, if the attempt were made to suppress all the boisterous behavior of the young people, they might retaliate by defacing property, teasing pets, and other forms of nuisance.

What young people sometimes call "the hypocrisy about marijuana" is an example of compromise law in action. Formal law makes possession of marijuana illegal, even though penalties for its possession may vary from state to state and even from locality to locality within states. Law enforcement (work group) personnel are charged with eliminating the possession of marijuana, but it is still used extensively in all communities. Possession and use is a fairly widely accepted value among many groups. An operational compromise is worked out whereby some users are caught and fined from time to time, but few determined efforts are put forth by law enforcement agencies to stamp out possession and use of marijuana. This is because, if the law were rigorously enforced, it would threaten many local groups, some of whose members are users. These groups would in turn withdraw their support for local law enforcement efforts, and the interests of all the individual members of the groups would therefore be threatened. A compromise goes into effect that maintains the illegality of possession of marijuana, which pleases some groups but prevents its rigorous enforcement against possession, which pleases others.

Laws against possession are enforced only when the informal rules governing possession are flagrantly violated, as when people have a huge party that is obvious to the neighborhood or when persons are apprehended with large amounts of other drugs. Compromise law ensures that all groups "keep their place" in relation to the others. Deviations from these rules of place are punished swiftly and severely.

With this brief description of the four types of groupings that comprise the informal organizations of the local community and the two types of informal laws that govern their interrelationships, let us now turn to a discussion of the interaction of formal and informal organizations in the local community and to some of the implications of the interaction for welfare programs.

Face-to-Face Groups and Welfare Organizations

We stated that formal organizations function to meet the goals of the overall society and that informal organizations exist to meet the goals of individuals. We also stated that it is in the local community where services of welfare organizations are delivered, and this is also the place where informal groups are found. Put another way, the local community is where the goals of society and individual goals intersect. When the goals of formal organizations coincide with goals of informal organizations, events proceed smoothly. When there are differences between the goals of formal and informal organizations, conflicts arise. If some accommodation is not worked out, the result will be continuous controversy and a feeling on the part of many persons that the community has serious problems for which there is no solution. The differences in goals between formal welfare organizations and informal organizations in the local community form one of the primary reasons for the controversial nature of welfare programs. Human services workers often find themselves caught in the crossfire, so it is important for them to understand the forces that give rise to these controversies. Only then can work procedures be accommodated to these differences to achieve the best results with the least amount of personal cost. Some examples of the differences that can arise between formal and informal organizations follow.

Work Groups

For several decades the government has operated a variety of work and training programs for unemployed persons. These programs have been financed from federal and state sources, either through departments of labor or departments of welfare. Unemployed persons are usually enrolled in these programs, given a stipend, and then put through a specified period of training; but often, when the period of training is over, few of the graduates of the programs find jobs that utilize their training because the local 'work groups control entry into semiskilled and skilled occupations. These groups do not want the competition generated by work and training programs because it interferes with their own chances to get the limited number of jobs available. Local work groups also have representatives in local government that can place limitations on the type of work and training programs fielded at the local level and thus minimize competition and threats to the employment of the individual members of the local work groups. Trainees often remain unemployed after their period of training is finished, although sometimes a local government will initiate public work programs to ensure that trainees will have some sort of employment.

The conflict exists because formal organizations are concerned with unemployment as a social issue, whereas local work groups are concerned with unemployment as it affects the groups' individual members.

Residential Groups

In recent years there has been a movement to decentralize various programs for care and rehabilitation of the developmentally disabled, the mentally ill, and offenders. Legislatures have passed laws making this possible, and federal agencies make funds available for small care homes to be established in local communities. However, residential groups often have resisted this development with determination and persistence. They sometimes express fear of the effect that the establishment of care homes would have on property values, the safety of children, the maintenance of the area, or the reputation of the neighborhood.

The following newspaper editorial illustrates the power that local residential groups can exert when they are opposed to the provisions of formal law, which formal organizations are expected to enforce:

Where's the Proof of Hazard?

It's dismaying to see emotion and fear winning out over a new state law designed specifically to rescue reason. But apparently that's happening in the case of a controversial group home for emotionally disturbed adults that has been proposed for the Town of Genesee. The case is an important test of the value of the new law.

Residents of the Waukesha County subdivision where the home would be located have raised every imaginable objection—including the argument that neighbors would be so hostile that the home's residents wouldn't want to live there. That ploy seems on the verge of working.

The chairman of Waukesha County's Unified Services Board, which still must approve the group home, says approval isn't likely. Why? Because, she says, neighbors are so unreasonably frightened of the idea. In short, if neighbors of such a proposed group home raise a big enough stink, they can block it.

That's exactly what the new state law was intended to prevent. The new law says such homes for handicapped, disturbed and certain other troubled persons cannot be kept out by local opposition or shut down later unless a danger to the health, safety or welfare of the community can be shown.

We could understand county authorities withholding approval if such proof could be offered by a community. But it has not been. It's shocking to think that sheer unreasoned fear, or maybe just a pretense of fright, might thwart the law.[9]

Leisure Groups

Human services personnel who work in hospitals and correctional settings often must deal with individuals who abuse alcohol. Police either arrest or bring to hospitals those who are seriously intoxicated. Courts sentence individuals to probation, prison, or special programs because of disruptive or dangerous behavior resulting from the use of alcohol. Individuals lose driving privileges and other freedoms if convicted of excessive alcoholic consumption.

Hospitals, rehabilitation centers, and correctional agencies, all are charged with the goal of "treating" alcoholics to restrict their use of alcohol. The goal is to control disruptive or dangerous behavior. Welfare programs often support these special treatment programs to further this goal.

However, the use of alcohol is an important component of the behavior of leisure groups. Programs are often organized by taverns, clubs, and fraternal societies in which the use of alcohol is encouraged. Drinking involves status, because, when an individual reaches the legal drinking age, then he or she can assume full membership in the leisure groups that encourage the use of alcohol. Thus, although drinking is defined as a problem by formal welfare organizations, its use is a mark of distinction among many leisure groups. Accordingly, alcoholic treatment programs have done little to eliminate the social problems that arise from the use of alcohol.[10]

Peer Groups

Welfare organizations have in recent years developed policies that permit the payment of costs for abortions under some circumstances. They have been assisted in the development of this policy by such national organizations as the Planned Parenthood Federation and the National Organization of Women. Nevertheless, when welfare organizations attempt to deliver these services, they often run into opposition from peer groups whose intense beliefs can sometimes make it impossible for the agency to provide the desired service in the community. As long as these peer groups remain active, making payments for abortions by welfare agencies will continue to be beset with difficulty and controversy, regardless of what the federal or state laws may say or what agency policy might be.

Informal Laws and Welfare Organizations

Representative Law

Representative law is an agreed-upon (or representative) standard of the community. As such, it can work even beyond a single local community when the interests of local groups from a number of communities coincide. The two examples of the operation of representative law that follow illustrate the difficulties that human services personnel may encounter when attempting to deliver services in a local community.

In 1972, the Wisconsin State Council of Criminal Justice, with the support of the federal Law Enforcement Administration Agency, recommended that the state's large penal institutions be closed down in favor of smaller community treatment centers. These formal state and federal organizations had impressive facts and statistics to back up their recommendations. The governor accepted their concepts. An almost new state correctional facility was sold to the federal government. The School for Girls was closed, and efforts were undertaken to shut down the large maximum-security prison in Waupun, a city in central Wisconsin.[11]

These members of the various federal and state organizations, many of whom were human services professionals, failed to take into account the powerful force of representative law. They assumed that formal laws and bureaucratic regulations would automatically prevail. They also thought that the local communities would accept their facts and figures and concepts even as the governor had done. They did not realize that there was a general agreement among local groups that convicted offenders of both sexes and of all ages should be removed from the community.

At this writing, the battle is still being waged. Efforts to establish local treatment centers have failed. When the centers were proposed for residential areas, groups of homeowners objected. When the centers were proposed for location in a business district, business groups objected.

Recently there was a proposal to create a residential school for delinquent girls in a defunct secretarial school building in Milwaukee, Wisconsin. This was to have been a closed facility; the girls would not be permitted to leave the school grounds without supervision. Most of the girls would be from the area. The proposal met with fierce opposition from local residential and work groups and eventually was dropped. At present, because the large State School for Girls had been closed, there is no place where girls under eighteen years of age can be sent other than to jails or county detention centers.

While the various local groups were arguing that they did not want facilities for criminal offenders located in their communities, groups in the city where the prison is located agreed that the closing of the prison would have a disastrous effect on the local economy, which in turn would affect all aspects of community life. They were able to develop coalitions with community groups in other parts of the state and became so powerful that efforts to close the prison were abandoned. So the operation of representative law supported the opposition to the location of the facilities in some locations, while at the same time prevented the prisons closing in the community that depended on the prison for its economic life.

In this example, representative law, agreed to by a number of community groups, nullified the effects of formal rules and regulations. Not even the prospect of financial subsidies could alter its effects.

Perhaps you may be thinking, "Well, that is a prison. Anybody can understand that a prison might be opposed by local groups." But keep in mind the example of residential groups opposing the establishment of small care homes for the developmentally disabled. For the human services professional, this opposition is often difficult to understand.

Nonetheless, opposition often exists, and, when a sufficient number of local groups agree that the formation of the small care homes is not in their interest, for example, through representative law they can obstruct or even prevent the operation of formal state or federal law.

A 1977 Associated Press release talks of opposition by residential groups to the formation of a home for the retarded in "an otherwise tranquil Boston neighborhood of tree-shaded single homes." "Property values will fall," says one of the founders of a group called Coalition to Maintain our Neighborhood, or C'MON. "Some of them [the retarded] may be sexually aggressive." This coalition was made up of representatives from residential, peer, leisure, and work groups from the neighborhood discussed in the article.

> C'MON allies complain that neighborhoods are not consulted about the establishment of houses for the retarded. The group also claims that the houses are virtually unregulated and that non-profit groups operating them could turn them over for profitable resale once they rid themselves of retarded tenants.
>
> Mrs. Abby Gould—director of community affairs for the retarded division [sic] of the State Department of Mental Health—said about deinstitutionalizing the retarded, "We've had maybe a half dozen lawsuits since 1939, and we've won them all. But we've never had such a vitriolic suit" [as the one begun by C'MON to prevent the establishment of the home].
>
> She continued, "But if we don't resolve this issue here, it could result in a series of federal lawsuits that could make life very uncomfortable here for a lot of people."[12]

Even though members of the formal organizations charged with the care of the retarded have won court case after court case, this still does not stop the operation of representative law among the local groups in communities that perceive the policies and services of these organizations as a threat to the prerogatives of the individual members of the local groups.

Compromise Law

Compromise law operates when the interests of a number of informal groups in the community are not in agreement about certain issues as they would be in the cases cited in the section on representative law. It also develops between the formal organizations and the informal community groups. Several examples follow.

Work groups are often opposed to welfare assistance programs because of the taxes they impose and because they seem to be a subtle threat to the value of work. At the same time, as we mentioned earlier, these work groups will resist the entry of the unemployed into competition for jobs even though this might reduce the cost of public assistance. A compromise is developed that permits welfare assistance programs to continue. Under this compromise, welfare recipients do not suffer extreme deprivation, but neither do they threaten the occupations of the work groups concerned. This compromise keeps social circumstances from changing to any marked degree in spite of the stated goals of many of the formal programs.

Job training programs often work under the same compromise. For instance, federal regulations governing the operation of the Comprehensive Employment and Training Act (CETA) program do not allow trainees to work at private, profit-making companies, for, as the following newspaper article states, the trainees would then be "displacing regular unsubsidized employes."

U.S. Probes Work Aid Program

The US Labor Department is investigating allegations that CETA participants in Milwaukee's Work Assistance Program have been assigned to work at private, profit-making companies, contrary to federal regulations.

Wages for those in the Work Assistance Program, set up for welfare recipients, are paid through the federal Comprehensive Employment and Training Act. The Work Assistance Program is administered for the county by the Jewish Vocational Service and a consortium of social service and rehabilitation agencies.

The companies in question are Ben Turick, Vaporized Coatings and General Electric.

Marion C. Smith, of the Labor Department's Chicago office, wrote Mary Ellen Powers, director of the county's CETA office, for information concerning the number of CETA workers, the amount of CETA funds, the number of unsubsidized employes and the wages paid at Ben Turick and Vaporized Coatings. The letter also asked how many unsubsidized workers had been employed in the jobs that CETA workers now do.

Ben Turick makes industrial rags. Some CETA workers in the Work Assistance Program have been assigned to Ben Turick by Goodwill. Smith asked in the letter how rent was paid for the space used by Goodwill in the Ben Turick building.

He also asked who issued the paychecks to CETA participants at Vaporized Coatings and, if JVS issued the checks, to what account these funds were charged.

Smith said allegations had been made that CETA workers are or were performing work that would normally be performed by private industry, thereby displacing regular unsubsidized employees.

Although the allegations were made specifically about General Electric, Smith said the allegations could be broadened to cover every sheltered workshop in which CETA workers were placed by rehabilitation agencies participating in the Work Assistance Program.

IN CHARGE OF WORKSHOPS

The rehabilitation agencies in the Work Assistance Program—such as JVS, Curative Workshop, Goodwill Industries, De Paul Rehabilitation Hospital—all run sheltered workshops. The work at the shops is provided through contracts with private industry, such as General Electric. Work Assistance participants are assigned to the workshops as part of the program.

Because of these allegations, Smith asked for a list of every workshop in which contracted work is done and in which CETA participants have worked since the beginning of the Work Assistance Program. He also asked for the names of the private employers with which the Work Assistance Program contracted for the workshops.

"I would like to impress upon you the serious nature of the above charges," Smith said in the letter.[13]

This article illustrates the existence of the compromise betweem formal organizations and informal local groups. It shows how easy it is for human services personnel to upset the fragile balance between the two even though they probably had no intention of breaking the law.

As stated previously, most welfare programs deal directly or indirectly with some aspect of the family. This is not surprising since the composition and operation of the family is the major concern of any society. Families who receive welfare services are always in violation with one or more of the rules of the members of the local grouups who do not receive welfare. They deviate from the rules of work since no one in the family is permanently gainfully employed. They deviate from the rules of leisure groups if members of the family on assistance have too much leisure or if this leisure is used in unacceptable ways. Ethnic minorities are sometimes considered deviates from the standards of local face-to-face groups simply because of their racial characteristics.

There is seldom consensus among all groups about the meaning of these normative differences. One group may consider a characteristic as deviant whereas another not only considers the characteristic acceptable but even assigns high value to it. For instance, although many groups give high value to being self-sufficient because of employment, there are also groups who devalue the importance of employment. This happens in areas where unemployment is high, and individuals seek other means to support themselves and their families. Sometimes they turn to prostitution, gambling, or burglary. These individuals are often highly valued by their group when their endeavors meet with success.

We will consider prostitution for further discussion because prostitution is regulated by compromise law and also because human services personnel often are involved in programs designed to assist and rehabilitate prostitutes.

Some community groups regard prostitution as an economic activity, whereas others regard it as reflecting a total deviation from moral standards. There is no consensus: some groups would like to see prostitution eliminated, others would like to see it legalized, and still others would like to see it approved as a respectable occupation.

In most places in the United States, prostitution is illegal, but it exists. The forms of delivery have been modified from the "houses" of the Victorian times to the present-day independent operators and their agents. Most prostitutes (both male and female) get into "the life" because they are unable to obtain other kinds of work that pay as well, so prostitutes generally come from the poorer segments of the community. However, prostitution would not be a profitable economic activity if the prostitutes' services were not sought by members of the more affluent segments of the community. Thus prostitution is illegal and in violation of the formal law, but, as long as the participants know and observe the rules of compromise law, the activity is condoned.

When compromise law is violated, the violators are swiftly punished. For instance, a prostitute who solicits in the wrong area of town will probably be taken into custody and punished directly, according to formal law. Purchasers of services are not usually taken into custody or even fined, but when they are caught they do incur a certain amount of censure by the local groups of which they are members. The law enforcement agencies will sometimes initiate a "crackdown," on prostitution, but then, when they pick up too many of the more influential members of the community, compromise law reasserts itself.

Compromise law operates in this case to prevent a modification of the relationships of local groups to each other. Those who violate compromise law threaten the rights and obligations of all the groups and their members that have a stake in prostitution, whether they desire to use it, control it, or eliminate it.

In the section on peer groups we described how peer groups can deter the introduction of abortion payment programs by welfare agencies. The controversy surrounding abortion shows what happens when compromise law is challenged.

For many years abortion was illegal. Women had abortions anyway, and little was said or done about it except when an abortionist killed too many clients, thereby coming to the attention of the authorities. Then he or she was convicted and fined or put in prison. Many groups thought this compromise was working against women who wanted safe abortions, and over the years they formed coalitions that became powerful enough to challenge the compromise law on abortion. This resulted in a change in the formal laws on abortion that many other groups were not prepared to accept. So they formed coalitions of their own so that their view of what the formal law should be would receive consideration. A new compromise is yet to be worked out, and, while the process is going on, stability is upset and conflict between various groups is very much in evidence. At this point, it is not clear what the outcome of the struggle will be. However, it is certain that, whatever permanent changes are effected, none of the contending parties will completely achieve their separate aims, either to prevent abortion completely or to make abortion completely socially acceptable.

Summary

This chapter describes some of the structures and processes whereby the goals of society and the goals of individuals are coordinated so that the expectations of both can be met, even though at times only minimally. Formal organizations reflect the goals of society; informal organizations reflect the goals of individuals. These intersect at the community level, and the extent to which they are accommodated determines whether a smooth flow of events and services evolves or disagreements, obstructions, frustration, and conflict develop.

Representative law and compromise law function to strike a workable accommodation between societal goals and individual goals. They are often more powerful than formal, statutory law, as the examples show. However, as they work in the local community, they serve most of the time to make it possible for both societal and individual interests to be met so that the situation does not develop into an either/or circumstance, where one side eliminates the interests of the other. In this sense, then, representative and compromise law are powerful forces for maintenance of social stability.

The human services worker, as a member of the formal organization is expected to make the formal rules, regulations, and laws work. On the other hand, the worker deals with individuals in the local community and cannot escape the force of informal rules and codes. So, in a sense, the worker is caught in the middle, often faced with difficult if not incompatible choices. To prevent being caught in highly controversial situations that they do not understand, to lessen frustration when plans go awry, to keep from feeling that it is not possible to make progress in some circumstances, it is important for human services personnel to understand the manner in which the society works out its accommodations between societal and individual goals and expectations.

Chapter 7 will deal with the complexity of the worker's task. It describes the responsibilities of the human services professional as he or she mediates the goals of society and the expectations of the individual so that the welfare services given can meet individual needs but continue to receive the support of society that provides the resources that makes welfare programs possible.

References

1. Moore, W. *Social Change*. Englewood Cliffs, N.J.: Prentice-Hall, 1963, pp. 62, 63.

2. Hewitt, J. *Self and Society*. Boston, Allyn, 1979, pp. 106, 107.

3. Klapp, O. *Currents of Unrest*. New York: Holt, 1972, ch. 1.

4. LaPiere, R. *A Theory of Social Control*. New York: McGraw-Hill, 1954, ch. 5.

5. Milgram, S. *The Individual in a Social World*. Reading, Mass.: Addison-Wesley, 1977, pp. 154-155.

6. Douglass, J. *Defining America's Social Problems*. Englewood Cliffs, N.J.: Prentice-Hall, 1974, ch. 6.

7. LaPiere, R. Op. cit., pp. 318–320.

8. Ibid., pp. 320–322.

9. *Milwaukee Journal*, September 16, 1978, part 1, p. 8.

10. Hartjen, C. *Possible Trouble: An Analysis of Social Problems*. New York: Praeger, 1977, ch. 6.

11. *Milwaukee Journal*, May 28, p. 3; July 21, 1972, p. 5.

12. "Home for Retarded Youths Draws Heavy Fire in Boston", *Milwaukee Journal*, November 25, 1977, part 1, p. 9.

13. *Milwaukee Journal*, November 4, 1979, part 2, p. l.

chapter/ 7

The Impact Point: The Human Services Professional

So far we have been discussing four major elements that must be taken into consideration if one is to understand the functioning of welfare programs:

1. the society
2. the individual
3. community groups
4. the services themselves

We pointed out that these are closely related to each other and interdependent but that they are not necessarily dependent upon each other in a systematic fashion. Events can take place that modify the characteristics of welfare programs that do not affect the characteristics of the society. The relationship among the four elements is usually apparent, but it is not a one-to-one relationship.

It is the human services worker who must integrate these elements so that he or she can hold a position in the organization, deal with the community groups and with his or her fellow workers, and provide services to the recipients. Therefore, because these relationships are uneven and unpredictable workers are often faced with uncertainties as to just how they fit into the welfare organization, how they conceptualize welfare services, and how they should make services available to their clientele. When these uncertainties arise, the situation is said to be *problematic*.

Social Problems or Problematic Situations?

Talking about "social problems" has become so popular that the real meaning of the words has been lost. Strictly speaking, for something to be called a social problem, it should affect every member of society equally. This is seldom the case. For the most part, what is defined as a problem by one segment of society can be seen by another segment as unimportant or by another as advantageous. Thus we have situations that are problematic for an individual or for a group but that are not, overall, social problems. Advocates of change frequently try to demonstrate that a specific problem does affect everyone equally and that everyone should equally desire a solution. This is why ad campaigns state, "Crime (or poverty or pollution) is everybody's business."

This lack of agreement on what is or what is not a problem can itself contribute to the intensification of the problematic situation.

James Rule discusses the differences between social problems and problematic situations in his book, *Insight and Social Betterment*:

> the language of social science itself may distract attention from the *conflictual nature* of troubled social conditions. We often speak of "social problems," for example, as though they were conditions which everyone deplores. Yet most troublesome social conditions are not really "problematic" in this sense. Such conditions almost always involve oppositions of interests between two or more parties. They are problematic because what helps one party hurts the other and because these antagonisms have unpleasant repercussions for the rest of society. What pass for "racial problems" in contemporary America are the symptoms of conflict between supporters and opponents of more privilege for blacks. The "problem" of pollution reflects a division of interest between those who profit from polluting activities and those who do not. Social science faces few authentic social problems, in the sense of conditions which hurt everyone equally. More often, *problematic social conditions are those where help to one set of interests can only mean harm to others.*[1] [emphasis added]

Human services workers often find that they represent the battleground where the conflicts are taking place. They are employed by organizations that are supported by the society and that therefore have as a primary goal the maintenance of the social order. Yet the worker serves clients who may feel that they are the victims of the society and therefore demand that the worker help them to profit more from the operation of society. If a worker accedes to this demand, he or she will sooner or later come into conflict with elements of society that perceive this action to be a threat to their self-interest.

When welfare organizations attempt to modify local programs, they often encounter resistance, as we pointed out in Chapter 6. Almost every day the news media cite examples of this. Human services workers are usually in the forefront of the attempt to carry out the objectives of welfare organizations, be it to establish a halfway house in a residential area, to expand the activities of the neighborhood center, to establish foster homes in an area where they have not previously existed, or to eliminate a service where funding has been cut off. The worker is caught in the middle of the conflict. And, if the personal inclinations of the worker tend in a different direction, the worker is in a three-way bind. As an example, think of the worker who is supposed to be promoting foster homes in an area that does not want them and who personally believes that young persons should be taken from their natural parents only in the most extreme circumstances.

So, because of the nature of welfare programs, human services workers frequently are in the midst of *problematic situations*. This is at the same time a challenge and a source of stress. It is a challenge because the worker is in a position to work for maximum convergence between divergent forces and thus possibly be able to effect sufficient change to diffuse the conflict and improve the situation for his or her clients. It is a source of stress because of the difficulty involved in being constantly in the throes of problematic situations where routine is not easily established and where, no matter what the worker does, one party or another is dissatisfied.

Human services workers often come into the profession because of their perception of certain issues as "social problems." They are frequently disheartened at the resistance they meet when others do not agree with their definitions. It is very important for the human services worker to learn the difference between "social problems" (which they will rarely encounter) and "problematic situations" (in which they will often find themselves embroiled).

Learning to Anticipate Problematic Situations

In the industrial society great debate arises over the means of integrating the functions of that society, because the atomization that accompanies technological specialization creates difficulty in ensuring that all parts of the society work well together. In America, continuing efforts are expended to see that economic forces do not destroy the security of individuals, that government does not take away freedom, that families continue to meet the needs of all members, and that all persons in the society obtain a share of the products of industrialization and therefore enjoy at least a minimum standard of living, however that standard may be defined.

Growing up in an industrial society almost always requires that sooner or later persons move outside the tightly knit community to which they were introduced at birth. When this happens, persons experience the shock of finding out that, for everything previously held to be good and true, there are other differing views about the same issues held by nice, likeable, intelligent persons. People who, for whatever reason, interact with others who hold differing views soon learn that no value is as absolute as they had originally thought. As one learns to relate to other persons who represent other views, one begins to find out that it is difficult to tie things together so that they make sense. It begins to seem difficult to know for sure what one should think about a particular issue.

In the modern industrial society, radio, television, and newspapers keep people constantly informed about events that would have escaped notice before the invention of electronic communications. There is a constant barrage of information about the amount of unemployment, plans for welfare reform, welfare fraud, inflation, lack of resources for the aged, cutback of welfare services, complaints about coddling the poor, resistance to establishment of community-centered services, evidence of overcrowding in welfare institutions. Most of these have little immediate effect on the vast majority of persons who learn about them through the media, although over a period of time they may have an impact.

People are often heard to ask why communications people cannot tell just once about things that are going well. Media people are well aware of the difficulties. Still, to them "good news is no news"; when things are going well, meanings are clear and most persons agree about the course of action. Then few persons are interested in reading or listening to what might be said. Anyway, reporters add, there are so many problems that must be solved about which people need information that little time or space is left over for something else. Furthermore, under the principle of equal time, the media must present all sides of the issues by all the contending groups. This makes it even more difficult for the reader or listener to know who or what to believe. Whatever a political, scientific, business, community, professional, or minority group leader may say, someone else can be quoted as disagreeing. The issues are rarely completely settled.

When things begin to seem confusing, they also begin to take on the characteristics of a problematic situation. Because of the confusion, many today perceive life to be full of problems.

And yet most persons wish to continue to claim their share of the benefits made possible by industrialization despite the confusion, complexity, inequality, and perception of problems that accompany industrialization. In the final analysis, most people are willing to choose the complexities of life over the rigors of life that were accepted with a sense of fatalism and equanimity in the so-called "simpler" times.

Problematic situations may be a way of life, especially in the area of welfare programs; however, one should not get the impression that society is hopeless because it contains many problematic situations. This is far from the case. In fact, the reverse is true, because only in problematic situations is there the possibility for change. When there is consensus that a given situation or condition is satisfactory, there is no opportunity to change that situation or condition. For many years it was accepted that women were the property of their husbands. Even the women themselves fought little against this definition. As recently as 1850 it was possible for a husband in England to sell his wife to another man, as described in Thomas Hardy's novel, *The Mayor of Casterbridge.* It was equally acceptable for parents to sell their children to factories. If either of these practices were attempted today, reaction would be violent and swift. But these changes came about only when the consensus broke down, because then only could those who sought new ways gain the chance to be heard.

It is important for human services workers to anticipate (but not with despair) that they will often be the impact point between varying societal and individual goals. This anticipation can serve a twofold purpose. First, it can stimulate the worker to equip himself or herself with the necessary skills to create the convergence necessary to keep a balance among the divergent elements that exist in the context of welfare programs. Second, this anticipation can help the worker to be sensitive to the possibilities for change that may arise. In this way recipients can be better served and the society that supports the services can be assured that the social order will be maintained and perhaps even enhanced, and workers will have positive feelings about their jobs.

We will now turn to a discussion of the characteristics of some of the problematic situations in which human services workers find themselves. We will pay particular attention to those situations that may or may not seem to the worker to be problematic but that in fact are often seen as problematic by the recipients of services.

The Problematic Nature of Values—Altruism

Webster's defines *altruism* as the regard for and devotion to the interests of others. Altruism is manifested in society in two contradictory forms:

1. generalized altruism
2. interpersonal altruism

Altruism becomes problematic when people interact with each other in terms of the latter while perceiving their interaction in terms of the former.

Generalized Altruism

In our society altruism has been generalized into an ethic. Individuals are taught, especially through religious teachings, that we are all "members of the family of man" and that all persons should be their "brother's keeper." The *Bible* strongly emphasizes this generalized ethic of altruism and teaches that it should be extended to all human beings as unconditionally as possible. This generalized concern for others is expressed not only in Judeo-Christian tradition, but it is also a part of many of the Eastern religions. In philosophy, Immanuel Kant speaks of the "categorical imperative" wherein individuals are supposed to do good whether or not God exists.[2] In psychology, L. Kohlberg describes the sixth stage of moral development, which he calls postconventional morality, as that in which an effort is made by persons to be guided by the same kind of "abstract ethical principles."[3]

This inclusive ethic of generalized concern for others is widespread and constitutes an important motivation for many who enter the welfare field. Generalized altruism is also a major ethic underlying what welfare services purport to do. Why then does the idea of doing good sometimes work in ways that make it scarcely recognizable when compared with its original aim?

Interpersonal Altruism

People like to think that their altruism is totally unselfish, but this is rarely the case as humans must live together in order to survive. This necessitates the formation of associations with others, and, if every member of a group were to insist on his or her own desires being met on each and every occasion, the result would be chaos and the breakdown of the group. To ensure survival of both the individual and the group, accommodations must occur. Each member of the group gives and each receives in return. This results in a modification of self-centered egoism. This modification operates to ensure both the survival of the individual in the group and of the group itself. Thus, in the final analysis altruism can be self-serving.[4]

Altruism does not operate to any degree between members of groups and other individuals who are not considered to be members of the group, and all groups have boundaries with some people who are "in" and some who are "out." There are always the "we's" and the "they's."[5] The discernment of who is or who is not a member of a certain group varies in strength from the strongest feeling of membership in primary groups to weaker feelings of membership in secondary groups. The stronger the feeling of group membership, the more discernment there is of differences between members and nonmembers.[6]

Time and space, however, permit persons to hold membership in only a limited number of groups (as stated in Chapter 6). Thus, one's personal concern for others tends to be limited to the groups in which one has membership. When altruism is generalized into an ethic and individuals think that they have developed a feeling for others, all too often the others for whom they have concern are those who have characteristics similar to their own. People will tend to feel affinity for persons whom they may not know but who are of the same religious faith, are members of the same occupational group, are of the same ethnic background, come from the same geographical region, are of the same sex, or share a similar handicap. On the other hand, people may often feel competitive, hostile, superior, inferior, or merely neutral toward individuals who do not share similar characteristics and therefore fall outside their sphere of concern.[7]

In other words, it is much easier to have concern for others if those others are somewhat like the individuals who desire to be altruistic. Because so many people who think they are operating according to the generalized ethic of altruism do not recognize that they are, in fact, operating on the basis of interpersonal altruism, their next step is often an effort to make those persons for whom they are supposed to have concern similar to themselves.

This is a major force that lies behind the effort of so many human services workers who attempt to manipulate welfare recipients into developing characteristics that are valued by those who care for them. People who need welfare assistance find that assistance much easier to obtain if they can convince the human services workers that they are honest, thrifty, healthy, clean, family oriented, employed, religious, proud of their neighborhood, respectful of property, and law abiding at all times. If they are not, they will find that much of welfare assistance is oriented toward enabling them to acquire these characteristics.[8]

This is not to say that there is anything wrong with these characteristics. Indeed, our society could not operate if the majority did not agree that they have value. The danger is that, when altruism takes this direction, it is often used only as a method of control, as a way of singling out those who will receive attention from those who will not.

It is important for human services workers to be aware of the ease with which interpersonal altruism can be confused with or even substituted for generalized altruism. It is the sort of thing that is often easy to see in others and very difficult to recognize in one's self.[9] Interpersonal altruism, masquerading as generalized altruism, is a major force contributing to problematic situations existing in welfare services.

The Problematic Nature of Values—Individualism

The altruistic value of being one's "brother's keeper" is contradictory to the individualistic value of "God helps those who help themselves." People are taught from early childhood that the responsibility for what happens to any individual rests squarely on that individual and therefore that success or failure is only a matter of individual effort. Happiness or disatisfaction is also a function of individual attitude.[10]

The simultaneous operation of the values of individualism and altruism produces a friction (particularly in the context of welfare services) that causes problematic situations. Most human services workers have worked hard to advance themselves. They have struggled to obtain an education, to find a position in a welfare organization, and then to work for advancement in that organization. They see themselves as strong evidence of the payoff of the value of individualism. And yet they must constantly deal with persons who are either unaccepting of the value of individualism or for whom the myth has gone awry.

Often, when the worker is faced with the choice of carrying out services that may benefit the client but are unpopular to persons with differing perspectives toward welfare services, the worker can encounter a problematic situation. If the worker chooses to work for what he or she sees as the best interests of the client, this effort may not produce acceptance from others with whom the worker must interact. Worse yet, the worker's chances for advancement may be threatened. In this case, the rewards of altruism are few, but the rewards of individualism (at least the worker's individualistic effort for self-improvement) are great.

The simultaneous existence of these two values puts the worker in the most difficult problematic situation of all. It is nearly impossible, given the pressures that exist in these situations, for workers to make choices that benefit the client when that altruistic choice runs counter to the benefit of the welfare organization, the society, the community, and particularly the worker himself or herself. The strength of the value of individualism in American society is such that persons will seldom make choices that will negate the effects of efforts for their own personal well-being, even though in so doing the welfare of clients is compromised. The dilemma produced by this problematic situation is continuous for human services workers.

The Problematic Nature of Special-Interest Groups

Welfare programs excite the interest of the general public. It is therefore certain that coalitions will be formed that are made up of persons who have a particular interest in influencing the character of welfare programs. These special-interest groups are seldom in agreement about their approach. Often more energy is consumed in competing with each other over what the nature of services should be than is directed toward actually molding welfare services in the pattern that they advocate. Human services workers are compelled to deal with many special-interest groups, groups that are frequently able to exert sufficient influence to alter the characteristics of the welfare services and, thus, to alter the responsibilities of the human services worker as well. Workers have to be careful not to alienate too many of the special-interest groups, no matter how heartily they wish they could, because workers need support (both financial and emotional) for themselves and for the continuance of services. They find that the support of the special-interest groups is particularly important when a service is to be discontinued, strengthened, or initiated.[11, 12]

Five types of special-interest groups relate to welfare services:

1. detractors
2. advocates
3. supporters
4. providers
5. recipients

Even the names suggest that the worker may expect difficulties, for he or she must at times deal with all five at once in connection with the responsibilities of the job. The major reason for difficulty is that these special-interest groups act toward welfare services according to differential and conflicting applications of criteria. These special-interest groups relate to welfare services according to their own unique perceptions in relation to the following:

1. attitudes toward the poor
2. resources available for services
3. power to control services
4. information available about services
5. the time frame of reference

The human services workers who understand the issues in which they will become involved as they deal with special-interest groups, all mixing and matching their own definitions of criteria will be better prepared to deal with the problematic situations that will inevitably arise. It should be remembered that these special-interest groups are not mutually exclusive and that membership of an individual is not limited to only one of these groups. For example, advocates might also be supporters, providers, or even recipients, although they will seldom be all at the same time.

First we describe the types of special-interest groups; then we discuss the criteria that these groups use in their approach to welfare services.

Detractors

Detractors are a diverse lot. They are members of religious groups, economic and political groups, taxpayer groups, local community groups, and so forth. They may be conservative or liberal. Religious groups who are opposed to welfare usually are so for moralistic reasons, because they feel that it defiles the sanctity of work, the family, or the procreative process. Many conservative groups do not wish to see political units of society using public monies for welfare. If they favor services at all, they do so in the "residual" rather than in the "institutional" sense. (See Chapter 2.) Taxpayer groups oppose welfare services because they resent having the government take their money and use it to support programs that they say are simply "give-aways" or "a subsidization of laziness" or "a reward for not working." Some work groups oppose certain welfare programs because they see in them a threat to job security.

Most detractors of welfare are harshly critical of the present welfare system, but few would wish to disband it completely. Still, there are some who would do so if they had the power.

Advocates

Advocates are the individuals and groups that favor the existence of welfare services in some form or another. They may be somewhat critical of the present system, but they believe that it is important to provide aid and assistance to the poor.

Advocates are as diverse a lot as the detractors. They include religious groups, commercial groups, employee groups, lobbies, welfare rights groups, philanthropic foundations, and the welfare organizations themselves. Their motives can range from generalized altruism to specialized self-interest. Religious groups tend to be the most altruistic in their support for welfare services, whereas employee groups in welfare organizations who are interested in maintaining their jobs tend to have continuity and conditions of employent uppermost in their minds. But, for whatever reason, these groups do not wish to see welfare programs weakened, and they provide powerful support for the continuation of services.

Supporters

Supporters are the groups or individuals who provide the financial resources that make it possible for welfare programs to operate. They include taxpayers who finance the public agencies; labor groups, business groups, local committees, and neighborhood groups that contribute to United Fund budgets; and religious groups that fund the services operated by religious organizations. Motives range from the most involuntary to the most voluntary, from direct taxation to the contribution placed in the offering plate during a religious service.

It should be kept in mind that organizations and groups that provide financial support may have within their membership both detractors and advocates of welfare services and that, while the advocates are probably in the majority, the balance may be very close.

Providers

Providers are the individuals and groups that operate the welfare programs. They furnish the labor. They range from administrators to janitors, from full-time professional personnel to part-time untrained volunteers. They are in contact with all the factions such as the politicians, the business persons, religious leaders, and, of course, the many categories of clients. They are responsible for the delivery of a wide variety of services.

Recipients

These are the individuals who receive the services of the welfare organizations. They range from the aged on Social Security, either in their own homes or in nursing homes, to children with no identifiable natural parent. They might be the law breakers or the mentally ill, the persons or families who are not economically self-sufficient, or the physically handicapped. How recipients see themselves in relation to society has much to do with how they view welfare services and how they will act toward what these services provide. Some see in these services the support that prevents them from experiencing calamity or that helps them over a rough time. Others see welfare as a societal invention that controls them and prevents them from bettering their personal or social condition.[13]

Operational Criteria of Special-Interest Groups

Human activity depends on meaning. When individuals agree on the meaning of what they experience in the world about them, they can agree on activities in which they should engage to achieve mutual satisfaction. When definitions differ, those who agree with each other band together to oppose those whose definitions differ. The more severe the differences in definition, the more intense the competition or conflict.[14] The degree of intensity determines the amount of effort that must be expended by the human services worker to maintain continuity and stability of welfare services.

The special-interest groups will hold varying definitions or attitudes to many different things, the most important of which are discussed in the following paragraphs.

Attitudes Toward Poverty

The differing attitudes toward poverty among the special-interest groups probably generate the most difficult problems with which human services workers must deal. Special-interest groups differ in their explanations of poverty as to whether it is societally caused or individually caused. They differ as to what should be the nature of welfare programs to deal with poverty.

They differ as to what should be the major thrust of welfare programs—economic assistance or social services or a combination of both. They differ in their perceptions of the poor, whether they are poor because of a lack of opportunity or a lack of appropriate personal characteristics. They differ as to whether the poor should be punished or supported. The conflicts that result from these differences in attitudes often prevent workers from achieving a feeling that their efforts have contributed toward the solution of any of the social or individual conditions that constitute poverty and underprivilege.

Resources Available

How much of all goods and services should be allotted to the various categories of the needy is a controversial subject. Economists disagree as to how much surplus is available, and the people who are not specialists are inclined to even more disagreement. Advocates say that as a wealthy nation we have resources available to aid the poor. Detractors feel that if there is any surplus it should go to those who worked hard to create it.

There is also argument about whether funds should be given in direct maintenance or be used to provide personal services and as to what the ratio of one to the other should be. Thus there is disagreement as to how much money dependent families should receive, what stipend should be available to the elderly who have insufficient retirement funds, and what kind of facilities should be made availabble to the ill, the crippled, or the criminal offenders. The type and amount of resources and services dispensed to recipients of welfare depends upon which special-interest group can gather support for its definition.

Power

As special-interest groups compete with one another, each attempts to force the others to accept its own definitions so that welfare programs will be operated in accordance with their definitions. How successful this is depends on the power that any one group is able to exert over the others. It also depends on the perception that each group has of the power of the other. Services are usually formulated and imposed without consideration of the reaction of the recipients, for most special-interest groups perceive welfare recipients as having little power. Therefore few pains are taken to involve the recipients in deliberations on the nature of welfare services. Taxpayer groups try to influence their political representatives to keep welfare costs down, while welfare advocate groups try to convince political representatives that the support should at least be maintained as it is and, preferably, expanded.

Information

All special-interest groups have information based on research, tradition, opinion, personal experience, and so forth that they wish to dispense to the general public, because what the general public hears over a period of time has an important impact on what they believe and will support. Special-interest groups compete for the means to disperse their ideas, and this can be done only by obtaining the support of mass communication. Media personnel talk to those whom they perceive to have the most credibility. One might think that the media would perceive human services workers or actual recipients as having credibility, but in fact the media tend to get information from public officials, business executives, and high-status experts. These members of special-interest groups have the most power to attract the attention of the media.

Time Frame of Reference

Special-interest groups have differing time references.[15] Taxpayer groups tend to see time in terms of a past period when taxes were lower and services were less extensive. They wish that those "good old days" would return, but there are also those who are aware that the "good old days" were not so good for everyone. For instance, advocates of expanded services to children recall that children were once employed in sweat shops, mines, and factories and worked under deplorable conditions, or that eight- and nine-year-olds were put to work doing jobs that were considered too unpleasant for the older employees. These individuals or groups are likely to resist any attempt to permit young people to work.

Some groups think that the movement to give women rights equal to those of men is a modern invention designed to destroy the family. They feel that it would be better to encourage women to be homemakers and child bearers as they supposedly have been since before the dawn of history. People with this perspective support welfare services that reward women who stay home and care for their children. They are often opposed to day-care services and public funding of abortion.

Still other groups try to anticipate a future time when it is hoped resources will be more equitably distributed than they are today. These groups often hold the opinion that assistance should be tied not to work but to income. If income falls below a certain minimum, regardless of the circumstances, a grant from public funds should be made to that individual or family.

The Worker—the Impact Point

And so it goes. The special-interest groups stand by their definitions, trying to convince others of the correctness of their recommendations. Sometimes one is successful, sometimes another. Most of the time a compromise is reached so that no one group loses out completely in the struggle for the achievement of minimum goals with which all can exist even if they don't agree.

The problematic nature of the situation in relation to special-interest groups is not lessened by the fact that human services workers are themselves members of one of the groups and have an affinity or antipathy for some of the others. It is difficult to work under constant criticism, to have to listen to persons who say that programs would be more effective if their suggestions were heeded, and to deal with recipients who question the services provided and the credibility of the provider.

There is a question that naturally arises at this point. Given all these special-interest groups, each having its own approach to welfare and creating problematic situations, how can the programs function at all? Yet it is apparent that services are provided, resources are made available, human services workers keep their jobs, and clients are served. The services do function reasonably well. Nonetheless, there is often a continuing sense of frustration on the part of the workers and a feeling that services could and should be improved. The effort required to maintain the structure of welfare services and to keep the process of assistance intact requires workers to exert more individual and collective effort than would be the case if the situation were less problematic.

Summary

Human services workers deal with few authentic social problems because their work does not benefit *all* members of society *equally*. Human services workers deal primarily with problematic situations, in that they are concerned with assisting one segment of the population, namely, the poor. Other segments of the population often perceive this assistance as being inimical to their own interests. These differences in perceptions give rise to special-interest groups that attempt to influence welfare programs in a variety of ways.

Human services workers are constantly dealing with the problems that are generated by these special-interest groups. This often is a source of stress and contributes to occupational turnover. The human services worker who anticipates that he or she will encounter these problematic situations can equip himself or herself with the necessary skills to maintain a working balance among the diverse interests that exist in the field. He or she can also become sensitive to the possibilities for change that may arise, because, when the attitudes of the groups in power can be modified or when the power relationships among the groups are changed, the human services worker has an opportunity to make welfare programs more effective.

Chapter 8 is the first of three chapters that will present a description of the three major types of welfare programs provided by human services professionals.

References

1. Rule, J. *Insight and Social Betterment.* New York: Oxford, 1978, p. 7.
2. Durant, W. *The Story of Philosophy.* New York: Time Books, 1933, ch. 6.
3. Kohlberg, L., and Gilligan, C. "The Adolescent as Philosopher," *Daedalus* (Fall 1971): 1051–1086.
4. "Our Selfish Genes," *Newsweek*, October 16, 1978, p. 118.
5. Yinger, M. *A Minority Group in American Society.* New York: McGraw-Hill, 1965, ch. 2.
6. Wilson, G., and Ryland, G. *Social Work Practice.* Boston: Houghton, 1949, p. 44.
7. Shibutani, T. *Society and Personality.* Englewood Cliffs, N.J.: Prentice-Hall, 1962, pp. 341–354.
8. Ryan, W. *Blaming the Victim.* New York: Random House, 1971, pp. 114–118.
9. Hirsch, F. *Social Limits to Growth.* Cambridge, Mass.: Harvard U. P. 1978, pp. 78–82.
10. *Ibid.*, pp. 80, 81.
11. Kaufman, H. *Politics and Policies in State and Local Governments.* Englewood Cliffs, N.J.: Prentice-Hall, 1963, ch. 3.
12. La Piere, R. *Social Change.* New York: McGraw-Hill, 1965, ch. 5, 6.
13. Feagin, J. *Subordinating the Poor.* Englewood Cliffs, N.J.: Prentice-Hall, 1975, ch. 3.
14. Hewitt, J. *Self and Society.* Boston: Allyn, 1979, pp. 105–110.
15. Douglass, J. *Defining America's Social Problems.* Englewood Cliffs, N.J.: Prentice-Hall, 1974, ch. 5.

part/two
Categories of Programs

In the next three chapters we will discuss the major types of welfare programs that are available to individuals and groups:

1. programs for economic maintenance
2. programs for personal improvement
3. programs to mitigate economic and social differences

Programs for economic maintenance, that is, programs that provide money or goods to individuals who are eligible to receive them under the rules of a particular program, will be discussed in detail in Chapter 8. Programs for personal improvement, which are often closely linked to programs for economic maintenance, are discussed in Chapter 9. For instance, a mother who receives a support check from the welfare department, will probably also be receiving attention from human services professionals. Some might be teaching her to manage her money better; a nurse might visit the home to assess the health of her children; a social worker or a psychologist might be giving her information on how to be a more effective mother; the mother may be receiving job training. This is only a partial list of many services potentially available. However, few if any of these services would be available to the mother were she not receiving economic maintenance services. On occasion, services for personal improvement are given separately from services for economic maintenance, but more frequently they go hand in hand.

Programs for mitigating economic and social differences are discussed in Chapter 10. These programs are designed to lessen the disparity of *groups* (not individuals) who have few of the material possessions or lack social position felt to be necessary for a satisfying life in contemporary America. For example, when a human services professional works with a neighborhood group to encourage the members to clean up their surroundings or to request increased services from the city for their neighborhood such as rat control, police protection, and so on, the worker is providing a service to mitigate economic and social differences.

The first two topics discussed in Chapter 8—definitions of poverty and theories of the causes of poverty—are also important to the understanding of Chapters 9 and 10. Definitions of poverty are used to develop the criteria by which individuals are tested to determine whether or not they are eligible for services from welfare programs. These definitions are functional; that is, they deal with what is in operation at the present. The definitions of poverty are used to position individuals relative to the lowest levels on the stratification continuum. A definition of poverty offers no explanation as to why an individual is poor. It is used only to sort out who needs assistance and who (according to the definition) does not.

In contrast, the theories of the causality of poverty offer explanations as to why some individuals occupy the lower ranks in the stratification continuum. There are a number of theories about why and how this happens. The three that are most relevant to the understanding of welfare programs in operation in the United States today will be discussed in the second section of Chapter 8.

chapter/8
Programs for Economic Maintenance

Definitions of Poverty

The oldest definition of poverty is that condition in which individuals cannot furnish for themselves sufficient resources to sustain life. This is an *absolute* definition of poverty* because it describes poverty as a lack of absolute resources to meet absolute needs. It is not too difficult to agree on the elements of this definition because it can be readily ascertained when individual resources have fallen below the minimum necessary to avoid starvation or when exposure to the elements reaches the point at which life might no longer continue.

This definition of poverty was used almost exclusively until the late 1950s, at which time three other definitions began to come into use to define the point at which people should be considered poor.[1] The newer definitions, which are *relative*, have not supplanted the earlier, long-standing one but they have added to it, giving four definitions of poverty. The three most recent

* See Chapter 4, p. 51.

definitions of poverty are relative as noted because the people in these definitions are considered poor in their material resources relative to the material resources of some other segment of the society.[2] These definitions emerged when it became generally accepted that welfare programs of economic maintenance had for the most part eliminated the grinding poverty that killed people, even though inequality of distribution of resources throughout the society was still very evident.

The first relative definition describes poverty as that situation in which an individual lacks the material resources that are necessary to provide an "adequate" diet, housing, health, and so on. It is not as easy to agree upon what amounts and types of food are necessary to provide "adequate" nutrition as it is to agree upon how much food is necessary to sustain life. The same difficulty arises between what constitutes "minimal" and "adequate" housing, "minimal" and "adequate" clothing and so on.[3]

The second relative definition of poverty concerns the standard of living. Currently this is described in terms of the income deemed necessary to support a single person, a married couple, a family with four children, and so on over a period of time. In the present inflationary period, the income necessary to provide the minimum adequate standard of living changes almost from week to week; it also varies from region to region in the nation.*

The most relative definition is that which defines the poor as anyone at the bottom of the socioeconomic scale.[5] Under this definition, people, regardless of their resources, will be perceived as being poor (and will perceive themselves to be poor) if they have less than do others about them. For instance, if many families have three automobiles, those with only two will be perceived as (and will feel) somewhat deprived, those with only one will feel more deprived, and those with no automobile at all will feel (and be perceived as) destitute even if good public transportation is available.

The continuum of definitions of poverty from the most absolute to the most relative poses a dilemma for the development of programs for economic maintenance. Each of the definitions has advocates. There are those who think that programs should operate to prevent only extremes of physical suffering from lack of resources for basic needs. At the other end of the range are those who wish to accomplish a redistribution of the wealth of society by income transfers that would wipe out the existing socioeconomic distinctions. Presently, most programs for economic maintenance take as their official definition of poverty the first relative definition, that is, the programs attempting to furnish resources that will provide the minimum "adequate" living requirements.

The technique whereby the definitions are put into effect is called the "means test" or "eligibility test." Although federal guidelines underpin all means tests for economic assistance, the tests still vary from program to program and from state to state.

* For a detailed discussion of the variety of formulas used to define a minimum standard of living, see Komisar.

The definitions of poverty are based on societal goals, not on individual needs. When put into operation, they can be a source of frustration to both the human services professional and to the recipient of welfare services as the following newspaper article demonstrates.

Rewards of Honesty—Gifts Conflict With Welfare

Honesty paid off for 16-year-old John Thompson of Norfolk recently, but only for a little while. Though he needed new shoes and trousers and had no lunch money that day back in October, he didn't keep the $40 he found on a schoolbus floor. He gave it to the driver, and the owner got it back.

After people heard and read about Thompson's honesty and about his mother's poverty, gifts began to pour in, including $1,000 from a Norfolk postman. Donations totaled about $1,500, which, the state said, made the Thompsons ineligible for welfare.

According to Virginia requirements, families with more than $1,500 in personal or real property can't receive food stamps, and those with more than $400 in resources can't receive Aid to Dependent Children grants. Carolyn Thompson, who is divorced and jobless, says she was told that if she wanted to continue receiving such aid, she would have to spend some of the money that had come in as a result of her son's honesty. So she bought a 12-year-old car for $175, and some related expenses consumed all but about $300 of the donations.

Joann Stauffenberg, a welfare-eligibility worker, says that "what we personally feel has no control over the law. You still have to abide by the law."

Mrs. Thompson says that at first she was overwhelmed with gratitude at receiving the gifts, but the welfare rules have made her wonder "if it would have been better if we hadn't received it at all. Everything is so confusing. I just figure that God giveth, and the devil taketh away."[6]

The Causes of Poverty

Three explanations of why people are poor underlie most of the welfare programs presently in existence in the United States:

1. stability theory
2. subcultural theory
3. opportunity theory

Stability theory emphasizes the permanence of poverty with little change possible in either its extent or its character. This theory is important to the understanding of the programs that provide economic assistance. The other two theories—subcultural theory and opportunity theory—allow for the possibility of change, although they offer different ideas as to how this can be achieved. They are fundamental to the understanding of programs that provide the poor with services that are supposed to help them move up on the stratification continuum.

Stability Theory

Many theorists believe that society tends toward a continued centralization of wealth and other forms of economic power rather than toward equality. They point out that history supports this conclusion in that no socioeconomic-political system up to this time has demonstrated any other trend. According to this point of view, persons are poor and unemployed because for some reason they are unable to obtain the resources and the power to change their situation. The poor tolerate these conditions because they have no choice and because they realize that it is in their own interests to cooperate with the more powerful. Also according to this theory the wealth is in the hands of the few, the society exists to meet the goals of these fortunate few, and the poor and underprivileged are exploited. Economic welfare services exist not to redistribute the wealth but to provide just enough economic resources to the poor to prevent them from disturbing the social order.[7][8]

According to this point of view, inequality is inevitable under the present economic system. According to the stability theory, economic welfare assistance must be a permanent part of the socioeconomic landscape because there is and will always be a coterie of industrial poor.[9] This is not to say that the same persons or groups must always be members of the coterie but only that the coterie will always exist. In practice, however, it is recognized that those presently in the grip of poverty find it nearly impossible to move up the stratification continuum. Thus membership in this coterie of industrial poor is also fairly stable.

Subcultural Theory

This theory states that, when persons are unable to support themselves adequately, it is mainly because they lack certain personal attributes that enable them to find and keep a job. Persons lack these attributes because they are absent in the groups with which these persons interact; that is, they are absent from their subculture. Some of these weaknesses in their subculture might be the following:

1. Lack of future orientation. A person who wants to be economically self-sufficient must be able to exert effort toward a reward that exists in the future, not in the immediate present, even if it only means working for a week to receive a paycheck at the end of that period. To be really successful, however, a person must also be able to postpone satisfaction for some years to receive even greater rewards. Subcultural theorists state that this lack of future orientation prevents some groups in the American society from finding and holding jobs.

2. Lack of understanding of the surroundings. Many people move to the cities from rural areas or from other countries and do not understand how to cope with their new location. Although they may have been able to hold jobs before they moved, now they cannot determine how to find work. Until these "immigrants" understand their surroundings, the subcultural theorists say, they will not be able to care for themselves economically.

3. Lack of basic job skills. This is closely related to the second point. When persons do not understand the nature of their surroundings, they are unable to develop the skills that are needed to obtain and hold a decent job. Often lack of education or of job training contributes to this cultural "deprivation."

4. Lack of appropriate family circumstances. Subcultural theorists point out that some groups in the American society have families in which the male adult is not present, so the female not only must bear the brunt of childrearing but also take economic responsibility for the family. These are commonly called "matriarchal" families. It is difficult for a single adult to assume all the responsibiilties for the family that two persons usually do, especially if that person is also handicapped by the other lacks discussed in 1, 2, and 3.

The subcultural theory of poverty places a heavy burden of responsibility on the groups identified as having these negative economic attributes. These negative attributes place these groups in an unfavorable position in relation to the rest of society, leading to the conclusion that these groups could be economically successful if they would modify their "subculture." This theory places the burden of responsibility for change on the groups and on the individuals that comprise these groups; it permits the rest of society to form negative stereotypes of these groups and a negative impression of welfare services that are predominantly focused on groups with some of these characteristics. This theory presumes that meaningful work is available for all who desire work; the impediment lies in those who are marginal to the majority culture.[10] [11]

Opportunity Theory

The opportunity theory of poverty assumes that most people want to work and are able to do so, but often work is not available to them at the right time and in the right place. It is therefore important for some segment of society to provide job opportunities. If persons who are employed live in areas in which jobs are scarce, then jobs must be created and these people must be given economic assistance until the jobs are available. If jobs already exist, then the unemployed must be given the opportunity to work at these jobs, perhaps by training programs that help them to acquire new skills, by providing transportation, and so on. If jobs are available, the unemployed must be encouraged to take these jobs, even if the jobs require minimal skills and pay below the minimum wage.

The opportunity theory of poverty assumes a more positive social attitude toward the various groups of the unemployed than do the first two theories presented. It assumes that welfare services will be temporary for the most part and also that there is an unevenness in the availability of jobs according to region and according to time. According to this theory, unevenness can be managed through societal intervention, and, in the long run, all that want to work will find work and stay at it. Both this theory and the subcultural theory of poverty assume that in time the extremes of inequality can be eliminated and the existence of a nearly universal class assured.

Both the subcultural and opportunity theories of poverty presume that economic assistance will be necessary only until either the negative economic subculture of those on welfare is modified or until opportunities are guaranteed for those who require them. The subcultural theorists urge that welfare organizations' develop positive cultural characteristics for those with whom they deal; the opportunity theorists urge welfare organizations to assist in creating employment opportunities and enabling the unemployed to take advantage of the opportunities when they occur. From this point of view, welfare services can be classified as *preventive* because they operate to prevent the necessity for long-term economic assistance to a permanent group of welfare recipients.[12] [13]

To summarize, stability theory emphasizes the permanence of poverty with little change possible in either its extent or character. Subcultural theory allows for the possibility of change because it views people who are poor as different from those who are not poor and states that change in the extent and character of poverty is possible when the persons who are poor are taught to be more like those who are not poor. Opportunity theory also allows for the possibility of change and, furthermore, places the responsibility for the modification of poverty on the social structure rather than on the individual.

Development of Programs for Economic Maintenance

Before we describe the present programs for economic maintenance, we will review some of the important developments leading to them. Prior to the Civil War, the primary means of providing for the poor was to indenture them to work for the well-to-do, to place them in one of a variety of institutions created for them, or to export them from the local community.

Indenture was the arrangement whereby poor persons bound themselves to a master for an agreed-upon length of time, after which they would be free. Under indenture the poor person would receive the minimum necessities and sometimes a small wage from the master for his or her labor. The term "indenture" arises from the practice of drawing up an agreement and then cutting it in two parts, the cut consisting of wavy lines, or "teeth." The indentured person received one half of the paper, the master the other. When the servant was freed, he or she received the master's half. When proof of freedom was demanded, the former servant had to furnish both matching pieces of paper. A pauper could be forced into indenture. Children were often indentured by poor parents who received either a lump-sum payment or a percentage of the annual wages of the child. The practice of indenture had for the most part disappeared by the beginning of the twentieth century.[14]

Poor persons were also often placed in prisons or in almshouses, later known as "poor farms," and lived under terrible conditions. Men, women, and children of all ages, the handicapped, the mentally ill, and the retarded, all were crowded together. The common name for this type of provision was "indoor relief." This form of care for the poor had a long history, and "poor farms" persisted as a major form of care from the early eighteenth century until the latter part of the 1930s.[15]

Poor persons were also often driven out of town so the members of the local community would not have to support them. Those who were "warned" wandered from locality to locality. The mortality rate among them was high. Many were forced toward the frontier because so few communities would tolerate their presence. Variants of this practice continue to the present day even though the U.S. Supreme Court in 1969 declared residency requirements to be obsolete.[16] Even so, some states still subvert the Supreme Court decision, and the federal government requires a residency test for eligibility to receive assistance through the Work Incentive Program (WIN).[17]

Without exception, the earliest programs for economic maintenance were based on the "cultural" theory of causation and the "absolute" definition of poverty, but many of the nation's leaders began to realize that there were forces outside the control of the individual that determined whether or not he or she was poor or self-sufficient. There was some support for the emerging practice of "outdoor relief," the furnishing of economic assistance to persons in their own homes. Again, this was a gradual development because, as we just stated, removal and institutionalization persisted for many years after the Civil War. The period of reform that swept the nation around 1900 was initiated partially because the waves of immigration from Europe spawned such terrible poverty in the nation's cities that it was impossible for the many poor persons to be cared for in institutions.

During this period private organizations concerned with the poor sprang up in the large cities. These organizations concentrated on giving services to the poor in their own homes. They worked to improve employment conditions, housing, education, and health services.[18] During this period human services professionals were acquiring experience in the local public and private welfare agencies. This experience provided the background that would enable them to design and carry out the massive national programs for economic maintenance that were inaugurated during the 1930s.

The Great Depression jolted American society into the realization that poverty was not solely the result of individual weakness or guile. When, by 1933, one quarter to one third of the work force was unemployed, there was fear of mass disorder.[19] It became clear that local piecemeal approaches to poverty would not suffice and that the federal government would need to develop large, broadly based programs to prevent a large-scale threat to national stability. This resulted in the passage, among other programs, of the

Social Security Act in 1935. The Social Security Act initiated the first system of insurance against the hazards of unemployment. The Civilian Conservation Corps provided jobs for thousands of young men. The Agricultural Adjustment Administration assisted the rural poor, especially the farmers. The Public Works Administration created jobs for the unemployed in building post offices, roads, court houses, and other public facilities. The Federal Emergency Relief Act made large sums of money available to the states and counties to provide economic maintenance for the unemployed.[20]

By the beginning of World War II, many of these programs had been dismantled. Most of the public programs that remained were administered by the states rather than by the federal government. There was a major retrenchment of the programs of direct economic assistance to the poor. The only direct relief that remained during this period was for special categories— the old, the blind, and the orphaned. Until the 1960s there was little provision for the able-bodied poor who could not find employment.[21]

Then, in the 1960s, welfare programs increased dramatically again. Piven and Cloward state that

> the welfare explosion occurred in all regions, and in both urban and rural counties. But the explosion was far greater in urban areas; and among those urban areas it was a handful of the most populous Northern cities that showed the largest rises. . . . Most of the increase occurred all at once, in just a brief period after 1964.[22]

They attribute this "explosion" of programs for economic maintenance to the revolution in agriculture that displaced thousands of black Americans from their rural surroundings and drove them to the northern cities. The threats to social stability that arose from this urban migration and the rising importance of black power dictated a response similar to the enactment of programs for economic maintenance that resulted from the Great Depression of the 1930s.[23]

Income Transfers

Resources made available to the poor always come from some other sector of society. Sometimes these resources come from "giving," as when people give Thanksgiving or Christmas baskets to needy families, give money to be used by United Way agencies, or give goods to be dispensed through organizations such as Goodwill, the Salvation Army, or the St. Vincent dePaul Society. Private giving of this sort is sporadic and does not provide consistent support. For this reason, economic assistance for the poor has been taken over by the publicly supported agencies. Thus, most resources for the poor come from taxation in which the government takes money income away from those who have it and distributes it through the various economic maintenance programs.

The next section of the chapter will describe some of the developments in the *public* programs for economic maintenance utilized in our society.* The

* Examples of specific programs are detailed in Document 8.1 at the end of this chapter.

procedures whereby resources are transferred from one segment of the society to another are classified today under the general caption, *income transfers.*

There are two categories of income transfers: cash and in kind.[24] *Cash* transfers involve the collection of money from one segment of the population and the allocation of that money to another segment. Cash transfer may be *direct, indirect, credit,* or *insurance.*

A *direct* cash transfer is the payment of money to a person who qualifies to receive that money. Examples are an assistance check given to the mother of dependent children, a subsidy check given to a farmer for keeping land out of production, or a monthly Social Security payment.

An *indirect* cash transfer is the lowering of required payment, usually taxes, through devices such as deductions. Examples are the income tax deduction given for dependent children and the tax deduction allowed for interest on loans.

Credit as an income transfer is money loaned at lower rates than can be found in the marketplace. This would include advances of funds to repair homes in central cities, loans to homeowners at low interest rates after their homes have been destroyed by fire, earthquake, or some other "act of God," and guaranteed loans to students or to large companies.

Insurance becomes an income transfer when it is offered to individuals at a lower rate than can be found from the insurance industry. Veterans' insurance is an example of this type of transfer.

Transfers *in kind* are resources that are furnished directly to the beneficiary, with the sponsoring agency paying for resources furnished. Examples of transfers in kind are (1) food—which is either furnished directly as through a Christmas basket or through the food stamp program; (2) clothing—which may be furnished through a Goodwill store or bought at a regular store and paid for by the agency; (3) housing—which is furnished directly in some cases, such as an apartment in a public housing project for a mother with dependent children; and (4) medical equipment (such as glasses, crutches, braces, wheelchairs)—as when the sponsoring agency pays the bill directly instead of giving the money to the recipient and letting him or her pay the bill.[25]

It is commonly assumed that all income transfers involve taxing income away from the affluent segments of the society and then allocating it to the less affluent segments. This is not necessarily the case, because what actually happens depends on the type of taxation and the nature of the income transfer.

Taxation can be either "regressive" or "progressive." Regressive taxation (such as sales and property taxes) is so named because the taxes are collected at the same rate throughout the population. Thus they take a proportionately larger share of a poor person's income than they do of a wealthier person's income. Progressive taxation (such as the income tax) increases in rate as the income of the taxpayer goes up. In theory, at least, it takes a proportionately larger share of the income from the wealthier segments of the population than it does from the poorer segments.

Income transfers consume a large part of the federal budget. Depending on how transfers are defined, they accounted for from 35 to 45 per cent of federal expenditures for fiscal 1977 or from $137 billion to over $170 billion.[26] As we will see, only a small portion of these income transfers go to persons on welfare. Income transfers as well as taxes can be regressive. This is the case in which large tax credits or other types of transfers are given to business. Regressive income transfers tend to concentrate wealth in the business sector of society, especially if accompanied by substantial regressive taxation.

We will not mention income transfers to business any further in this chapter. But other types of income transfers not commonly thought of as welfare will be discussed because these income transfers are lumped together in most discussions of the federal budget and provide ammunition to opponents of welfare on the grounds that they are funds transferred to the poor. It is important for human services professionals to understand that income transfers to persons who have never experienced poverty and to business are more than 12 times greater than are the amount of transfers that are usually termed welfare.[27]

Lawrence and Leeds sum up the complications of trying to separate income transfers to the poor from other income transfers as follows:

> It is difficult to see how the nation's welfare programs can be simplified and rationalized without a basic understanding of the myriad other programs also distributing benefits to various segments of the population. While many of these income transfer programs serve the lower-income population generally, others are beamed at special groups such as farmers, veterans, Indians, disaster victims, the elderly, or the disabled. To the extent that many of these programs provide benefits to middle- and upper-income individuals, one might question the necessity of such expenditures, postulating instead that less would be better spent if it were focused on those in greater need. Thus, while all such programs contribute, in varying degrees, to the alleviation of distress, no overriding theme or theory unifies them at present . . .
>
> At the federal level, many programs are small enough or specialized enough or so divorced from legislative authority that they have escaped analysis and scrutiny. A number of such programs do not even appear as separate line items in the Federal Budget; their costs are lumped together with other expenditures. Many of the largest programs—those with well-organized constituencies like farmers, veterans, or the aged, and often with their own very protective Congressional committees—have been deliberately excluded time and time again from consideration in conjunction with "welfare reform."[28]

Contemporary Programs for Economic Maintenance

Besides having to sort out income transfer programs concerned with welfare from those that are not, there is the problem of classifying the programs of economic maintenance so that they will make sense. There are several ways of doing this, but none of them really does the job. For instance, an obvious method of classification would be by *source of support*. But this has limitations, because, although it is relatively easy to document the federal sources of support, it is another matter to try to identify the sources of support from the states, not to mention the private sources of funds. Then, too, everything gets mixed up because many programs receive support from several sources at the same time.

Another scheme of classification is by the amount of *financial need* that recipients must demonstrate to be eligible for assistance. Although this would not be impossible, it is complicated by the fact that programs requiring demonstration of need, or a "means" test, are scattered throughout the various levels of bureaucracy. Programs are often mixed up with other programs that also transfer income but that have no means test connected with them. Furthermore, in most cases, the means test is only one of the tests applied to determine eligibility.

The food stamp program illustrates the problem. It is located in the U.S. Department of Agriculture, but at the state and local levels it is frequently administered by the departments of welfare. The food stamp program requires a means test, but food stamps are frequently made available in conjunction with other programs such as Aid to Families with Dependent Children (AFDC), which is administered by the Department of Health and Human Services.* AFDC has a different means test than does the food stamp program. To complicate matters further, within the Department of Agriculture there is a massive income transfer program that has no means test connected with it, namely, the price support program of payments to farmers for withholding land from production.

Medicare and Medicaid programs also illustrate how complicated it is to attempt to classify programs according to financial need. These programs are administered by the Department of Health and Human Services (DHHS). Medicaid is based almost solely on demonstration of need, whereas Medicare has two other tests—age and work history.

While demonstration of need remains an important criterion for eligibility for an income transfer, it breaks down as a method for classification because it is by no means the sole criterion. The definition of need varies from program to program, and furthermore government agencies often administer many different income transfer programs, some of which require a means test and some of which do not.

Programs for economic maintenance might be classified by the *agency that administers them,* but to do so can also create confusion rather than clarity. Most services are actually handled by outlets in the local communities. However, personnel in the local outlet may be employed by the state,

---

* Prior to June 1980, the Department of Health and Human Services was known as the Department of Health, Education and Welfare (HEW). As of June 1980, the educational functions of the former HEW were consolidated into a separate department, called the U.S. Department of Education.

federal, or local government. Programs can be designed and funded at the federal level, modified and provided with additional funding at the state level, and then actually handled by an agency at the local level. For instance, try to classify programs under the Social Security Act by administering agency. The Old Age and Survivors Insurance program is administered by the Social Security Administration, which is strictly a federally administered and funded program, with no state or local administrative or funding connection. On the other hand AFDC is also under the Social Security Act, but it has nothing to do with the Social Security Administration and is administered by county or state employees and sometimes by both.

Another problem in classification is that the vocabulary varies from program to program and from agency to agency. Lawrence and Leeds state, "A confusing array of schemes and definitions is in use throughout the federal bureaucracy to describe those income transfer programs which are variously referred to as comprising the nation's income maintenance, income security, public welfare or social welfare system." They sum up the whole problem by saying, "the multiplicity of approaches does not permit facile classification."[29]

Since there is so much inconsistency, overlap, and confusion in the funding, administration, and eligibility requirements for programs of economic maintenance, we can be somewhat arbitrary in our selection of classification standards. Thus we will describe the federal programs for economic maintenance according to two classifications: (1) by programs, number served, and dollars expended and (2) by the societal values used to determine eligibility.

For the purposes of this discussion, we will confine our examination of economic maintenance programs to those for which the federal government is the source of funding. This covers the bulk of funds expended and the major types of programs. How these programs are translated into action varies from state to state and even from county to county. It would be impossible to provide complete information on how all programs function throughout the country, but for illustration we have included in Document 8.1 at the end of the chapter an inventory of social insurance and income assistance programs peculiar to a single state, Wisconsin. This inventory includes all federal programs and shows how the federal programs are put into use in combination with state support.

We will define the special terms used to describe the programs as the terms are introduced. However, a more complete listing and definition of special terms used in connection with welfare programs can be found in the Glossary.

Classification by Program, Number Served, and Dollars Expended

Table 8.1 lists the major federally supported *income transfer* programs for individuals in fiscal 1977. The grand total of all these programs comes to $195.53 billion. Since the total federal budget for 1977 was nearly $400

Table 8.1 / Major Federal Income Transfer Programs, Fiscal Year 1977

Program and Number Served	Expenditures in Billions
1. AFDC and AFDC-U* (over 10,700,000 recipients in over 3,150,000 families)	$ 6.12
2. Supplemental Security Income (4,400,000 monthly)*	5.30
3. Social Security	
Disability insurance (4,500,000 monthly)	11.63
Retirement insurance (20,500,000 monthly)	52.36
Survivors insurance (7,500,000 monthly)	18.89
	82.88
4. Food programs	
Food stamps (over 17,000,000 monthly)*	5.47
School lunch (27,000,000 children)	2.21
Other (8 programs)	1.19
	8.87
5. Medicaid (over 24,000,000 annually)*	9.86
6. Medicare	
Hospital insurance (6,000,000 annually)	15.31
Supplementary med. ins. (15,000,000 annually)	6.33
	21.64
7. Federal–state unemployment insurance (about 10,000,000)	13.49
8. Manpower and public employment (15 programs)*	7.11
9. Railroad Retirement Board	
Disability ins. (over 100,000 monthly)	.55
Retirement ins. (300,000 monthly)	2.25
Survivors ins. (400,000 monthly)	1.03
Unemployment ins. (average 20,000)	.18
	4.01
10. Civil Service Commission	
Disability pensions (about 300,000 monthly)	1.69
Retirement pensions (800,000 monthly)	6.37
Survivors pensions (over 400,000 monthly)	1.21
Health benefits (over 1,000,000 covered)	.43
	9.70
11. Defense Department	
Military disability retirement (over 140,000)	.98
Military nondisability ret. (close to 1,000,000 monthly)	7.23
Military survivors benefits (over 40,000)	.12
	8.33
12. Veterans Administration	
Department of Medicine and Surgery	
(21,296,650 recipients)	4.32
Department of Veterans Benefits (7,986,200) annually	13.90
	18.22
GRAND TOTAL of these items	$195.53

* Need is a primary qualifying factor.

Adapted from William J. Lawrence and Stephen Leeds, *An Inventory of Federal Income Transfer Programs, Fiscal Year 1977*. White Plains, N.Y.: The Institute for Socioeconomic Studies, 1978.

billion, it can be seen that income transfers are a substantial portion of the monies the federal government disburses each year.

The six items in Table 8.1 with an asterisk are programs that require demonstration of need for qualification for economic assistance. The total cost of these programs came to $23.86 billion in 1977. Other programs such as those listed under the Social Security heading have demonstration of need as one factor for qualification, but other factors such as work history, nature of disability, or age of survivors weigh equally to need in determination of eligibility.

Note that the programs with an asterisk in Table 8.1 are scattered among several agencies. The AFDC program is in the Department of Health and Human Services. The food stamp program is in the Department of Agriculture, whereas the various manpower and public employment programs are in the Department of Labor and in the Department of Health and Human Services.

Of the twelve major programs listed, only five can be considered "welfare" or "public assistance" programs. These are the programs of AFDC, Food Stamp, Medicaid, Supplemental Security Income, and Manpower and Public Employment. The cost of the programs comes to $14 billion, or approximately 7 per cent of the total amount of income transfer programs listed in the table. We omitted Medicare from this list, because Medicare has no means test connected with it. Furthermore, it provides medical care, is connected with Social Security, and has less of the connotation of welfare or public assistance than do the other programs.*

Table 8.1 also shows the large numbers of individuals who are recipients of income transfers, for the figures in parentheses in each program category give the number of cases served. This does not mean that you can simply add up these numbers to find how many people get income transfers, because the numbers often include individuals who were served by more than one program. Nevertheless, the numbers indicate that a substantial portion of the U.S. population is involved in the receipt of income transfers. Many of these programs are noncontroversial, such as those for war veterans, even though the outlay of funds is greater for veterans than for those programs considered to be "welfare" programs. Economic assistance to veterans is less controversial than "welfare" programs; this is because, even though many veterans are needy, they are not all confined to the lower ranks of the stratification hierarchy as are the poor. Veterans can be found at all levels of society. Economic assistance programs for veterans are therefore judged in most cases, by "service to country" rather than by "need," even though in many cases, such as medical care and pensions, the type of assistance may be identical. Even in those instances in which "need" may be a factor for a veteran to qualify for financial assistance, such as a home loan, the income test is based on criteria different from those used in welfare programs. Furthermore, when assistance is given, it is not perceived by the public as "welfare."

* Document 8.1, pp. 139, 140.

Classification Criteria to Determine Eligibility

Whereas Table 8.1 shows the dollar amounts of income transfers from federal sources and the numbers of individuals served, Table 8.2 (see p. 124) shows the criteria under which individuals qualify for income from federal sources.

There are three major criteria around which programs for economic maintenance are presently constructed:

1. work
2. resources
3. altruism

Economic assistance is extended to individuals in the United States when they qualify for this assistance by "evaluations" related to these criteria. Table 8.2 lists the major income transfer programs that were available in fiscal year 1977 grouped under these three evaluative criteria. Note that the programs are spread throughout a number of federal departments and subunits within departments. Note also that, on the one hand, a single department may utilize a number of tests but that, on the other hand, a single test may be used in programs located in a number of departments.

The criteria of work, resources, and altruism around which the tests for eligibility are devised reflect the values of the larger society toward which the programs for economic maintenance are oriented. As we stated in previous chapters, *work* is a highly held value in America. Therefore, if an individual has had a history of work, when he or she cannot support himself or herself, the society takes responsibility to furnish economic assistance based on the amount and type of work the individual has previously performed. *Survival* and *adequate resources* are also important social values, and, when some members of the society fall below a certain minimum, these individuals are assisted by programs established for them. The programs based on minimum resources are not as generous, however, as are those based on work. We shall see in Chapter 9 that those who receive economic assistance under the minimum resources test are placed under strong constraints to work so that they will not need economic assistance any longer than is necessary.

The criterion of altruism exists because of a concern developed by the society toward some special groups, members of which are often unable to furnish minimum resources for themselves. These special groups can receive economic assistance on a long-term basis. Examples are crippled children, alcoholics, or those who receive assistance because of their being the victims of some catastrophic event. The last group receives assistance only long enough to bring them through the crisis. Victims of discrimination are another example of the special groups who receive economic assistance because of the value of altruism.

Though we have divided the programs to emphasize the different values backing up requirements for eligibility, we do not mean that individuals may

Table 8.2 / Classification of Economic Assistance by Value Test, Fiscal Year 1977 (in billions)

Work		*Resources*	
Health Education & Welfare		Agriculture	
Social Security Admin.		Food and nutrition service	
Old age benefits	$ 52.36	Food stamps and donations	5.5
Disability insurance	11.63		
Survivors insurance	18.89	Health Education & Welfare	
Medicare	21.64	Social Rehabilitation Service	
Coal miners disability	.94	Medicaid	9.86
		Aid to Families with	
Labor		Dependent Children	6.12
Employment and Training Admin.		Aid to Blind and Disabled and	
Unemployment insurance	13.49	Old Age Assistance	.01
Employment Standards Admin.		Work Incentive Program	.37
Longshoremen's compen-		Social services	2.64
sation	.01	Office of Education	
		Student loans, grants,	
Railroad Retirement Board		work study programs	.75
Railworkers insurance	4.01		
		Housing and Urban Development	
Department of Defense		Housing for the needy	2.39
Retirement, disability, and			
survivors insurance	8.33	Labor	
	131.30*	Employment and Training Admin.	
		Job training	1.41
		Job opportunity	.85
		Legal Services Corporation	
		Legal services to the poor	.13
		Small Business Admin.	
		Job creation for the	
		unemployed	.05
			30.08*

* Totals may not add due to rounding.
NM–Not meaningful.
Adapted from William J. Lawrence and Stephen Leeds, *An inventory of Federal Income Transfer Programs, Fiscal Year 1977.* White Plains, N.Y.: The Institute for Socioeconomic Studies, 1978.

Altruism		Minimum Income (Proposed)
Action		Negative income tax
Vista	.02	
		Universal grant payment
Agriculture		
Farm assistance	.68	Grant payment to special groups
School lunch	2.20	
Milk	.18	
Community Services Admin.		
Community development	.40	
Health Education & Welfare		
Mental Health Admin.		
Mentally ill	.23	
Alcoholic	.06	
Drug abuse	.16	
Health Services Admin.		
Crippled children	.10	
Migrant workers	.03	
Office of Education		
Disadvantaged students	.02	
Social Rehabilitation Service		
Cuban refugee	.07	
Indo-Chinese refugee	.10	
Housing and Urban Development		
Riot victims	NM	
Flood victims	.18	
Small Business Admin.		
Disadvantaged businessmen	.01	
Veterans Admin.		
Veterans benefits	13.90	
Health Education & Welfare;		
and Interior		
American Indians	.46	Total expended for all
	18.80*	classifications $180.64*

qualify for only one program. Programs for American Indians* illustrate the confusing manner in which these tests are applied. There are special programs for American Indians in the Department of Health and Human Services in its two subunits, Health Services Administration and the Office of Human Services, and in the Department of Interior and its subunit, the Bureau of Indian Affairs. These programs apply the altruism test. Participation in these special programs does not exclude individuals from receiving benefits from any other program for which they may qualify or from receiving benefits simultaneously from several programs in multiple governmental units.

Because an individual may often receive economic assistance from several different units of the federal government, that individual often has to deal with human services professionals from *each* of these units of government.

Work Test

The strength of the value that underpins programs for economic maintenance is often reflected by the amount of resources devoted to the programs. Table 8.2 shows that the programs for economic maintenance that receive the most funds are those related to work. In fiscal 1977, $131.30 billion was spent for work-related programs for economic maintenance. These programs were in four administrative units of the federal government. This is three times the amount spent for all the other programs combined. These programs are usually called insurance programs because the individuals eligible for benefits from these programs are presumed to have earned them, even though as in the case of military benefits they have made no contributions from wages to the program.

Individuals qualify for assistance for programs under the work test only after they have worked for a certain period of time that varies according to the specific program. For instance, the old age benefits available under the Social Security Administration of the Department of Health and Human Services require a person to be at least sixty-two years of age and to have worked for a specified number of "quarters" to be eligible for all the benefits of the program. The benefits are cash payments that are designed to offset the loss of income caused by retirement. Retirement benefits for military personnel listed under the Department of Defense, on the other hand, are available when the individual has worked for 20 years, and these benefits have no age requirement attached to them.

Not only is there a hierarchy of importance associated with programs for economic assistance regarding work, but there is also a hierarchy of qualifications according to financial resources related to the various programs. An obligation on the part of society is presumed to exist for all those who have worked throughout their careers, especially if they have not accumulated the resources to support themselves when they can no longer work. At the present time, almost all occupations are covered by Social Security, which provides

* Native Americans is the preferred term for this group, however, American Indians is still the official term.

a minimum income for the necessities after a person retires. Social Security, however, requires that persons receiving the benefits earn no more than the maximum allowed, an amount that varies depending on economic conditions. Benefits also vary according to the dependents of the former wage earner.

The requirements to qualify for benefits from the Department of Defense for career members of the armed forces are quite different. One need only serve twenty years. Upon retirement, the individual receives a set amount, usually around one half of regular pay, which is not related to the number of dependents or to the amount of income earned at another job. A military retiree can receive full benefits and work full time at another job, even a government job. This situation leads to the conclusion that work in the military is considered more important than work that qualifies one for Social Security benefits, at least as far as programs for economic assistance are concerned. In general, a program called an *insurance* program carries little of the negative connotations connected with programs that have no direct work test history involved. They are seen by the general public as payments that individuals have *earned*, because they have contributed to the production of goods and services of the society and thus have an *entitlement* even if the amount paid out far exceeds the amount contributed. Individuals receiving benefits from these programs do not hesitate to apply for them. In fact, they urge increased benefits for they feel that the benefits they receive are a result of their long-term commitment to the work ethic. There is a minimum of controversy surrounding income transfers based on the work test, because both society and the recipients see these programs as supporting the goals of the society and as maintaining the social order. They are not seen as challenging to the general distribution of goods and services within the society, but rather as providing the means for individuals to meet their expectations for survival, comfort, and respect in a socially approved fashion. Most persons, however, are unaware of the large federal retirement and disability programs for rail workers, longshoremen, and coal miners unless they are involved with these lines of work.

Resources Test

Column 2 of Table 8.2 lists income transfers that are made to those persons who have insufficient resources to maintain themselves. Presently these programs are scattered among eight administrative units of the federal government. Fewer persons are served through programs related to the resources test than through programs related to the work test (Table 8.1). The amount of money spent for these programs is roughly one fifth of that spent for programs shown in column 1 of Table 8.2. People also receive assistance for shorter periods of time in programs using the resources test than they do under the work test programs.

All the programs under the resources test require an investigation of the income and assets of the applicants before assistance is given. This is done at the time of application and is usually repeated at intervals during the period that the individual is receiving assistance. If the investigation results in the conclusion that the applicant has so few resources that he or she falls into a poverty category that is used by the program, the applicant will be certified "needy" and qualify for assistance. In contrast to the programs under the work test category, many of the programs under the resources test give assistance in kind rather than in cash.

For instance, for an applicant to be eligible for benefits from AFDC in Milwaukee, Wisconsin in 1979, the applicant had to meet the following income and assets requirements:

1. Own no more than one state-registered automobile.
2. Own only one home of reasonable value, in which the recipient lives.
3. Have no more than $1,500 in other total assets.
4. Have an income less than the established need on which the family allowance is based. For an eligible family of four persons the family allowance is $492. Food stamps may be permitted in addition.

In addition, an adult applicant, upon becoming a recipient of benefits under AFDC, had to enter the work incentive program (WIN). This is a work training and employment program designed to put AFDC recipients to work, to remove them from the AFDC rolls or at least to minimize the amount of benefits required. Recipients must take the first job offered if they are to remain eligible for benefits under AFDC.

Programs for economic maintenance under the work test are not usually defined as "welfare" programs, whereas programs under the resources test usually are so defined. These programs are sometimes called "handouts," "give-aways," or "rewards for laziness" by those who oppose them. These perjorative labels are based on the opinion that persons receiving economic assistance because of lack of resources related to unemployment are motivationally deviant in some way. This is the reason why so many of the programs listed in column 2 of Table 8.2 have as a major objective the placement of the recipients into employment. There is constant controversy about the level of assistance that is given the recipients for there is fear that, if the support from these programs is too high, the recipients will have no desire to return to work. To assure that the "handout" is not excessive, when the recipient does locate work, the amount of wages that he or she receives is deducted from the amount of assistance given. This is usually done without consideration of any of the other factors that might be involved in the scarcity of resources the individual has experienced. In many states it is difficult for families to qualify for economic assistance if the adult male is present in the home, for this signifies in the public mind that the family is poor only because of the unwillingness of the adult male to work.

It is in this classification of welfare economic maintenance programs that the clash between the materialistic and humanistic values is most marked. The materialistic value states, "An honest day's pay for an honest day's work." The humanistic ethic states, "We are our brother's (and sister's) keepers." The result is a compromise wherein those without resources are not left to starve but are given a defined minimum to keep them from "feeling too comfortable," with conditions placed on them so that they will be forced to work if at all possible.

Incidentally, we included student loans, grants, and work study programs in this category because these forms of economic assistance are directly related to resources and not to work. Either the parents or the applicant must certify their lack of resources to pay for college. The program exists because of the assumption that a college education will make the individual a more economically productive member of society. These are not commonly defined as "welfare" programs because they are oriented primarily to young people whose parents are in the main economically self-sufficient.

Finally, we listed the program fielded by the Small Business Administration called job creation for the unemployed to further illustrate the preoccupation with work that exists in the society. This program was established to ensure that, once the recipients of economic assistance are trained, the opportunity will be there for them to work. This is done through the provision of subsidies, low-interest loans, and contracts.

When an adult member of a family comes to the public welfare agency for economic assistance because of lack of employment, the first procedure to take place is the determination of whether the family falls into the official definition of poverty used by the agency. The official definition usually utilizes the "adequate resources" definition of poverty to determine eligibility.

When the family is certified for assistance, other programs may come into play. Food stamps may be made available, administered by the Department of Agriculture. The family will usually receive some services for personal improvement that we will discuss in Chapter 9. The family will probably receive Medicaid (DHHS) and possibly some housing assistance under the Department of Housing and Urban Development. Of course, if the father is not in the home, the mother is required to become economically self-sufficient as soon as possible. Thus she will be enrolled in either the WIN program in the Department of Health and Human Services or in the job training program in the Department of Labor. She then will be expected to use the services of the job opportunity program or perhaps the job creation for the unemployed program.

Altruism Test

Only about one tenth of the total expenditures in Table 8.2 is distributed to recipients on the basis of the altruism test. The programs utilizing the altruism test are listed in column 3 of Table 8.2.

In addition to the programs for American Indians, which we mentioned earlier, assistance is also given to farmers, to businessmen, and to migrants. School lunches and milk are furnished to the young because there is concern over their nutrition. Vista and community development programs provide assistance (usually benefits in kind) to poor neighborhoods to help the individuals who reside therein to improve their surroundings. Since there is concern about the condition of the mentally ill, the alcoholic, and the drug addicted, they are defined as being economically dependent on society through no fault of their own for they are "ill." They must therefore be cared for until they are "cured" and reemployed. Crippled children comprise one of the earliest groups with which the society felt general concern.[30] Veterans are given a broad array of economic assistance because of the special concern they engender for the service they performed in the protection of the country, especially during times of war.

Proposals for Modification of Programs for Economic Maintenance

There are a number of proposals for economic maintenance that are different from the programs now in existence in that all are a form of guaranteed income. They are usually grouped under the following headings:

1. negative income tax
2. universal grant payment
3. grant payment to special groups[31]

In its basic outline, the *negative income tax** provides that every family receive a minimum guarantee of money. If the family had no income of its own, the federal government would pay the entire amount upon the filing of an income tax return. Work incentives would be built in so that the federal government's share would not diminish directly in relation to the amount earned. At a certain earnings point acheived by the family, the subsidy would be cut off and the family would be on its own, judged to be economically self-sufficient.

The *universal grant payment* is a subsidy from the government paid to individuals regardless of their financial circumstances or social status. Therefore, if the grant program were designed for every adult in the society, every adult would receive a given sum of money for a designated period. This money would be available whether or not people worked, were poor or millionaires, were male or female, recently achieved their majority, or were past their retirement. A program such as this would lead to a major redistribution of the wealth of the society.

Grant payments to special groups are usually classified according to age. The two groups most frequently mentioned under this proposal are the young and the aged. Those who qualify would receive periodic grant payments regardless of financial resources. A form of this proposal, the Townsend Plan, was first advocated in the 1930s. Under the Townsend Plan each person age

---

* See Document 8.2, p. 145, for a specific proposal on the use of the negative income tax.

sixty and over would receive a grant of $200 per month provided that he or she would not work and that the $200 (a substantial amount of money in 1934) was spent within the month in which it was granted.

None of these proposals has been adopted because they (1) violate the value of work and (2) threaten the stability of the distribution of wealth. It is feared that the negative income tax would devalue the incentive to work. The redistribution of wealth that would result from a universal grant would be so radical that the proposal is not even discussed seriously at the present time. The grant payment to special categories is resisted for the same reasons that the negative income tax is resisted, plus the fear that if it were granted to children the birth rate would increase significantly.[32]

There have been attempts to modify the current programs for economic maintenance by Presidents Nixon, Ford and Carter. These proposals are mainly modifications of programs now in existence, except that they all advocate the introduction of a form of the negative income tax. The proposal by President Carter under consideration by Congress in 1979 would establish the minimum "adequate" income for a family of four at $7,200. President Carter proposed to guarantee every family a minimum income of 65 per cent of that amount. The minimum income floor is limited however to families; single persons or childless couples are not eligible under President Carter's proposal.* The proposals for a negative income tax by Presidents Nixon and Ford were not enacted, and it is doubtful that President Carter's similar proposal will receive favorable treatment, although modifications of existing programs have been adopted that bring them closer to a form of guaranteed income. For instance, AFDC recipients can now keep a percentage of their earnings. This can be considered a type of negative income tax (NIT). Proposals for a guaranteed annual income (GAI) would include more of the working poor who presently earn too much to qualify for public assistance but still earn less than the poverty level. Conservatives and liberals generally agree that this needs to be done; they also agree that it would be too costly to implement.

The American society is presently strongly oriented toward stability in the distribution of wealth and privilege among its members. Work is also an important value. These two values combine to ensure that the current programs for economic maintenance will remain as they are for the foreseeable future. Most of the funds will continue to be alloted to those who meet the work test, less will go to those who meet the resources test, and the least of all will go to those who meet only the altruism test. In general, although the value of altruism plays a part in programs for economic maintenance, it is secondary to the values of work and stability of distribution of wealth. The only probable change will be in the technical details necessary to adjust programs to situational factors while preserving the original character of the programs.

* See Document 8.2, p. 145.

Summary

We explained in Chapter 2 that American society is stratified into ranks characterized by differences in occupations and availability of resources. Those with the lowest rankings by occupation and assets receive benefits from the programs for economic assistance that are usually defined as "welfare." The resources for these programs are obtained through various kinds of income transfers.

There are also income transfers and programs for economic maintenance designed for people who are not ranked as poor. These are not called "welfare."

The income transfers for the poor are usually controversial. They are constantly under scrutiny. Critics demand either that they be eliminated or that less money be allotted to them even though the expenditures for these programs are only about 7 per cent of all federal income transfer programs. Although proposals for change have been made, it is probable that the programs for economic assistance will continue in their present form, expanding and contracting depending on the general economic circumstances of the society.

In many cases, individuals receive economic assistance from several different units of government, and therefore individuals often have to deal with human services professionals from a number of these units of government if they are to receive the benefits for which they are eligible.

If, in reading this chapter, you find it difficult to make sense out of the patchwork nature of programs for economic maintenance, imagine how incomprehensible it seems to the needy, most of whom come to the agencies with little or no prior knowledge of the confusing system on which their very lives may depend.*

Documents—Programs for Economic Maintenance

This section presents two documents that relate to the material discussed in the chapter: (1) a description of the specific social insurance and income maintenance programs in the United States in fiscal 1977 and (2) excerpts from President Carter's *Message to Congress* on welfare reform of August 6, 1977.

The first document is adapted from *An Inventory of Social Insurance Programs and Income Assistance Programs: United States 1977* published in 1979. This is the first of nine working papers of the Welfare Reform Advisory Committee to the Wisconsin Department of Health and Social Services. It formed the basis for the *Wisconsin Welfare Reform Study Report and Recommendations* of the Advisory Committee, published in 1979.

The second document, *Message to Congress*, illustrates official thinking about the current state of affairs of welfare programs and includes proposals

* See also Document 8.2, p. 143.

to modify them. What is unique about the proposals contained in the President's *Message* is the recommendation for the establishment of a guaranteed income. As we mentioned earlier, however, each president since President Nixon has advocated the establishment of a minimum guaranteed income.

The *Message* also illustrates one of the initial steps in the complicated process of the implementation of ideas into welfare programs. The president sends his messages to Congress. Congress then considers the suggestions and adds and deletes as it sees fit as it proceeds with the legislative process. Then, after the statutes are placed on the books, it is the responsibility of the appropriate federal department to develop its implementing rules and regulations that the states must follow to deliver services that adhere to the mandates of the law. Examples of the later steps in the process, the implementing rules and regulations, and a state plan are presented at the end of Chapter 9.

Document 8.1 / An Inventory of Social Insurance Programs and Income Assistance Programs: United States 1977

SOCIAL INSURANCE PROGRAMS

The social insurance programs are designed to meet the income needs of persons (or dependents of persons) who have exhibited a substantial attachment to the labor force. In general, they are considered a right accruing to eligible persons. Ordinarily, they are not income tested and, in most cases, they are financed through segregated financing systems (e.g., payroll taxes).

Some social insurance programs provide an income cushion to individuals (and families) who suffer a loss of income through no fault of their own. These include:

1. *Workmen's Compensation* provides support for persons whose income loss is a direct result of their work activity.
2. *Unemployment Insurance* provides temporary income support for persons whose employment is terminated through no fault of their own.
3. *Veterans Compensation* provides income support for those whose capacity to lead productive lives is substantially diminished as a result of their service in the armed forces.

Other social insurance programs provide income support and in-kind benefits to persons who are no longer expected to provide for their own needs. Included among these programs are:

4. *Old Age, Survivors Insurance* provides income support to persons who because of age or loss of the primary wage earner are no longer able to support themselves. *Disability Insurance* provides long-term income support for those whose ability to *continue* to support themselves is terminated by a permanent physical and/or psychological disability.

From *An Inventory of Social Insurance Programs and Income Assistance Programs: United States 1977*. Madison, WI: Department of Health and Social Services, 1979. p. 1-31.

5. The *Railroad Retirement* program provides income support to those who have worked for an appropriate time in a covered employment activity (i.e., the Railway System).
6. The *Medicare* program provides low-cost health insurance to those who are no longer expected to work (e.g., the aged).
7. The *Black Lung* program provides income support for those who can no longer work because of a specific employment-related disability.

WORKMEN'S COMPENSATION

Benefits under Workmen's Compensation will reach an estimated $6.7 billion in FY 1977. Every State has enacted workmen's compensation laws to provide financial protection against loss of income, medical expenses, or death due to injuries on the job. The first law was enacted in 1908—a law passed by Congress covering Federal civil service employees. Similar laws were enacted subsequently by the States. Programs generally are administered by State departments of Labor or independent workmen's compensation boards. Most State programs are financed entirely by employers. Coverage of employees varies from State to State, but coverage is provided for about 85 percent of employees nationwide.

Generally, for an individual (or his family) to qualify for benefits he must have sustained an injury or been killed in performing his duties, but the injuries must not have arisen due to the employee's gross negligence, willful misconduct, or intoxication. Some States cover certain occupational diseases. Benefits are payable to a disabled worker and, in the case of death, to the worker's survivors. Some States pay dependent's benefits. There are no income or assets tests under most laws. Benefits are paid in the form of periodic cash payments, lump-sum payments, medical services to an injured worker, and death and funeral benefits for worker's survivors. Most States also provide rehabilitation services or benefits. Benefit levels for temporary disability are about two thirds of a worker's weekly wage in most States. Death and permanent disability benefits vary widely among States.

UNEMPLOYMENT INSURANCE

In FY 1977 an estimated $14.3 billion will be paid to an estimated 11 million beneficiaries. Unemployment Insurance was enacted in 1935. Unemployment Insurance was added for Federal civilian employees in 1954, and ex-servicemen in 1958. Amendments in 1970 and 1971 provided for extended benefits during periods of high unemployment. 1974 legislation established a temporary program of emergency benefits beyond the extended benefits program, in 1958, 1961, 1971 and 1974.

Legislation enacted in 1976 extended coverage to 40 percent of farm workers, to State and local government employees, and to certain domestic workers. (Overall, coverage is expanded from a pre-amendment 87 percent to a new 97 percent of total employment.) This also raised the Federal payroll tax temporarily from .5 to .7 percent and the taxable earnings base permanently from $4,200 to $6,000.

UI is financed by Federal and State payroll taxes on employers. These taxes are deposited to individual State accounts within Federal UI Trust Fund accounts. States draw on their accounts as necessary to pay benefits; Congress appropriates funds from the Trust Fund for Federal and State administrative expenses. The program is administered by the Department of Labor's Employment and Training Administration through State employment Security agencies and their local offices. The Federal government finances administration of the programs and half the extended benefits from its .5 percent payroll tax on covered employers.

The specific requirements for UI benefit eligibility are established by individual State laws. In general, however, a claimant must have earned a specified amount of wages in covered employment or have worked a certain period of time within his "base period," or both, to qualify for benefits. A claimant must be able to work, be available for work, and be free of any disqualifying factor (e.g., voluntary separation from work). Benefits are available to individual workers and, in eleven States, to their dependents.

Claimants employed less than a full week and earning less than the amount of their weekly benefit for total unemployment may receive partial benefits in most States. A claimant's earnings, less specified disregarded amounts, are deducted from the partial benefits to which the worker is entitled. Neither earnings of other family members nor unearned income from investments is considered in determining eligibility or benefit amount. Benefits are reduced or denied a claimant who receives workmen's compensation in 24 States; social security, in 12 States, pension benefits from his base period employer in 22 States (from *any* employer, in 13 States).

Benefits are paid weekly in cash. Weekly benefit amounts and duration are established by the individual States and vary, within certain minimum and maximum limits, with the worker's past wages and work experience during his base period. Currently, minimum weekly benefits range from $5 in Hawaii to $35 in Indiana. Maximums range from $63 in Texas to $174 in Connecticut (including dependents' allowances). In most States the maximum duration of benefits is 26 weeks. In periods of high unemployment, either nationally or within a State, an extended benefit period may be "triggered," allowing a claimant to draw half again the number of benefit weeks his work experience allows, up to a maximum of 39 weeks in all.

Because of recent high unemployment, a temporary emergency benefits program provides still another 13 weeks' benefits should extended benefits be exhausted, and 13 weeks beyond that (for a total of 65 weeks) in especially high unemployment States.

All worker beneficiaries are subject to a work test—they must be able to work and be available for work. They may be disqualified from benefits for refusal to apply for or to accept suitable work without good cause.

VETERANS COMPENSATION PROGRAMS

In FY 1977 an estimated $5.7 billion will be paid to an estimated 3.5 million beneficiaries (2.3 million veterans and 1.2 million dependents and survivors). Service-connected disability and death benefits programs were enacted in 1917. Dependency and indemnity compensation (DIC) was enacted in 1956. The programs are financed through open-ended Federal appropriations providing for direct payments to beneficiaries. They are administered through regional offices of the Department of Veterans Benefits, Veterans Administration.

For disability benefits a veteran must have contracted a disease, suffered a non-misconduct injury, or aggravated an existing disease or injury in the line of active duty, and have been discharged under conditions other than dishonorable. Death compensation and DIC benefits are available to a widow, child, or dependent parents of a veteran whose death was due to service. There are no income tests for a disabled veteran, his wife, or children, but parents' income is considered in determining their dependency. Similarly, there is no income test for widows or children, but benefits to parents of a deceased veteran are income-tested (again to determine dependency).

Disability benefits payable as cash are determined by: (1) the percentage of impairment; (2) marital status and sex of spouse; (3) number of entitled children; (4) dependency of parents; (5) need for special care; and (6) certain anatomical losses or loss of use of limbs or bodily functions. Benefits are extended for wives, children, or dependent parents only if the veteran is entitled to compensation for a disability rated at 50 percent or greater.

Under the death compensation and DTC programs, benefits are paid monthly as cash. The size of benefits is determined by: (1) the number of eligible children; (2) the sex and health of the surviving spouse; (3) the number, marital status, health, living arrangements and income of dependent parents; and (4) under DIC, the pay grade of the deceased veteran. There are no work tests under these programs.

OLD AGE, SURVIVORS, AND DISABILITY INSURANCE (OASDI)

In FY 1977 an estimated $81.9 billion will be paid to an estimated 33.1 million beneficiaries. Old age insurance was enacted in 1935, survivors insurance in 1939, and disability insurance in 1956. OASDI is federally financed by payroll taxes on employers and employees which are maintained in Federal trust funds. It is administered by the Federal government (Social Security Administration), with the contracting out of disability determinations to State vocational rehabilitation agencies.

About 90 percent of the nation's labor force works in employment covered by OASDI. For each calendar quarter of covered employment during which workers earn at least $50, they are credited with a "quarter of coverage." Full retirement benefits are available to workers at age 65, provided they have sufficient quarters of coverage (40 or in some cases less). Survivors benefits are payable to dependents of deceased workers. Disability benefits are payable to workers who have 20 quarters of coverage out of their last 40 and who are found sufficiently disabled to be unable to earn a significant amount from employment for at least 12 months. Benefits also are payable to wives or dependent husbands of primary beneficiaries, children who are under 18 or who are 18-22 and full-time students, and some parents and grandchildren.

Benefit eligibility and payment amounts are not affected by receipt of *unearned* income, with the exception of beneficiaries entitled to both disability and workmen's compensation benefits (combined benefits may not exceed 80 percent of the worker's average current earnings before he became disabled). *Earned* income is subjected to the "retirement test." Under this test beneficiaries are allowed to earn up to $3000 a year without benefit reduction. $1 in benefits is subtracted for each $2 of earned income above $3000. Regardless of the amount of annual earned income, full benefits are payable for any month where earnings are $250 or less, and for all months beginning at age 72.

Benefits are paid monthly in the form of checks issued by the Treasury. Benefit amounts are calculated according to a formula which is applied to a worker's average monthly earnings over his lifetime which were subject to the payroll tax. The five lowest years of earnings are dropped from the computation. Dependents of living workers receive 50 percent of the worker's benefit, subject to a family maximum. Aged widows receive 100 percent of the worker's benefit amount, and surviving dependent children receive 75 percent (again subject to a family maximum). Workers coming on the rolls at age 62 through 64 receive permanently reduced benefits. Benefit levels are weighted to give workers at the lower end of the benefit scale (minimum is currently $108) a higher wage replacement ratio than workers at the high end of the benefit scale (maximum is currently $387). The current average benefit to retired workers is $224;

the current average to aged couples is $372; and the current average to disabled workers is $242. Benefits are automatically adjusted each year by the increase in the cost of living. There are no work requirements as such under OASDI, but disabled beneficiaries must accept vocational rehabilitation services should their condition warrant them.

RAILROAD RETIREMENT, DISABILITY AND SURVIVORS INSURANCE

In FY 1977 an estimated $3.6 billion will be paid to an estimated 1.0 million beneficiaries. The Railroad Retirement Act of 1937 provided for payment of retirement and disability annuities; amendments in 1946 provided for survivor benefits; 1951 amendments added spouses benefits; and 1966 amendments added a supplemental annuity program. The Railroad Retirement Act of 1974 remade the program into a two-tier system, with Tier I being social security benefits based on combined railroad and non-railroad employment and Tier II a supplemental benefit based on railroad employment alone. The program is administered by the Railroad Retirement Board. Tier I benefits are financed by a combination of employer/employee payroll taxes, Federal general revenue funds, and transfers from social security trust funds. Tier II benefits are financed by an employer tax on the number of hours worked.

Tier I retirement benefits are payable to workers having at least 10 years of railroad employment. Retired workers may receive full benefits at 65, or at 60 with 30 years' or more service. Reduced benefits are available to retirees having less than 30 years service, at ages 62-64. Disability benefits are payable to those having 12 months' railroad retirement out of the last 30. Tier II retirement benefits are payable at age 60 with 30 years' service. Disability benefits are payable.for the permanently and totally disabled who have completed 10 years' service, and for the occupationally disabled after 20 years' service. An aged wife of a retired worker may receive a benefit, as may an aged widow, a widow with dependent children in her care, and dependent children.

Entitlement to benefits is subject to a strict retirement test. Workers, spouses, or survivors may not receive benefits for any month in which they are employed by the railroad industry. Eligibility for a Tier II benefit is permanently lost if a beneficiary works for the railroad after retirement. The social security component of benefits is subject to the social security retirement test (see above). The form of benefits is monthly cash payments. Annuities are composed of Tier I benefits (as computed under the social security benefit formula on the basis of an employee's combined railroad and non-railroad earnings) and Tier II benefits (based on railroad service only). Spouses generally receive one half of the primary worker's amount. There is no work test under railroad retirement.

MEDICARE

In FY 1977 an estimated $21 billion will be paid to or on behalf of an estimated 20.8 million beneficiaries. Medicare was enacted in 1965 to cover the medical expenses of the aged. Coverage was extended to disability insurance beneficiaries and chronic renal disease patients in 1972. Medicare is composed of two programs—hospital insurance (HI) and supplemental medical insurance (SMI). HI is financed by payroll taxes levied on employers and employees which are maintained in a Federal Trust Fund. SMI is financed by a combination of beneficiary premiums ($7.20 per month) and Federal general revenue financing, all maintained in a Federal trust fund. The programs are administered by the Social Security Administration, which contracts the certifications of health care providers to State health agencies, and contracts the payment of claims to intermediaries such as Blue Cross plans and private insurance companies.

To be eligible for HI individuals must be: (1) 65 or over and entitled to social security or railroad retirement benefits; (2) disabled and eligible for social security or railroad retirement benefits for 25 or more consecutive months; or (3) chronic renal disease patients who have social security coverage. SMI coverage is available to any of the above who enroll for it and pay the monthly premium. Coverage and payments focus on the individual as a filing unit. There are no income tests or assets tests as a condition for eligibility, or as a condition for the amount of benefits paid. Benefits are usually in the form of payments to third parties (e.g., hospitals, physicians) for expenses covered under Medicare, although in some cases cash payments are made to beneficiaries as reimbursement for medical bills already paid by the individual.

Under HI, payments are made to providers of services (e.g., hospitals) for up to 90 days of in-patient hospital care per benefit period (subject to a $104 deductible and $26 per day co-insurance for the 61st through 90th day), 100 days post-hospital extended care per benefit period (subject to $13 per day co-insurance for the 21st through 100th day), and 100 post-hospital home health care visits per year. Under SMI, payments are made (subject to a $60 per year deductible and 20 percent co-insurance) for physicians' and surgeons' services, out-patient hospital services, and home health care visits (100 per year with no co-insurance).

There are no work requirements in medicare.

SPECIAL BENEFITS FOR DISABLED COAL MINERS (BLACK LUNG PROGRAM)

In FY 1977 an estimated $950 million will be paid to 480,000 beneficiaries. The Black Lung Program was enacted as a part of the Coal Mine Health and Safety Act of 1969. It is financed through open-ended Federal appropriations from general revenues. The Social Security Administration handled all claims through June of 1973, after which the handling of most new claims was transferred to the Department of Labor. SSA continues to make benefit payments and adjustments for all claims under its original jurisdiction, and also takes new claims under contract with the Department of Labor.

To receive benefits an individual must be: (1) a coal miner totally disabled due to pneumoconiosis (black lung) arising out of employment in a coal mine; or (2) a widow, orphan, dependent parent, brother, or sister of a coal miner who was totally disabled from black lung at death or whose death was caused by black lung. Miner's and widow's benefits are increased where there are dependents. Benefits of miners are subject to the social security retirement test on all earned income (i.e., benefits are reduced by $1 for each $2 of earned income above $3000 per year). Unearned income is disregarded, with the exception of a dollar for dollar reduction against any State workmen's compensation payments, unemployment compensation, or State disability insurance payments received because of the miner's disability.

Benefits are paid monthly in the form of checks. The basic benefit payable to a miner or widow is currently $205.40 per month. This benefit is increased by 50 percent if the miner or widow has one qualified dependent, 75 percent for two dependents, and 100 percent for three or more dependents. There are no work requirements for benefit eligibility.

INCOME ASSISTANCE PROGRAMS

In general, the income assistance programs provide income support and/or in-kind benefits to those individuals and families who meet the following criteria: (1) they are lacking substantial independent income; (2) they meet the non-financial eligibility requirements which may apply; and (3) their needs cannot be met through the array of social insurance programs. In general, these programs do not require that recipients (or their dependents) have exhibited a substantial attachment to the labor force or its socially defined equivalent (e.g., the Armed Forces). In addition, these programs are generally characterized by the fact that they are financed by general as opposed to segregated revenues. Finally, these programs are not considered a right by virtue of previous contributions to a segregated fund (e.g., payroll taxes). Rather they are intended to provide an income floor under which no one is expected to fall.

There are several income assistance programs which essentially provide cash transfers to eligible recipients.

1. The *Aid to Families with Dependent Children* program provides income support to children and their eligible caretakers who are deprived of normal support. This usually means the absence of the normal wage earner but may (at the state's discretion) include intact families where the male caretaker is currently unemployed and meets other eligibility criteria.
2. The *Work Incentive Program* (WIN) is a subprogram designed to assist AFDC recipients in securing employment.
3. The *Supplementary Security Income* program provides income support to those persons who would be eligible for social security (OASDI) if they had met the contributory requirements for this major social insurance program. In effect, this program covers the aged, disabled, and blind persons.
4. The *General Assistance* program provides income support (and in-kind benefits) to individuals who are in need and not eligible for a major Federal/State income support program. This program is entirely financed at the State and/or local level. Therefore, its availability and generosity is locally determined.
5. The *Relief to Needy Indian Persons* is a State program which provides income support to eligible Native Americans who reside on reservation lands.
6. The *Veterans Pensions* program provides income support to needy persons who have served a prescribed tenure in the Armed Services.
7. The *Earned Income Tax Credit* provides a tax refund to eligible low-income persons. The transfers are limited to families with earnings of $8000 or less, with the amount of the transfer dependent upon the level of income.
8. The *Homestead Credit* is a State program which provides a cash transfer in the form of a refundable tax credit to low-income persons not on AFDC.

Other Income Assistance programs are designed to meet specific needs (e.g., food, fuel, education, etc.) of low-income persons. In general, these programs are provided on an in-kind basis.

9. The *Food Stamp Program* provides a form of voucher which can be redeemed for food items. The program is essentially available to all persons who meet the income criterion.
10. The *Special Supplemental Food Program* provides food supplements to low-income pregnant or lactating women, infants, and children up to 5 years old who suffer from nutritional deprivation. Benefits are in-kind.

11. The *Medicaid* program provides health assistance to low-income persons who meet the nonfinancial eligibility criteria of the AFDC or SSI programs, and to those who meet the income criterion in those states which opt to cover people not actually eligible for either AFDC or SSI.

12. *Housing Assistance* involves several programs. In general, these programs provide subsidized public housing and/or subsidies to persons to purchase shelter. As with other programs, this form of assistance is income-conditioned.

13. *Fuel Assistance* programs provide low-income people a variety of services to lessen the impact of the high cost of energy and to reduce energy needs.

14. *Basic Opportunity Grants* provide income support to low-income post-secondary students in order to pursue a higher education. Most of the benefits are directed toward defraying tuition costs, but some portions can be used to offset related educational costs.

Of the fourteen income assistance programs, we will describe in detail only AFDC; it is the major program in the number served, in expenditure, in complexity, and in attention it receives from the public.

AID TO FAMILIES WITH DEPENDENT CHILDREN (AFDC)

Aid to Families with Dependent Children is a federally-established income maintenance program in which all 50 states voluntarily participate. Currently, AFDC is one of Wisconsin's largest public assistance programs. The responsibility for funding the AFDC program is shared by the federal and state governments, with the federal government providing approximately 59 percent of the funds and the state providing the remaining 41 percent. In Wisconsin, prior to the 1973-75 biennium, counties were responsible for providing a portion of the non-federal share of AFDC costs. Effective January 1, 1975, however, the entire local share of the cost for the AFDC program was assumed by the State, with some counties continuing to pay a portion of additional costs of administration which are above the State allocation.

In addition to sharing the responsibility for funding the AFDC program, the Federal and State governments are jointly responsible for determining program policies. Major program guidelines as well as a number of specific policy directives are established at the Federal level. Within the Federal guidelines, each State has some flexibility to determine eligibility criteria, payment levels and the types of families to which AFDC will be granted.

Eligibility for AFDC is based upon three major criteria: family composition, resources, and income.

1. *Family composition.* According to this criterion the following types of families are eligible for AFDC:

    a. *An adult living with at least one child under 18*: The adult must be a natural parent of the child or an authorized relative to whom the care of the child has been awarded (NLRR). The child must have been "deprived of support" because a parent is dead, disabled, incapacitated, or not present in the home. In some States, including Wisconsin, families with unemployed fathers are also eligible.

    b. *A woman who is pregnant*: The woman must have been deprived of support because the father is dead, disabled, incapacitated, or not present in the home. A woman and her unborn child are a one-person family for AFDC. Once the child is born they become a two-person family.

c. *A child in a foster home or in a licensed child care institution*: The child must have been placed there with court approval, the State or the county and the child must have come from a family that was receiving AFDC or that was eligible to receive AFDC.

d. *An 18-year-old high school student*: The student must have received AFDC immediately prior to his or her 18th birthday. This segment of the program is *totally State funded*. This program was passed into Law in the 1978 Wisconsin Annual Review Bill, AB-1220, and has not been implemented yet.

2. *Resources.* In addition to family composition, AFDC eligibility is based on certain asset and resource limits. Wisconsin's regulations establish a limit of $1,500 in liquid assets (i.e., cash, checking and savings accounts, stocks, bonds, etc.) per family. There are some assets exempted from such limit (e.g., one home, one car, or another registered vehicle).

3. *Income.* Family income, both earned and unearned, is also considered in determination of eligibility for AFDC. Unearned income includes payments received through social security, retirement funds, etc., and is considered in its entirety in the determination of eligibility for AFDC. Earned income, on the other hand, is subject to a deduction to reflect "work-related expenses." In Wisconsin, the deduction for work-related expenses is set at either 18 percent of gross earned income or the amount of actual expenditures, whichever is greater. Work-related child care expenses are paid in full if an applicant is found to be eligible for AFDC.

Under Federal regulations, each state is required to develop an AFDC assistance standard which reflects the financial needs of AFDC recipients. While the standard represents a payment goal, States which are unable to provide the level of assistance reflected in the standards may set actual payment levels (i.e., family allowances) at a percentage of the standard. There is an assistance standard for every family size in each of four areas in Wisconsin. Currently the maximum allowable grant is 88% of the standard.

If a family's budgetable income (i.e., total income minus work-related expenses) is less than the sum of the AFDC standard for the appropriate family size and area plus any work related child care expenses, that family will be eligible for AFDC.

In addition to meeting the eligibility criteria for income, assets and family composition, single parents of children 6 and over and unemployed fathers must also participate in the work incentive program (WIN), and single parents must cooperate in efforts to establish paternity and to collect child support payments. All child support payments must be assigned to the State. In fiscal year 1977-78 the child support program in Wisconsin collected approximately $22 million in payments for AFDC recipients.

Like the determination of eligibility, the determination of AFDC grant size is based on budgetable household income (which includes both earned and unearned income). Unearned income is treated in the same way as it is in the determination of eligibility in that it reduces the amount of the AFDC grant dollar for dollar.

Earned income, however, is subject to several "disregards." In 1969, the Federal government established the "$30 plus one third" earned income disregard policy to provide an incentive for AFDC recipients to secure employment. Under this policy, the first $30 of earned income plus one-third of the remainder is disregarded (not counted as budgetable income) in the determination of the amount of the AFDC grant. An additional deduction of 18 percent of gross earned income (or the amount of actual expenditures if greater than 18 percent) is made to account for work-related expenses. Day care expenses are also excluded. For purposes of determining AFDC grant size, budgetable income is subtracted from the maximum allowable grant for the appropriate family size and area, and the difference is the amount of the AFDC grant.

Document 8.2 / From President Carter's Message to Congress

THE WHITE HOUSE
To the Congress of the United States

As I pledged during my campaign for the Presidency I am asking the Congress to abolish our existing welfare system, and replace it with a job-oriented program for those able to work and a simplified, uniform, equitable cash assistance program for those in need who are unable to work by virtue of disability, age or family circumstance. The Program for Better Jobs and Income I am proposing will transform the manner in which the Federal government deals with the income needs of the poor, and begin to break the welfare cycle.

The program I propose will provide:

- Job opportunities for those who need work.
- A Work Benefit for those who work but whose incomes are inadequate to support their families.
- Income Support for those able to work part-time or who are unable to work due to age, physical disability or the need to care for children six years of age or younger.

This new program will accomplish the following:

- Dramatically reduce reliance on welfare payments by doubling the number of single-parent family heads who support their families primarily through earnings from work.
- Ensure that work will always be more profitable than welfare, and that a private or non-subsidized public job will always be more profitable than a special federally-funded public service job.
- Combine effective work requirements and strong work incentives with improved private sector placement services, and create up to 1.4 million public service jobs. Forty-two percent of those jobs may be taken by current AFDC recipients. Those who can work will work, and every family with a full-time worker will have an income substantially above the poverty line.
- Provide increased benefits and more sensitive treatment to those most in need.
- Reduce complexity by consolidating the current AFDC, Supplemental Security Income (SSI), and Food Stamp programs, all of which have differing eligibility requirements, into a single cash assistance program, providing for the first time a uniform minimum Federal payment for the poor.
- Provide strong incentives to keep families together rather than tear them apart, by offering the dignity of useful work to family heads and by ending rules

From *President Carter's Message to Congress August 6, 1977*. Washington, D.C.: The White House; Office of the White House Press Secretary, 1977. p 1–12.

which prohibit assistance when the father of a family remains within the household.
- Reduce fraud and error and accelerate efforts to assure that deserting fathers meet their obligations to their families.
- Give significant financial relief to hard-pressed State and local governments.

THE NEED FOR REFORM

In May, after almost four months of study, I said that the welfare system was worse than I expected. I stand by that conclusion. Each program has a high purpose and serves many needy people; but taken as a whole the system is neither rational nor fair. The welfare system is anti-work, anti-family, inequitable in its treatment of the poor and wasteful of taxpayers' dollars. The defects of the current system are clear:

- It treats people with similar needs in different fashion with separate eligibility requirements for each program.
- It creates exaggerated difference in benefits based on State of residence. Current combined State and Federal AFDC benefits for a family of four with no income vary from $720 per year in Mississippi to $5,954 in Hawaii.
- It provides incentives for family breakup. In most cases two-parent families are not eligible for cash assistance and, therefore, a working father often can increase his family's income by leaving home. In Michigan a two-parent family with the father working at the minimum wage has a total income, including tax credits and food stamps, of $5,922. But if the father leaves, the family will be eligible for benefits totalling $7,076.
- It discourages work. In one Midwestern State, for example, a father who leaves part-time employment paying $2,400 for a full-time job paying $4,000 reduces his family's income by $1,250.
- Efforts to find jobs for current recipients have floundered.
- The complexity of current programs leads to waste, fraud, red tape, and errors. HEW has recently discovered even government workers unlawfully receiving benefits, and numbers of people receive benefits in more than one jurisdiction at the same time.

The solutions to these problems are not easy—and no solution can be perfect; but it is time to begin. The welfare system is too hopeless to be cured by minor modifications. We must make a complete and clean break with the past.

People in poverty want to work, and most of them do. This program is intended to give them the opportunity for self-support by providing jobs for those who need them, and by increasing the rewards from working for those who earn low wages.

PROGRAM SUMMARY

The Program for Better Jobs and Income has the following major elements:

- Strengthened services through the employment and training system for placement in the private sector jobs.
- Creation of up to 1.4 million public service and training positions for principal earners in families with children, at or slightly above the minimum wage through State and local government and non-profit sponsors.
- An expansion of the Earned Income Tax Credit to provide an income supplement of up to a maximum of well over $600 for a family of four through the tax system, by a 10% credit for earnings up to $4,000, a 5% credit for earnings

from $4,000 to the entry point of the positive tax system, and a declining 10% credit thereafter until phase-out. A major share of the benefit will accrue to hard-pressed workers with modest incomes struggling successfully to avoid welfare.

- Strong work requirements applying to single persons, childless couples and family heads, with work requirements of a more flexible nature for single-parent family heads with children aged 7 to 14. Single-parent family heads with pre-school aged children are not required to work.
- A Work Benefit for two-parent families, single-parent families with older children, singles and childless couples. The Federal benefit for a family of four would be a maximum of $2,300 and, after $3,800 of earnings, would be reduced fifty cents for each dollar of earnings.
- Income Support for single-parent families with younger children and aged, blind or disabled persons. The Federal benefit would be a base of $4,200 for a family of four and would be reduced fifty cents for each dollar of earnings.
- New eligibility requirements for cash assistance which ensure that benefits go to those most in need.
- Fiscal relief to States and localities of $2 billion in the first year, growing in subsequent years.
- Simple rules for State supplements to the basic program, in which the Federal government will bear a share of the cost.

PROGRAM DETAIL
EMPLOYMENT SERVICES AND JOB SEARCH
A central element of this proposal is a new effort to match low-income persons with available work in the private and public sector. It will be the responsibility of State and local officials to assure an unbroken sequence of employment and training services, including job search, training, and placement. Prime sponsors under the Comprehensive Employment and Training Act, State employment service agencies, and community-based organizations will play major roles in this effort.

JOBS FOR FAMILIES
A major component of the program is a national effort to secure jobs for the principal wage earners in low-income families with children. The majority of poor families—including many who are on welfare for brief periods of time—depend upon earnings from work for most of their income. People want to support themselves and we should help them do so. I propose that the federal government assist workers from low-income families to find regular employment in the private and public sectors. When such employment cannot be found I propose to provide up to 1.3 million public service jobs (including part-time jobs and training) paying at the minimum wage, or slightly above where states supplement the basic Federal program.

This program represents a commitment by my Administration to ensure that families will have both the skills and the opportunity for self-support.

This new Public Service Employment Program is carefully designed to avoid disruptive effects to the regular economy:

- Applicants will be required to engage in an intensive 5-week search for regular employment before becoming eligible for a public service job. Those working in public service employment will be required to engage in a period of intensive job search every 12 months.

- In order to encourage participants to seek employment in the regular economy, the basic wage rate will be kept at, or where states supplement, slightly above, the minimum wage.
- Every effort will be made to emphasize job activities which lead to the acquisition of useful skills by participants, to help them obtain employment in the regular economy. Training activities will be a regular component of most job placements.

The development of this job program is clearly a substantial undertaking requiring close cooperation of all levels of government. I am confident it will succeed. Thousands of unmet needs for public goods and services exist in our country. Through an imaginative program of job creation we can insure that the goals of human development and community development are approached simultaneously. Public service jobs will be created in areas such as public safety, recreational facilities and programs, facilities for the handicapped, environmental monitoring, child care, waste treatment and recycling, clean-up and pest and insect control, home services for the elderly and ill, weatherization of homes and buildings and other energy-saving activities, teachers' aides and other paraprofessionals in schools, school facilities improvements, and cultural arts activities.

EARNED INCOME TAX CREDIT

The current Earned Income Tax Credit [EITC] is an excellent mechanism to provide tax relief to the working poor. I propose to expand this concept to provide benefits to more families and provide relief to low- and modest-income working people hard hit by payroll tax increases, improve work incentives, and integrate the Program for Better Jobs and Income with the income tax system. The expanded EITC, which will apply to private and non-subsidized public employment, will have the following features:

- A 10% credit on earnings up to $4,000 per year as under current law.
- A 5% credit on earnings between $4,000 and approximately $9,000 for a family of four (the point at which the family will become liable for federal income taxes).
- A phase-out of the credit beyond roughly $9,000 of earnings at 10%. The credit will provide benefits to a family of four up to $15,600 of income.
- The credit will be paid by the Treasury Department and the maximum credit for a family of four would be well over $600.

WORK BENEFIT AND INCOME SUPPORT

I propose to scrap and completely overhaul the current public assistance programs, combining them into a simplified, uniform, integrated system of cash assistance. AFDC, SSI and Food Stamps will be abolished. In their place will be a new program providing: (1). a Work Benefit for two-parent families, single people, childless couples and single parents with no child under 14, all of whom are expected to work full-time and required to accept available work; and (2). Income Support for those who are aged, blind or disabled, and for single parents of children under age 14. Single parents with children aged 7 to 14 will be required to accept part-time work which does not interfere with caring for the children, and will be expected to accept full-time work where appropriate day care is available.

These two levels of assistance are coordinated parts of a unified system which maintains incentives to work and simplifies adminstration.

- For those qualifying for income support the basic benefit for a family of four with no other income will be $4,200 in 1978 dollars. Benefits will be reduced fifty cents for each dollar of earnings, phasing out completely at $8,400 of earnings. Added benefits would accrue to those in regular private or public employment through the Earned Income Tax Credit.
- An aged, blind, or disabled individual would receive a Federal Benefit of $2,500 and a couple would receive $3,750—more than they are now receiving. That is higher than the projected SSI benefit for either group—about $100 higher than for a couple and $120 higher for a single person.
- For those persons required to work who receive a Work Benefit, the basic benefit for a family of four with no other income will be $2,300. To encourage continued work, benefits will not be reduced at all for the first $3,800 of earnings and will thereafter be reduced by fifty cents for each dollar earned up to $8,400. Again, the Earned Income Tax Credit will provide added benefits to persons in regular private or public employment.
- We are committed to assure that inflation will not erode the value of the benefits, and that real benefits will be increased over time as federal resources grow. To preserve flexibility in the initial transition period, however, we do not at this time propose automatic indexing of benefits or automatic increases in their real value. (The figures contained in this message expressed in 1978 dollars will be adjusted to retain their real purchasing power at the time of implementation.)
- Single-parent family heads will be able to deduct up to 20% of earned income up to an amount of $150 per month to pay for child care expenses required for the parent to go to work.
- No limits are placed on the right of States to supplement these basic benefits. However, only if States adopt supplements which complement the structure and incentives of the Federal program will the Federal government share in the cost.

Eligibility rules for the Work Benefit and Income Support will be tightened to ensure that the assistance goes to those who are most in need.

- To reduce error and direct assistance to those most in need, benefits will be calculated based on a retrospective accounting period, rather than on the prospective accounting period used in existing programs. The income of the applicant over the previous six-month period will determine the amount of benefits.
- The value of assets will be reviewed to ensure that those with substantial bank accounts or other resources do not receive benefits. The value of certain assets will be imputed as income to the family in determining the amount of benefits.
- Eligibility has been tightened in cases where related individuals share the same household, while preserving the ability of the aged, disabled and young mothers to file for benefits separately.

STATE ROLE AND FISCAL RELIEF FOR STATES AND
LOCAL COMMUNITIES

Public assistance has been a shared Federal and State responsibility for forty years. The program I propose will significantly increase Federal participation but maintain an important role for the states.

- Every State will be assured that it will save at least 10% of its current welfare expenses in the first year of the program, with substantially increased fiscal relief thereafter.
- Every State is required to pay 10% of the basic Federal Income benefits provided to its residents except where it will exceed 90% of its prior welfare expenditures.
- Every State is free to supplement the basic benefits, and is eligible for Federal matching payments for supplements structured to complement and maintain the incentives of the Federal program. The Federal government will pay 75% of the first $500 supplement and 25% of any additional supplement up to the poverty line. These State supplements will be required to follow Federal eligibility criteria to help achieve nationwide uniformity.
- Where States supplement the income support they must also proportionally supplement the work benefit and the public service wage.
- There will be a three-year period during which States will be required to maintain a share of their current effort in order to ease the transition of those now receiving benefits. These resources must be directed to payment of the State's 10% share of the basic benefit, to supplements complementary to the basic program, and to grandfathering of existing SSI and partially grandfathering AFDC beneficiaries. The Federal government will guarantee a State that its total cost for these expenditures will not exceed 90% of current welfare costs. States can retain any amounts under the 90% requirement not actually needed for the mandated expenditures. In the second year of the program States will be *required* to maintain only 60% of current expenditures, in the third year, only 30%. In the fourth year, they will only be required to spend enough to meet their 10% share of the basic benefit.
- States will have the option to assist in the administration of the program. They will be able to operate the crucial intake function serving applicants, making possible effective coordination with social service programs. The Federal government will operate the data processing system, calculate benefits, and issue payments.
- The Federal government will provide a $600 million block grant to the States to provide for emergency needs. These grants will assist the States in responding to sudden and drastic changes in family circumstances.
- The Federal government will provide 30% above the basic wage for fringe benefits and adminstrative costs of the jobs program, and will reimburse the states for costs of administration of the work benefit and income support program.

In the first year of this program, states and localities would receive $2 billion in fiscal relief, while at the same time ensuring that no current SSI beneficiary receives a reduced benefit and that over 90% of current AFDC beneficiaries receive similar protection.

In subsequent years as current recipients leave the rolls and as the maintenance of State effort requirement declines from 90% to zero within 3 years, the opportunities for increased fiscal relief will grow.

Under our program for fiscal relief, States will be required to pass through their fiscal relief to municipal and county governments in full proportion to their contributions. Thus, for example, in New York State, where New York City pays 33% of the State's share, New York City would receive 33% of the State's fiscal relief or $174 million.

REDUCTION OF FRAUD AND ABUSE

The few providers and recipients guilty of fraud and abuse in our welfare programs not only rob the taxpayers but cheat the vast majority of honest recipients. One of the most significant benefits of consolidation of existing cash assistance programs is the opportunity to apply sophisticated management techniques to improve their operation. The use of a central computer facility will permit more efficient processing of claims, reduce the incidence of error in calculating benefits, and facilitate the detection of fraud. No longer will people easily claim benefits in more than one jurisdiction.

We will strongly enforce current programs directed at assisting local officials in obtaining child support payments from run-away parents, as determined by judicial proceedings.

We will ensure that the Department of Health, Education and Welfare will vigorously root out abuses and fraud in our social programs.

We will work for passage of current legislation designed to crack down on fraud and abuse in our Medicaid and Medicare Program. The administration of these programs will be a major challenge for federal and state officials. It provides a valuable opportunity to demonstrate that government can be made to work, particularly in its operation of programs which serve those in our society most in need.

IMPLEMENTATION

Because of the complexity of integrating the different welfare systems of the 50 states and the District of Columbia into a more unified national system, we estimate that this program will be effective in Fiscal Year 1981. Moreover, we recognize that the National Health Insurance plan which will be submitted next year must contain fundamental reform and rationalization of the Medicaid program, carefully coordinated with the structure of this proposal. However, we are anxious to achieve the swiftest implementation possible and will work with the Congress and State and local governments to accelerate this timetable if at all possible.

Given the present complex system, welfare reform inevitably involves difficult choices. Simplicity and uniformity and improved benefits for the great majority inevitably require reduction of special benefits for some who receive favored treatment now. Providing the dignity of a job to those who at present are denied work opportunities will require all the creativity and ingenuity that private business and government at all levels can bring to bear. But the effort will be worthwhile both for the individual and for the country. The Program for Better Jobs and Income stresses the fundamental American commitment to work, strenghtens the family, respects the less advantaged in our society, and makes a far more efficient and effective use of our hard-earned tax dollars.

I hope the Congress will move expeditiously and pass this program early next year.

Jimmy Carter

References

1. Douglass J. *Defining America's's Social Problems.* Englewood Cliffs, N.J.: Prentice-Hall, 1974. p. 134.
2. Ibid. p. 135.

3. Banfield E. *The Unheavenly City Revisited.* Boston: Little, Brown, 1974. p. 130.

4. Komisar, L. *Down and Out in the U.S.A..* New York: Franklin Watts, 1973.

5. Banfield, E. Op. cit. pp. 141, 142.

6. *National Observer,* February 5, 1977, p. 4.

7. Parker, R. *The Myth of the Middle Class.* New York: Liveright, 1972. pp. 14–16.

8. Lenski, G. *Power and Privilege.* New York, McGraw-Hill, 1966. pp. 41, 42.

9. Piven, F., and Cloward, R. *Regulating the Poor.* New York: Vintage, 1972. pp. 345–347.

10. Banfield, E. Op. cit., pp. 142–147.

11. Douglass, J. Op. cit., p. 55

12. Ibid., pp. 55, 56.

13. Harrington, M. *The Other America.* New York: Macmillan, 1963, ch. 1.

14. Trattner, W. *From Poor Law to Welfare State.* New York: Free Press, 1974. pp. 99, 107.

15. Axinn, J., and Levin, H. *Social Welfare A History of the American Response to Need.* New York: Dodd, 1975, pp. 14, 15.

16. Trattner, W. Op. cit., p. 20.

17. Axinn, J., and Levin, H. Op cit., pp. 2, 278.

18. Ibid., Ch. 4

19. Piven, F., and Cloward, R. Op. Cit., p. 49

20. Ibid., chap. 2, 3.

21. Ibid., p. 117.

22. Ibid., p. 189.

23. Ibid., pp. 196–198.

24. Lawrence, W., and Leeds, S. *An Inventory of Federal Income Transfer Programs, Fiscal Year 1977.* White Plains, N.Y.: The Institute for Socioeconomic Studies, 1978, p. 1, 2.

25. Ibid., pp.1,2.

26. Ibid., p. 2.

27. Ibid., p. 13.

28. Ibid., p. 14.

29. Ibid., p. 14.

30. Schenk, Q. *Development of Provisions for Education of Crippled Children in the United States,* 1951. Unpublished.

31. Schorr, A. "Alternatives in Income Maintenance," *Social Work* (July, 1966): 22–29.

32. Freeman, R. *Welfare Reform and the Family Assistance Plan.* Testimony before the Committee on Finance, U.S. Senate, January 27, 1972.

chapter/9

Programs for Personal Improvement

In Chapter 8 we discussed the provisions which have evolved in American society to provide economic assistance to those who are defined as having insufficient resources. These provisions transfer resources from the more productive sectors of society to the less productive sectors; these transfers are designed to be utilized by the individuals who make up the categories for which the programs were established. From this perspective, people are seen only as units of social categories, and little attention is given to each individual's unique characteristics. For instance, a young person who meets the social definition of being a dependent child becomes eligible to receive the economic resources available for dependent children. When he or she no longer meets this definition, he or she becomes ineligible for further assistance, even though that particular individual might still need assistance.

Fortunately there is more to welfare programs than this; it is recognized that it is also necessary to focus attention on the individuals who comprise the categories to assure that the services will be used to best advantage. Therefore hand in hand with economic assistance comes a variety of services. These services see the individual not merely as poor but as someone who can be helped in a variety of ways to become more productive and at the same time to achieve better interpersonal relationships. Human services workers are often involved with programs that are designed to help offenders see the value of giving up their criminal activities; to help the mentally or physically ill, or the crippled and the infirm to become better adjusted to their problems and to make the most of opportunities that might be available; to families so that they can better serve their individual members; to children so that they may grow up to be productive members of society with a minimum of psychological problems; and to the aged so that they and their families can better cope with the problems that must be faced when people grow old. These are all services for personal improvement because they are designed to help individuals improve their relationships, their opportunities, and their physical circumstances. Services are provided through counseling, therapy, job training, housing, day care centers, protective care, and institutionalized care.

Because the American society is primarily functionalist and equilibrium oriented, programs for personal improvement are designed to reshape the individual to fit into society rather than the reverse.

Claims Made for Services to Individuals

No individual can exist without a supportive society, nor can a society exist without the support of individuals. In fact, the well-being of the society and the well-being of individuals are mandatory to each other. This may seem to be so obvious that there would be no need for any further discussion. However, the argument over the relative importance of society versus the individual has been going on for thousands of years and will probably continue. As Seneca the Younger, the Roman Stoic, dramatist, and statesman, suggested, "We are members of one great body. . . . We must consider that we were born for the good of the whole." Herbert Spencer, the English philosopher, expressed the other extreme: "Society exists for the benefit of its members, not the members for the benefit of society."

That the individual should be considered subordinate to society has been accepted by many thinkers since Seneca. According to this body of thought, the individual functions to serve the best interests of society. It is assumed that individuals who face poverty do so not because of a malfunction in society, but, rather, because something is "wrong" with them. They must receive "treatment" to function adequately. They must be "trained" if they are young or "rehabilitated" if they are adults.

The opposite view is that society exists to serve individual interests. Thus, if individuals face poverty, it is because something is wrong with the way in which society operates. Individuals run into problems only because the society is "sick" and therefore cannot provide what individuals need, desire, or rightfully should have.[1]

William Ryan, in his book *Blaming the Victim*[2] discusses these two polarities of thought. He argues that, while most individuals are on welfare because society operates in ways that prevent them from receiving its benefit, most human services professionals regard those receiving welfare as being themselves responsible for their poverty.

Sometimes claims are made that through the provision of personal services, inequality and poverty will be eliminated from the total society.[3] This claim is made when factors associated with poverty are assumed to be the causal factors of poverty, a misinterpretation that was common when case work was accepted as a social work technique in the early twentieth century. The early social workers, as they visited the homes of their clients, noticed, for instance, that the poor have large families. Forgetting that many middle-class people and even some rich people also have large families, they began to see a factor that is frequently *associated* with being poor as the factor that *caused* poverty.[4]

Many people even today find it difficult to distinguish between associational relationships and causal ones. Poverty is often associated with such things as broken homes, drunkeness, criminal activity, substandard housing, or poor education, but none of these in and of themselves causes poverty.

The issue here is not the appropriateness of the services being provided by welfare organizations but, rather, the appropriateness of the claims being made for the results of the service. Services to individuals are often very helpful to the individuals, but such services have not eliminated poverty, and there is no evidence that they ever will, particularly now that poverty is defined in relative rather than in absolute terms.

Origin and Growth of Services

The Association for Improving the Condition of the Poor, established in New York in 1843, initiated one of the first organized attempts to deal with the poor on an individual basis. Led by Robert Hartley, the Association divided the city into 21 districts and 225 subdistricts, each of which was assigned a "friendly visitor" who was supposed to go to the home of every person asking for aid and evaluate the situation. The friendly visitor offered few services other than moral reeducation. The Association and similar ones that sprang up in other cities did accomplish some social reform, but they failed in another of their objectives, that of promoting cooperation among the many small relief organizations who competed among themselves for donations.[5]

Cooperation among these agencies began with the Charity Organization Societies, the first of which was formed in Buffalo in 1877. Within ten years, more than twenty-five larger cities had their own C.O.S. In the beginning these societies accepted the prevailing social philosophy that poverty was the fault of the individual, but the C.O.S. maintained the friendly visitor system, and, as the visitors came more and more into contact with the poor, they began to recognize that being poor was not something that happened simply because an individual was lazy or vice ridden.

They began to differentiate between those who were able bodied but did not work and those who worked but still could not provide minimum necessities for themselves and their families. Those who did not work were called the "unworthy poor"; those who worked but did not earn enough were called the "worthy poor." Services were concentrated on the "worthy poor."

It is to be kept in mind that the C.O.S. were private organizations and did not favor public poor relief (economic assistance) which they felt weakened the "moral fiber" of the poor. Their aim, instead, was to "rehabilitate" the "worthy poor" so that they might become self-supporting.

Rehabilitation could be carried out only after a careful investigation, analysis, and discussion of the poor person's condition or "case" had taken place and a plan formulated for the person's improvement. This came to be called "case work" and was first described as a method of personal services to the poor by Mary Richmond in 1917 in her book, *Social Diagnosis.*[7]

From the end of World War 1 to the 1960s, there was slow but steady growth in services for personal improvement, and, over the years, housing, health and psychological services, job training, legal aid, and so on became more and more a function of welfare agencies. During the Kennedy and Johnson administrations there was an explosion of social legislation that it was hoped would eliminate poverty once and for all. Most of the legislation provided for an increase in funding for the many types of services offered, so much so that the 1970s was characterized by a great outcry over the cost of welfare legislation enacted in the previous decade. Nonetheless, in a period of one hundred years, the concept of services for personal improvement became so accepted a part of welfare services that many came to think that such personal services were the most important function of a welfare agency.

The 1962 amendments to the Social Security Act led to the separation of personal services from economic assistance programs.[8] Presently, many employees of the public welfare agencies do only eligibility work. Then they refer clients to service specialists who are employed in other sections of the public agencies, in private agencies, or in private practice. However, before any referral can be made, the needs of the client must be evaluated and so, in fact, human services workers do more than the determination of financial need even when they are not responsible for providing services. How much the worker will do depends on the policy of the employing agency, the availability of specialized services in the particular area, and the education and occupational classification of the worker. The human services worker in a rural setting often provides a greater variety of personal services than does one who works in a large urban agency, where the services are more highly specialized.

The 1962 amendments created the Social and Rehabilitation Service within the federal Department of Health, Education and Welfare (now the Department of Health and Human Services). The 1962 amendments were a landmark in that they marked the formal entrance of public welfare organizations into the area of provision of personal services. This was done in part because private organizations were beginning to experience problems in financing their operations and so one of the provisions of the amendments was the "purchase-of-service" feature, whereby the public organization could pay private organizations for personal services that they would provide for the recipients of welfare services.

"Social services" were reorganized in the 1974 amendments to the Social Security Act, commonly called the Title XX amendments. These amendments embody the provisions for personal services that are in operation at the present time.*

It is important to keep in mind the distinction between the popular term"social security" and the Social Security Act. Social security generally refers to the payments to persons who retire that are made under the insurance provisions of the Social Security Act. But the Social Security Act also contains a number of provisions under which public assistance (economic maintenance) programs are authorized. It is to these public assistance programs that the Title XX amendments pertain, not to the insurance provisions of the Social Security Act.

Present Characteristics of Personal Services

The 1962 and 1974 amendments to the Social Security Act were based on two assumptions not previously a part of the public welfare provisions:

1. Personal services are necessary to enable the poor to become economically self-sufficient.
2. personal services are beneficial to members of the society other than the poor.

Assumption 1 is reflected in that portion of the Title XX amendments that makes those persons on public assistance eligible for social services without charge. Assumption 2 is reflected in that portion of the amendments that makes it possible for persons not on public assistance to receive personal services by payment of a fee established on a sliding scale. †

Table 9.1 illustrates the wide variety of personal services that can be made available under the Title XX amendments. All are related to the five objectives or goals that the services are expected to achieve. The services enumerated in Table 9.1 are without exception services to individuals. The emphasis is upon the functional characeer of the society, for the object of change is the individual, as the nature of the services provided illustrates.

* See Document 9.1, pp. 168-174.
† Document 9.3. p.191.

Table 9.1 / Title XX Program Goals and Services

Goal I	Achieving or maintaining economic self-support to prevent, reduce, or eliminate dependency.
Goal II	Achieving or maintaining self-sufficiency, including reduction or prevention of dependency.
Goal III	A. Preventing or remedying neglect, abuse or exploitation of children and adults unable to protect their own interests. B. Preserving, rehabilitating, or reuniting families.
Goal IV	Preventing or reducing inappropriate institutional care by providing community-based care, home-based care or other forms of less intensive care.
Goal V	Securing referral or admission for institutional care when other forms of care are not appropriate or providing services to individuals in institutions.

Goal I	Goal II	Goal III	Goal IV	Goal V
Diagnosis/ evaluation	Diagnosis/ evaluation	Diagnosis/ evaluation	Diagnosis/ evaluation	Diagnosis/ evaluation
Counseling	Counseling	Counseling	Counseling	Counseling
Day care	Chore services	Adoption services	Chore services	Court services
Education and training	Court services	Chore services	Court services	Education and training
Family planning	Day care	Court service	Day care	Family planning
Health related	Day services program	Day care	Day services program	Health related
Home and financial management	Education and training	Day services program	Education and training	Home and financial management
Housing	Family planning	Education and training	Family planning	Legal services
Sheltered employment	Health related	Family planning	Health related	Personal care
Transportation	Home and financial management	Health related	Home and financial management	Planning, placement and supervision
	Home-delivered or congregate meals	Home and financial magagement	Home-delivered or congregate meals	Special living arrangements
	Housing	Home-delivered or congregate meals	Housing	Transportation
	Legal services	Housing	Personal care	
	Personal care	Legal services	Planning, placement and supervision	
	Recreation	Personal care	Recreation	
	Transportation	Planning, placement and supervision	Special living arrangements	
		Protective payment services	Transportation	
		Recreation		
		Special living arrangements		
		Transportation		

Excerpted from *State Plan*. See Document 9.3, pp. 190, 191. See also Document 9.1, p. 168; and Document 9.2, p. 179.

We mentioned earlier it is possible for public funds to purchase services from private agencies through the provisions of the social service amendments to the Social Security Act. These amendments have served to blur the distinctions that previously existed between the private and public agencies. Public agencies now not only can deliver the services that previously were the preserve of private agencies but they can also provide financial assistance to private agencies through the purchase-of-service arrangements. These purchase-of-service arrangements have in many ways brought the private agencies under the control of the public sector because the services must be given according to the provision of the laws and rules and regulations of the various levels of government concerned. This has been a mixed blessing for private organizations. On the one hand the social service provisions were advantageous to them because it gave them access to the clientele served by the public agencies, from which they had been largely excluded since the Great Depression. On the other hand, they lost much of their independence and flexibility because they were now subject to the controls imposed by the social service amendments.

Categories of Individuals Receiving Services for Personal Improvement

The services provided under the social service amendments to the Social Security Act are aimed primarily at the following three categories of individuals:

1. those affected adversely by marketplace conditions
2. those affected adversely by cultural labeling
3. those affected adversely by their own personal characteristics.

The first two categories address conditions that originate outside the individual. They are societal in origin, because individuals cannot affect marketplace conditions or prevent discrimination against themselves. The third category addresses conditions that are attributes of individuals and relate to specific qualities that affect their personal competence to be self-sufficient.

Because these services are offered primarily under public auspices, the services are oriented toward the achievement of societal objectives. This means that, even though they are called services to individuals, they are *instrumental* in assuring that the individuals eventually cease to be eligible for the services and become productive members of the society. This is the case even when individuals are handicapped either at birth or from accident or disease following birth. The *ultimate* aim of all welfare services to individuals is to enable them to "pay their own way" insofar as this is possible.

Services to Deal with the Effects of Marketplace Conditions

Most of the services designed to deal with marketplace conditions focus on job training and job finding. This is because, even though societal conditions do not permit full employment, societal expectations require that all able-bodied adults participate in the work force. When adults are not working, they are caught between two conficting social forces, altruism and the work ethic. They are not allowed to starve, and they are constantly prodded to enter the labor force. Only one program of economic assistance, that of Old Age Assistance, does not have services connected with it that are supposed to push the individual into a program to enter or reenter the work force.

Personal service programs are often sold to the public with the claim that the unemployed will eventually become employed and that therefore, the need for welfare economic assistance will eventually be eliminated, but this has not happened.[10] The failure to realize the claims of social services to lessen unemployment of the poor has contributed to the frustrations of the general public with welfare programs. Their frustration focuses on the recipients of assistance, the workers who provide the assistance, and the programs themselves. The periodic tax revolts that sweep the nation are partly in response to this frustration. Because of the claims made for the results of personal services, human services professionals are under pressure to obtain employment for the poor.

Services to Deal with the Effects of Cultural Labeling

The stratification system of our society attaches names or labels to the various groups that occupy the various ranks, from the highest to the lowest. Members of the society are generally able to place individuals in the various ranks by knowing what the group labels stand for. This is not done only by occupational category but by other related labels as well. For instance, college graduates will generally be assumed to occupy some of the higher occupational categories, even though it will be necessary to know their specific occupational specialty to place them in a specific rank.

Likewise, labels are given to groups whose members are presumed to occupy some of the lower occupational ranks in society and who suffer economic disadvantages in part because of the ranks to which they are relegated. The groups currently receiving the greatest amount of discrimination in the marketplace because of cultural labeling are women, the poor, the handicapped, and the ethnic and racial minority groups.* It is difficult to estimate the dollar penalty in income for members of these groups, but

* For a full discussion of the phenomenon of the discriminatory effects of cultural labeling, see Milton Yinger's *A Minority Group in American Society*,[11] and de Lone's *Small Futures*.[12]

Schiller estimates that in 1973 black workers were penalized about $3,600 per year because they were members of a racial minority.[13] Many services for personal improvement are designed to overcome the effects of this sort of cultural labeling.

AFDC programs assist poor mothers who cannot earn enough to support their families. Human services workers associated with AFDC programs usually work with other human services workers connected with programs such as Headstart, Talent Search, or Upward Bound. These programs, under the auspices of a welfare agency or public school, furnish special educational services that aim to compensate for the inferior education that the poor and members of minority groups often receive.

Headstart is a preschool program based on the premise that people are poor because they are culturally deprived. The program is supposed to make up for the deficiency in the children's home life or cultural background. Its activities have generated much controversy.

Talent Search and Upward Bound programs provide special educational aids for capable older children of the poor or minority groups who might otherwise fall behind or drop out of school. Talent Search is for those with exceptional potential. It provides no instruction, tutoring, or financial aid, but it does give grants to institutions of higher education as well as to public and private agencies to assist them in the provision of services. Upward Bound provides academic instruction, career counseling, guidance, and a $30 a month stipend to children from low-income families with inadequate secondary school preparation.[14] Through these educational aids programs and others, human services workers have been successful in assisting the poor and members of minority groups to obtain a much better education than would otherwise be possible.

The movement to establish services for displaced homemakers illustrates the ongoing efforts to create new types of services for special groups.[15] Even though there are existing programs for which these women could qualify for assistance, advocates press for the creation of new centers in which displaced homemakers, most of whom are members of the middle class, can receive assistance, primarily through counseling, job training, or job finding.

The operation of cultural labeling is clearly evident in the case of the displaced homemaker. Advocates for the creation of these services want the public to accept the label of "displaced homemaker" as a special group that requires special assistance. The effort is also made by these advocates to get the public to understand that displaced homemakers are not to be labeled in such a fashion that they will be ranked with the "poor" who receive welfare services under the usual public assistance programs. Advocates work to get across the idea that displaced homemakers are not "poor" in the usual sense of social stratification. They are instead middle-class individuals who have fallen on hard times, and, with the help of special services, will likely be able to compensate for their misfortune and return to their previous places in society. This is something presumably not expected from the poor who make use of the regular welfare system.

Services to Deal with Effects of Personal Characteristics

Unlike the first two types of services, which deal with conditions external to individuals, this category is concerned with services that deal with characteristics pertaining to the individuals themselves. These services are related to an internal situation, that is, to personal characteristics.

These personal characteristics range from physical handicaps such as blindness, deformity, or minimum mental capacity to psychological handicaps such as lack of self-control, mental illness, or antisocial tendencies. These personal characteristics are considered to be the concern of human services professionals because they interfere with the ability of individuals to be self-sufficient. Individuals therefore receive services to enable them to take care of themselves to the fullest extent possible. Services range from assisting a person with limited sight to obtain needed glasses to various kinds of psychological therapy. Of course an individual who receives personal services of this sort may at the same time be receiving the kind of services mentioned in the other two categories.

The vocational rehabilitation program, which began under federal statute in 1920, is one of the earliest of public programs for services dealing with personal characteristics. This program was expanded with the Social Security Act of 1935. It furnishes such services as education, medical care, psychiatric care, family assistance if necessary, employment counseling, job training, and job finding to the physically handicapped; all programs are oriented toward enabling individuals to become self-sufficient.[16]

Services to the blind were some of the first to be developed under public auspices, for blindness was one of the first handicaps to be recognized to be severe enough to be a public responsibiltiy. Even before the enactment of the Social Security Act of 1935 in which the federal government assumed the responsibility to initiate nationwide services for the blind, twenty-nine states had passed special statutes for blind relief. Services to the blind include special education, furnishing of special equipment, job training, home services, and counseling services for personal problems. Similar services are available for the deaf and for deaf-mutes.

Developmental disabilities include handicaps to performance that may result from retardation, from physical handicaps and so on. Services involve physical therapy, special education, sheltered workshop, curative workshop, and counseling with the parents to enable them to adjust to the handicap that their children carry through life.*

Conditions defined as illnesses must be "treated." Medical services, psychological services, social work services, educational services, and legal services, with all their related technologies, are all brought to bear to render a "cure" for an individual with an illness. Mental dysfunction has been defined as an illness for some time. Alcoholism has recently been officially

---

* Programs for the handicapped were also discussed in the section on "Cultural Labeling," for personal characteristics that set people apart result in their being labeled as different. Personal characteristics can produce cultural labels.

reclassified from a crime to an illness. Drug addiction is in limbo at present for it is defined both as a crime and as an illness. Individual treatment programs for these "illnesses" are the most sophisticated of the services offered through welfare programs.

Family planning services are recent. They are sometimes available to families on AFDC as well as to other families who may be receiving support and/or services under some of the many programs we have discussed. At present family planning services include education in the use of contraceptives, spacing of children, size of the family, and responsibilities of the parents. They often do not include abortion services because of the controversial and problematic nature of these services.

Services to offenders and their families are also available either through services already described or through the services furnished by the courts, probation and parole, and the prisons or reformatories to which the offenders are sent. These services include job training, job finding, health care, assistance to families while the offender is incarcerated, and counseling of the offender to prevent repetition of the behavior that led to the original offense.

Schiller states that one of the most important of the personal characteristics associated with poverty is shown by the frequent "accusation" that the poor lack self-control and therefore do not limit the size of their families or maintain stable families.[17] Schiller also states that poverty precedes large families and family instability, even though a large portion of the services to families is oriented toward "treatment" of the adults and children to instill self-control so that the family can pull itself out of poverty.[18]

Unemployment is often considered to be a personal handicap, and counseling is considered to be necessary to get the individual to "want" to work. Children in poor families may need special counseling to help them to "want" to go to school. In this circumstance, family counseling often deals with the "handicap of being poor" and the consequent necessity to "treat" the poor.[19] This is in spite of Goodwin's work that showed that the poor tend to have a stronger work ethic than do most Americans.[20]

There are also a variety of services lumped under the heading of "social service" that include foster care, day care, protective care, homemaking, services to counter child abuse and neglect, adoptive services, institutionalization such as residential treatment, and alternatives to institutionalization when indicated. These services are provided *through* the public agencies: however, at times the actual service will be given *by* a private agency. When someone on welfare utilizes the services provided by private agencies, there is a "fee for service" charged under purchase-of-service agreements. This is charged by the private agency to the public agency.

Since about 1970 there has also been a rapid development of new agencies independent of both the private agencies and public agencies. These agencies are sometimes called "private vendors," because they furnish services such as residential homes, medical services, psychological services, or special educational services on a fee-for-service basis that is paid by public funds. These agencies exist as private profit-making businesses providing services to those under public care. These vendor agencies grew up because it was claimed that they could provide better services for less money than could the public and private agencies. There is considerable controversy as to the validity of this claim.

Some Techniques Utilized in Provision of Services

We will give only a cursory description of the two basic techniques utilized in the interaction between workers and their clientele. Training in the proper utilization of techniques makes up a major portion of the curriculum of schools that train human services professionals.

The two basic techniques are

1. the interview session
2. the group session

The *interview* session is a formal verbal exchange, a conversation with a purpose, between the individual who can provide a service and the individual seeking the service. In the context of welfare sevices, the worker may offer financial aid, information as to how that resource may be obtained, information about other resources available, explanations about rules that must be followed to receive the *aid*, and assistance to the recipient so that he or she may make best use of the resource. This assistance can be procedural or supportive. Procedural assistance helps the recipient to conform to the requirements of the organization; supportive assistance helps the recipient to overcome motivational, emotional, or social difficulties that he or she may be experiencing.

Sometimes a worker will see an individual only once; sometimes the worker will follow a particular client over a period of years. The worker's office is usually the setting for the interview, but interviews may also occur in other places, such as the home of the recipient.

Human services professionals utilize the interview session to accomplish the following:

1. The worker obtains information about the recipient's situation, why the individual is seeking service, and the nature of the service being sought. The worker attempts to find out as much as possible about the recipient's background and environment because this may have a bearing on the type of service offered and the manner in which the service can be delivered.

2. The worker assesses the ability of the organization to deliver the type of service sought and the ability of the recipient to utilize the service.

3. Determination is made as to whether the person is eligible to receive services from the organization.

4. The worker estimates the amount of involvement with the recipient that will be necessary to effect the transfer of resources.

5. The paperwork is handled. The worker assists the recipient to provide the information required from the recipient to receive assistance.

6. A determination is made of the psychological and social supports that the recipient needs to profit from the transfer of resources, the amount of training the recipient requires either to achieve personal satisfaction or to engage in income-producing activities, and the necessity for other organizations or other human services workers to become involved.

7. After formulating a plan of procedure, the worker goes over the plan with the recipient, listens to his or her reactions to the plan, and obtains the recipient's cooperation.

8. The recipient is placed in touch with other workers if necessary.

9. The worker is supportive of the recipient throughout the period that he or she receives the service.

10. As a worker sees a recipient over a period of time, evaluations are made of the progress of the recipient and of the results of the services given. When adjustments are necessary, the worker attempts to make them in cooperation with the recipient, other members of the organization, and with workers from other organizations that may be involved with the recipient.

The human services worker who carries out formal face-to-face exchanges with more than one individual is using the medium of *group techniques* to deliver services. This is done

1. when a number of recipients share similar concerns that can be dealt with simultaneously. This is sometimes done for the sake of efficiency.
2. when the recipient's relationships with other persons create difficulty and can likely be improved through the acquisition of skills, through modified perceptions of the individuals, or through a realization on the part of the recipient that greater satisfaction could be achieved through alteration of his or her behavior in relation to other persons.

An example of the first instance might be a human services worker getting together a group of mothers all of whom were receiving Aid to Families with Dependent Children to explain to them all at once the requirements for receiving or remaining eligible for assistance. The worker could also use this type of group to assist mothers to learn better ways of handling their children, taking care of their homes, or making their finances stretch. Not only can the worker save time by utilizing the group, but he or she can also utilize the members of the groups to assist, inform, support, or correct each other.

An example of the second use of the group might be with an AFDC recipient who could be having difficulty with her children. The worker would want to meet with the recipient and her children simultaneously to try to improve the situation for all. The worker might also attend sessions of other groups of which the mother is a member such as church groups, neighborhood groups, and clubs to elicit assistance from others in improving family relationships.

Children in AFDC families frequently have difficulties with teachers, school administrators, law enforcement authorities, or business personnel. The worker might meet with groups of these officials, sometimes even with the mother and/or her children present to try to resolve the issues. These are usually only one-session exchanges, but they may occur more often.

The human services worker should become familiar with the use of both the interview and the group session and be ready to utilize them flexibly in the best interests of the recipients.* The goal should be to enable recipients to make the best use of the resources available from welfare programs. Human services professionals who utilize only one technique may lose their flexibility. Techniques are important. However perfection of a technique should never be an end in itself; rather it should be the means by which services are delivered to recipients.

A Case in Point

The following example illustrates the interplay of external and internal conditions in the life of an individual who applies for economic assistance from a welfare agency and how personal services can be successful in enabling the individual to become self-sufficient. It also illustrates the limits of personal services.

Robert, an adult male, comes to the agency. He has been unemployed for an extended period and has exhausted his resources. His relatives were helpful for a while but they can no longer be counted on for support. Robert and his wife, Helen, have three children, ages two, ten, and eighteen. They live in a rented upper flat in a two-family dwelling. Because he is unable to pay the rent, Robert and his family are in danger of eviction. Robert has had to forego medical care for himself and his wife, for the ten-year-old has been ill and what money he had was spent on the child.

Robert sees a social worker who must decide how he might be best helped. Since the AFDC program is the largest of the public assistance programs and is oriented toward families, it might seem to be the logical one to utilize. However, in the state in which Robert lives, AFDC cannot be given to families in which an unemployed male head of the household is present. Robert is unskilled and has worked primarily in janitorial jobs, so the worker encourages him to enroll in a job training program. If he does so, he is told that, while he is in training, he and his family will be eligible to receive a stipend and that the family will also be eligible for public medical care and housing assistance. Robert agrees to enroll.

The social worker then refers Robert to another worker connected with the job training program. This worker takes care of the arrangements to enroll Robert in a program. These arrangements include testing for interests and skills, a physical examination, and checking Robert's eligibility for

* For a discussion of similarities and differences between the interview and the group session, see A. Kadushin, and Q. Schenk.[21]

support while in training. Meanwhile the first worker is checking into the circumstances of the rest of the family. This worker notes that Robert's wife has never worked outside the home and that the eighteen-year-old is doing well in school and may be eligible for student assistance when he graduates. The worker talks to the eighteen-year-old about going to a vocational school or having on-the-job training or perhaps even going on for higher education.

Robert enrolls in a course to train him to be a welder. The course lasts for three months. Robert works and studies hard and is encouraged by his progress. At the end of the training, another social worker finds Robert a job as an apprentice welder in a large manufacturing company in the area and informs him about his responsibilities to his employers and to his union. Robert is also given information on how to budget his income to care for his family.

Robert likes his job very much and is able to support himself and his family at a higher economic level than the family has ever enjoyed before. He does not need further support from the welfare program. He recognizes that, without the efforts of the human services workers in his behalf, he would have been unable to work through the difficulties he faced as a result of protracted unemployment. In this case, the human services professionals have assisted an individual and his family to solve a number of problems that resulted from a lack of financial resources.

Robert's case can be closed and success assured as long as marketplace conditions remain the same. In many cases persons like Robert no longer require assistance from human services professionals. But let us assume that Robert is affected by a change in market conditions.

Instead of providing continuous employment for Robert until he reaches retirement age, the plant where he works decides to shift its operation to another state and Robert is not eligible for transfer because he lacks seniority. Once again Robert finds himself unemployed and unable to find a job in the area even though he now has some skills. He finds some odd jobs, but these do not pay enough to support his family, and, when he reaches the low state of finances that prompted him to seek assistance in the first place, he returns to the agency. He looks for the worker who was so helpful, but he has gotten married and moved to another city. When the new worker tells him that the reason he is unemployed is that he doesn't have the skills necessary to land one of the jobs available in the area, Robert becomes very discouraged. He feels that the entire responsibility for his plight is placed on him, even though he has tried very hard to improve himself and to find employment. He begins to resist taking any further training, for, as he tells his wife, "What's the use. It won't pay off anyway." Robert's wife, Helen, then finds work as a clerk in a variety store but is unable to earn enough to support the family. The eighteen-year-old (now nineteen) who was attending college drops out because he can no longer afford to stay in school. He finds a job and contributes to the family finances, but he wants to get married and both Robert and Helen are reluctant to continue to receive support from him.

Robert lies around the house feeling miserable and occasionally doing an odd job. After several months he returns to the agency. The worker tells him that he might obtain a job paid for by the government under the public services employment program, but there is no guarantee that the job would last longer than a year. This does not seem to be much help to Robert so he returns home.

Helen is by now becoming desperate, so she goes to the agency to request assistance. The worker tells her that as long as Robert is in the home and is unemployed, there is nothing that can be done. She returns home and discusses what the worker has said. Robert decides to leave home so that his family can receive economic assistance under the AFDC program. He goes to another state where he works periodically and earns enough to support himself. Helen is now able to qualify for AFDC and receives support for herself and her dependent children. This includes housing, medical, and educational assistance. The human services worker also works out financial assistance for the oldest child so that he can return to college. For a time, Helen keeps her job in the variety store because the worker told her that she should do so since this saves the government some money. However, this doesn't do Helen much good, because the agency takes out of her assistance allowance nearly the equivalent of what she earns. Helen resents this and after a while finds a medical excuse for quitting her job. The worker then refers Helen to a clinic where she receives medical care and some counseling that is designed to encourage her to go back to work. It doesn't matter much to Helen, because she has given up trying to improve the conditions of her life. As far as she is concerned, she and Robert both did the best they could and nothing came of it. Helen never thought of herself as poor, but now she is beginning to believe that she and Robert *are* poor and that there is nothing they or anyone else can do about it. "That's just the way it is," she thinks. At present she is supported fully throught the AFDC program, because she still has a child under age six. Robert slips into town whenever he can to visit his family and gives them some money when he can. No members of the family or any of the neighbors would dream of telling the agency that Robert comes around; if they did, Helen would be in danger of losing her AFDC benefits.

This case example illustrates the relationship of external and internal conditions to individual behavior. It also illustrates how important the mix of these conditions is to chances for success that the human services professional has in improving a situation. When the worker and Robert saw the possibilities for permanent employment, they were able to do a good deal together to move toward a solution for Robert's problem. If the external market conditions had remained stable, Robert would have been able to escape the conditions of poverty that he and his family faced. However, market conditions in any given community do not remain stable, and Robert found himself out of a job because of circumstances beyond his or the human services worker's control. Because welfare organizations have no control over the externals that affect the Roberts of this world, all that the workers could do was to encourage Robert to keep trying and to try to minimize the effects of the loss of the job on Robert and his family. In the end, however, the only solution was for Robert to get his old job back, or one like it, and this was impossible. Thus the only resource the workers had was to enroll the family in an income maintenance program, a program that had requirements connected with it that did not assist in strengthening family relationships.

Human services professionals can often effect changes in individuals that assist them to improve their circumstances. Seldom, however, can human services professionals modify the external circumstances with which individuals must deal. The inability to modify the external circumstances of individuals comprises one of the major frustrations for human services professionals because the external circumstances with which the poor must deal cause a significant portion of their difficulty.* In Robert's case, the attainment of permanent employment was mandatory to his well-being. He was not able to adjust to the prospect of continued sporadic employment, and that was the only course of action open. In another situation, the workers might have been able to keep the recipient motivated sufficiently for him to continue the struggle for employment, but in Robert's case his solution was to give up the struggle in the face of what to him must have been insurmountable odds.

When faced with a situation such as that of Robert and his family (which is not all that uncommon), it is important that the human services professionals involved do not themselves become discouraged. Often the only resource that persons such as Robert have is the welfare organization and human services professionals. Were it not for the services that workers gave, Robert and his family would be in even more dire straits than those in which they eventually ended up.

Summary

This chapter deals with the emergence of public support of personal services. It was not until 1962 that federal provision was made for social services to complement economic assistance, although services for certain categories of the handicapped originated earlier. These services are presently contained primarily under the 1974 amendments to the Social Security Act known as Title XX.

Not only did the Title XX amendments direct the public agencies to provide social (personal) services to recipients, it permitted payments for services given by private agencies to recipients on a reimbursement basis. Also for the first time individuals not receiving economic assistance were allowed to receive services on a fee-for-service basis according to a sliding scale related to income.

These social services are oriented toward individual improvement. They are organized under five major objectives or goals. A variety of services is

* Note that we are speaking of the limits imposed by the confines of employment. However, through their membership on political action committees, professional associations, lobbying, and participation as citizens in community activities, human services professionals can have an impact on the external circumstances that place limits on what Robert and others like him can do.

authorized under these objectives, which utilize the skills of a number of human services occupational categories.

Individual behavior is related to an interplay of both external and internal conditions. Because the services provided do not deal in any significant way with external circumstances, there are limits to what can be accomplished. Human services professionals should be knowledgeable about the possibilities and limits of the services, so that they can be as helpful as possible to the individuals that they serve.

Documents—Programs for Personal Improvement

The three documents presented in this section relate to the programs discussed in Chapter 9: (1) excerpts from *Senate Bill 4082*, 93rd Congress, 2nd Session; (2) excerpts from the *Federal Register*; and (3) excerpts from a *State Plan*.

The excerpts from *Senate Bill 4082* show how Congress enacts laws. The final law as passed by both the Senate and the House of Representatives and signed by the president in 1974 is essentially the same as this bill. The bill contains the Title XX amendments to the Social Security Act of 1935. These amendments deal with the delivery of social services through public welfare agencies. The excerpts that we have included spell out the general purpose of the amendments, which is that the federal government will make grants to the states to deliver the social services that we described in the chapter. The excerpts then describe the general requirements that the states must meet to qualify for the federal funds authorized under the Title XX amendments of 1974.

The excerpts from the *Federal Register* illustrate how federal agencies implement federal statutes after they have been enacted by Congress. The excerpts contain samples of rules and regulations developed by DHEW (DHHS) that the states must follow if they are to receive federal funds for the services they offer under the Title XX amendments. A new set of rules and regulations is issued by DHHS each year. Those we cite here are the rules and regulations that the states must follow for fiscal 1977, the period from July 1, 1977 to June 30, 1978.

The excerpts from a *State Plan* illustrate the way in which one state, Wisconsin, met the requirements of DHHS rules and regulations for Title XX services. Upon approval of this plan by DHHS, the state implements the proposals according to the plan, and is reimbursed by DHHS according to the formulas for reimbursement. This process is repeated each year by all the fifty states.

The documents presented here and in Chapter 8 are *not* intended to give you up-to-the-minute information about the specifics of welfare programs that you should memorize. The specifics change from year to year and even within fiscal periods. At the time of this writing, for instance, Congress has failed to provide sufficient funds for food stamps, with the distinct possible result that, in a time of high unemployment, an increasing number of individuals and families may not be able to obtain the food they require.

The documents are included to give you an idea of the bureaucratic layers that comprise public programs, of which public welfare is an example. We mentioned in the previous chapter that the *President's Message* was a beginning step in the development and implementation of welfare programs. By coupling the *Message* with the documents presented here, you can see why it almost takes an archeologist to figure it all out. Layer after layer is piled on welfare recipients by government. You find the recipients at the lowest layer, and considerable effort must be expended to get to the bottom of it all. As you sift through these documents, remember that we have included highly excerpted material from a few sources for one year. Imagine trying to sort through the mountains of paper produced throughout the years that public welfare has existed. And this is only one part of a very large federal establishment!

DOCUMENT 9.1 / Senate Bill 4082

To amend the Social Security Act to establish a consolidated program of Federal financial assistance to encourage provision of services by the States.

Be it enacted by the Senate and House of Representatives of the United States of America in Congress assembled, That this Act may be cited as the "Social Services Amendments of 1974."

SEC. 2. The Social Security Act is amended by inserting at the end thereof the following new title:

TITLE XX—GRANTS TO STATES FOR SERVICES
APPROPRIATION AUTHORIZED
SEC. 2001. For the purpose of encouraging each State, as far as practicable under the conditions in that State, to furnish services directed at the goal of—

(1) achieving or maintaining economic self-support to prevent, reduce, or eliminate dependency,
(2) achieving or maintaining self-sufficiency, including reduction or prevention of dependency,
(3) preventing or remedying neglect, abuse, or exploitation of children and adults unable to protect their own interests, or preserving, rehabilitating, or reuniting families,
(4) preventing or reducing inappropriate institutional care by providing for community-based care, home-based care, or other forms of less intensive care, or
(5) securing referral or admission for institutional care when other forms of care are not appropriate, or providing services to individuals in institutions,

From *Senate Bill 4082* 93rd Congress, 2nd Session. Washington, D.C.: G.P.O., 1974. pp. 1–31.

There is authorized to be appropriated for each fiscal year a sum sufficient to carry out the purposes of this title. The sums made available under this section shall be used for making payments to States under section 2002.

PAYMENTS TO STATES

SEC. 2002 (a) (1) From the sums appropriated therefor, the Secretary shall, subject to the provisions of this section and section 2003, pay to each State, for each quarter, an amount equal to 90 per centum of the total expenditures during that quarter for the provision of family planning services and 75 per centum of the total expenditures during that quarter for the provision of other services directed at the goal of—

(A) achieving or maintaining economic self-support to prevent, reduce or eliminate dependency,

(B) achieving or maintaining self-sufficiency, including reduction or prevention of dependency,

(C) preventing or remedying neglect, abuse, or exploitation of children and adults unable to protect their own interests, or preserving, rehabilitating, or reuniting families,

(D) preventing or reducing inappropriate institutional care by providing for community-based care, home-based care, or other forms of less intensive care, or

(E) securing referral or admission for institutional care when other forms of care are not appropriate, or providing services to individuals in institutions,

including expenditures for administration (including planning and evaluation) and personnel training and retraining directly related to the provision of those services. Services that are directed at these goals include, but are not limited to, child care services, protective services for children and adults, services for children and adults in foster care, services related to the management and maintenance of the home, day care services for adults, transportation services, training and related services, employment services, information, referral, and counseling services, the preparation and delivery of meals, health support services, appropriate combinations of services designed to meet the special needs of children, the aged, the mentally retarded, the blind, the emotionally disturbed, the physically handicapped, and alcoholics and drug addicts.

PROGRAM REPORTING, EVALUATION, AND
ADMINISTRATION REQUIREMENTS

SEC. 2003. (a) Each State which participates in the program established by this title shall provide for the publication by the chief executive officer of the State or such other official as the laws of the State provide, within ninety days, or such longer period as the Secretary may authorize, after the end of each services program year (as established under the requirements of section 2002 (a) (3)), of a services program report prepared by the individual or agency designated pursuant to the requirements of section 2003 (g) (1) (C1) and, unless the laws of the State provide otherwise, approved by the chief executive officer which describes the extent to which the services program of the State was carried out during that year in accordance with the annual services program plan for that year and the extent to which the goals and objectives of the plan were achieved.

(b) Each State which participates in the program established by this title shall have a program for evaluation of the State's program for the provision of the services described in section 2002 (a) (1) which conforms to the description of the evaluation activities to be carried out by the State contained in its current final comprehensive annual services program plan.

(c) Each State which participates in the program established by this title shall submit to the Secretary, and make available to the public, information concerning the services described in section 2002 (a) (1) provided in the State, the categories of individuals to whom those services are provided, and such other related information as the Secretary may by regulation provide, at such times and in such form as he may by regulation provide. In establishing requirements under this subsection, the Secretary shall take into account other reporting requirements imposed under this title and other titles of this Act.

(d) Each State which participates in the program established by this title shall make available to the public, within one hundred and eighty days, or such longer period as the Secretary may authorize, after the end of each services program year (as established under the requirements of section 2002 (a) (3)), the report of an audit performed by—

(1) a private certified public accountant or auditing firm utilizing certified public accountants, the services of which have been secured in accordance with procurement standards prescribed by the Secretary,
(2) a publicly elected auditor utilizing certified public accountants, or
(3) an office representing the legislature of the State utilizing certified public accountantants,

of the expenditures for the provision of the services described in section 2002 (a) (1) during that year which sets forth the extent to which those expenditures were in accordance with the State's final comprehensive annual services program plan (as developed under the requirements of section 2002 (a) (3), including any amendments thereto, and the extent to which the State is entitled to payment with respect to those expenditures under section 2002. So much of the report as relates to the extent to which the State is entitled to payment with respect to those expenditures under section 2002 shall be submitted to the Secretary.

(e) Each State which participates in the program established by this title shall assure that the non-Federal share of the aggregate expenditures for the provision of services during each services program year (as established under the requirements of section 2002 (a) (3)) with respect to which payment is made under section 2002 is not less than the non-Federal share of the aggregate expenditures for the provision of those services during the fiscal year ending June 30, 1973, or the fiscal year ending June 30, 1974, with respect to which payment was made under the plan of the State approved under title I, VI, X, XIV, or XVI, or part A of title IV, whichever is less, except that the requirements of this subsection shall not apply to any State for any services program year if the payment to the State under section 2002, for each fiscal year any part of which is included in that services program year, with respect to expenditures other than expenditures for personnel training or retraining directly related to the provision of services, equals the allotment of the State for that fiscal year under section 2002 (a) (2).

(f) (1) If the Secretary, after reasonable notice and an opportunity for a hearing to the State, finds that there is a substantial failure to comply with any of the requirements imposed by subsections (a) through (e) of this section, he shall, except as provided in paragraph (2), notify the State that further payments will not be made to the State under section 2002 until he is satisfied that there will no longer be any such failure to comply, and until he is so satisfied he shall make no further payments to the State.

(2) The Secretary may suspend implementation of any termination of payments under paragraph (1) for such period as he determines appropriate and instead reduce the amount otherwise payable to the State under section 2002 for expenditures during that period by three percent for each of subsections (a) through (e) of this section with respect to which there was a finding of substantial noncompliance and with respect to which he is not yet satisfied that there will no longer be any such failure to comply.

(g) (1) Each State which participates in the program established by this title shall have a plan applicable to its program for the provision of the services described in section (a) (1) which—

(A) provides that an opportunity for a fair hearing before the appropriate State agency will be granted to any individual whose claim for any service described in section 2002 (a) (1) is denied or is not acted upon with reasonable promptness;

(B) provides that the use or disclosure of information obtained in connection with administration of the State's program for the provision of the services described in section 2002 (a) (1) concerning applicants for and recipients of those services will be restricted to purposes directly connected with the administration of that program, the plan of the State approved under part A of title IV, the plan of the State developed under part B of that title, the supplemental security income program established by title XVI, or the plan of the State approved under title XIX;

(C) provides for the designation, by the chief executive officer of the State or as otherwise provided by the laws of the State, of an appropriate agency which will administer or supervise the administration of the state's program for the provision of the services described in section 2002 (a) (1), including planning and evaluation;

(D) provides that the State will, in the administration of its program for the provision of the services described in section 2002 (a) (1), use such methods relating to the establishment and maintenance of personnel standards on a merit basis as are found by the Secretary to be necessary for the proper and efficient operation of the program, except that the Secretary shall exercise no authority with respect to the selection, tenure of office, or compensation of any individual employed in accordance with such methods;

(E) provides that no durational residency or citizenship requirement will be imposed as a condition to participation in the program of the State for the provision of the services described in section 2002 (a) (1);

(F) provides, if the State program for the provision of the services described in section 2002 (a) (1) includes services to individuals living in institutions or foster homes, for the establishment or designation of a State authority or authorities which shall be responsible for establishing and maintaining standards for such institutions or homes which are reasonably in accord with recommended standards of national organizations concerned with standards for such institutions or homes, including standards related to admissions policies, safety, sanitation, and protection of civil rights;

(G) provides, if the State program for the provision of the services described in section 2002 (a) (1) includes child day care services, for the establishment or designation of a State authority or authorities which shall be responsible for establishing and maintaining standards for such services which are reasonably in accord with recommended standards of national organizations concerned with standards for such services, including standards related to admissions policies for facilities providing such services, safety, sanitation, and protection of civil rights;

(H) provides that the State's program for the provision of the services described in section 2002 (a) (1) will be in effect in all political subdivisions of the State;

(I) provides for financial participation by the State in the provision of the services described in section 2002 (a) (1).

(2) The Secretary shall approve any plan which complies with the provisions of paragraph (1).

(h)(1) No payment may be made under section 2002 to any State which does not have a plan approved under subsection (g).

(2) In the case of any State plan which has been approved by the Secretary under subsection (g), if the Secretary, after reasonable notice and an opportunity for a hearing to the State, finds—

(A) that the plan no longer complies with the provisions of subsection (g) (1), or

(B) that in the administration of the plan there is a substantial failure to comply with any such provision,

the Secretary shall, except as provided in paragraph (3), notify the State that further payments will not be made to the State under section 2002 until he is satisfied that there will no longer be any such failure to comply, and until he is so satisfied he shall make no further payments to the State.

(3) The Secretary may suspend implementation of any termination of payments under paragraph (2) for such period as he determines appropriate and instead reduce the amount otherwise payable to the State under section 2002 for expenditures during that period by 3 per centum for each clause of subsection (g) (1) with respect to which there is a finding of noncompliance and with respect to which he is not yet satisfied that there will no longer be any such failure to comply.

SERVICES PROGRAM PLANNING

SEC. 2004. A State's services program planning meets the requirements of this section if, for the purpose of assuring public participation in the development of the program for the provision of the services described in section 2002 (a) (1) within the State—

(1) the beginning of the fiscal year of either the Federal Government or the State government is established as the beginning of the State's services program year; and

(2) at least ninety days prior to the beginning of the State's services program year, the chief executive officer of the State, or such other official as the laws of the State provide, publishes and makes generally available (as defined in regulations prescribed by the Secretary after consideration of State laws

governing notice of actions by public officials) to the public a proposed comprehensive annual services program plan prepared by the individual or agency designated pursuant to the requirements of section 2003 (g) (1) (C) and, unless the laws of the State provide otherwise, approved by the chief executive officer, which sets forth the State's plan for the provision of the services described in section 2002 (a) (1) during that year, including—

(A) the objectives to be achieved under the program,

(B) the services to be provided under the program including at least one service directed to at least one of the goals in each of the five categories of goals set forth in section 2002 (a) (1) (as determined by the State), together with a definition of those services and a description of their relationship to the objectives to be achieved under the program and the goals described in section 2002 (a) (1),

(C) the categories of individuals to whom those services are to be provided, including any categories based on the income of individuals or their families,

(D) the geographic areas in which those services are to be provided, and the nature and amount of the services to be provided in each area,

(E) a description of the planning, evaluation, and reporting activities to be carried out under the program,

(F) the sources of the resources to be used to carry out the program,

(G) a description of the organizational structure through which the program will be administered, including the extent to which public and private agencies and volunteers will be utilized in the provision of services,

(H) a description of how the provision of services under the program will be coordinated with the plan of the State approved under part A of title IV, the plan of the State developed under part B of that title, the supplemental security income program established by title XVI, the plan of the State approved under title XIX, and other programs for the provision of related human services within the State, including the steps taken to assure maximum feasible utilization of services under these programs to meet the needs of the low income population.

(I) the estimated expenditures under the program, including estimated expenditures with respect to each of the services to be provided, each of the categories of individuals to whom those services are to be provided, and each of the geographic areas in which those services are to be provided, and a comparison between estimated non-Federal expenditures under the program and non-Federal expenditures for the provision of the services described in section 2002 (a) (1) in the State during the preceding services program year, and

(J) a description of the steps taken, or to be taken, to assure that the needs of all residents of, and all geographic areas in, the State were taken into account in the development of the plan; and

(3) public comment on the proposed plan is accepted for a period of at least forty-five days; and

(4) at least forty-five days after publication of the proposed plan and prior to the beginning of the State's services program year, the chief executive officer of the State, or such other official as the laws of the State provide, publishes a final comprehensive annual services program plan prepared by the individual or agency designed pursuant to the requirements of section 2003 (g) (1)

and, unless the laws of the State provide otherwise, approved by the chief executive officer, which sets forth the same information required to be included in the proposed plan, together with an explanation of the differences between the proposed and final plan and the reasons therefor; and

(5) any amendment to a final comprehensive services program plan is prepared by the individual or agency designated pursuant to section 2003 (g) (1) (C), approved by the chief executive officer of the State unless the laws of the State provide otherwise, and published by the chief executive officer of the State, or such other official as the laws of the State provide, as a proposed amendment on which public comment is accepted for a period of at least thirty days, and then prepared by the individual or agency designated pursuant to section 2003 (g) (1) (C), approved by the chief executive officer of the State unless the laws of the state provide otherwise, and published by the chief executive officer of the state, or such other official as the laws of the Senate provide, as a final amendment, together with an explanation of the differences between the proposed and final amendment and the reasons therefore.

Document 9.2 / Excerpts from the *Federal Register**

The DHEW (DHHS) rules and regulations for Title XX for FY 1977 were published in the *Federal Register* 42, 20 (January 31, 1977): it begins by explaining some of the ways in which input from interested parties is to be obtained.

Title 45—Public Welfare
CHAPTER II—SOCIAL AND REHABILITATION SERVICE (AS-SISTANCE PROGRAMS DEPARTMENT OF HEALTH, EDUCA-TION, AND WELFARE
PART 228—SOCIAL SERVICES PROGRAMS FOR INDIVIDUALS AND FAMILIES: TITLE XX OF THE SOCIAL SECURITY ACT
FINAL REGULATIONS
Notice of proposed rulemaking was published in the FEDERAL REGISTER August 26, 1976 (41 FR 36156) revising existing regulations for the provision of social services under Pub. L. 93–47, Title XX of the Social Security Act. These proposed revisions represented the first comprehensive review of the Title XX regulations since the program began October 1, 1975. They were aimed at reducing the operational difficulties States encountered during the first program year. The final regulations which follow are issued after further consideration of the policies and changes proposed in the NPRM and of the comments received on these proposals.

Three hundred letters containing about 1400 comments were received from a broad range of respondents: private citizens, Governors, members of Congress, national and local health and welfare organizations, advocacy organizations, public

* Consult the Federal Register for the fine-print, complicated wording, and excessive jargon used in regulations drawn up by federal agencies to implement statutes. Revisions of these statutes occur at least annually and frequently semi-annually.
From *Federal Register* 42, 20. Monday, January 31, 1977, Part III. DHEW; SRS. "Social Services Programs for Individuals and Families" Washington, D.C.: G.P.O., 1977. p. 5842–5861.

and private provider agencies, provider agency organizations, State and local Title XX agencies, other State agencies, and colleges and universities. In addition, staff in each of the HEW regions arranged informal public meetings during September and October, 1976 in one or more States in each region to obtain additional discussion and comments. Summaries of comments received during these public meetings have also been carefully considered.

Pages 5843–5849 (not included here) discussed the various clarifications of wording and any additions and corrections contained in the rest of the document. On page 5848 (also not included) are listed the various sections that, upon publication, became the implementing rules for the fiscal year in which they were published.

SUBPART I—GENERAL PROVISIONS

Three changes have been made in this Subpart. In response to requests for clarification, (§ 228.90 (a) (2) adds language that clarifies the availability of FFP for medical examinations for eligible persons precedent to receipt of a service, such as an examination for a child entering day care.

Section 228.90 (a) (3) also adds the word "agency" to clarify that FFP is available for costs of State (and local) Title XX agency advisory committees. This clarification is made in response to questions concerning FFP for costs of local advisory committees.

Also in response to comments, § 228.91 clarifies that no FFP is available for goods or services provided in-kind by individuals. The purpose of these changes is to make explicit statements that will resolve continuing questions in these areas.

Part 228, Chapter II., Title 45 of the Code of Federal Regulations is revised to read as set forth below:

SUBPART A—SCOPE AND DEFINITIONS

228.0 Scope of program.
228.1 Program definitions.

SUBPART B—STATE PLAN REQUIREMENTS, REPORTS, MAINTE-NANCE OF EFFORT, COMPLIANCE

228.5   State plan requirements.
228.6   Appropriate State agency.
228.7   State financial participation.
228.8   Statewide operation.
228.9   Merit System.
228.10 Safeguarding information.
228.11 Residency requirements.
228.12 Standards for institutions or foster homes.
228.13 Standards for child day care services.
228.14 Fair hearings.
228.15 Amendments to State plan.
228.16 Submittal of State plan and amendments for approval by the Secretary.
228.17 Reports and maintenance of records.
228.18 Maintenance of effort.
228.19 Noncompliance.

AUTHORITY: Sec.102, 49 Stat. 47 (42 U.S.C. 1302).

The following are illustrative sections excerpted from the document. They detail some of Part 228, Chapter II, Title 45, Subpart A-"Scope and Definitions" as revised.

SUBPART A—SCOPE AND DEFINITIONS
§ 228.0 Scope of program
(a) Federal financial participation is available in accordance with title XX of the Social Security Act and this Part, with respect to expenditures under a State program for the provision of services, to low income individuals and families, directed at the goals of:
(1) Achieving or maintaining economic self-support, to prevent, reduce, or eliminate dependency:

(2) Achieving or maintaining self-sufficiency, including reduction or prevention of dependency;

(3) Preventing or remedying neglect, abuse, or exploitation of children and adults unable to protect their own interests, or preserving, rehabilitating, or reuniting families;

(4) Preventing or reducing inappropriate institutional care by providing for community-based care, home-based care, or other forms of less intensive care, or

(5) Securing referral or admission for institutional care when other forms of care are not appropriate, or providing services to individuals in institutions.

§ 228.1 PROGRAM DEFINITIONS

As used in this Part:

Act means the Social Security Act.

Administrator means the Administrator of the Social and Rehabilitation Service of the U.S. Department of Health, Education, and Welfare.

Categories of individuals means groupings of persons on the basis of common characteristics such as recipient status (AFDC, SSI, Medicaid), income level, age, physical or mental condition or any other characteristic that the State specifies in its comprehensive annual services plan.

Family means one or more adults and children, if any, related by blood or law, and residing in the same household. Where adults, other than spouses, reside together, each may be considered a separate family by the State. Emancipated minors and children living under the care of individuals not legally responsible for that care may be considered one-person families by the State.

Fiscal year means the Federal fiscal year unless otherwise specified.

FFP means Federal financial participation.

Geographic area means any identifiable area encompased within the State.

Indian tribal council means the official Indian organization, administering the government of an Indian tribe, but only with respect to those tribes with a reservation land base. This includes Inter Tribal Councils whose membership tribes have reservation status.

Indian tribe means any Indian tribe, band, nation, or other organized group or community, including any Alaska Native region, village or group as defined in the Alaska Native Claims Settlement Act (85 Stat. 688), which is recognized as eligible for the special programs and services provided by the United States to Indians because of their status as Indians, or any Indian Tribe, band, nation, or other organized group or community which is recognized as an Indian Tribe by any State commission, agency, or authority which has the statutory power to extend such recognition.

Medical or remedial care means care directed toward the correction or amelioration of a medical condition which has been diagnosed as such by a licensed medical practitioner operating within the scope of medical practice as defined by State law, and which care is provided by or under the direct supervision of such a medical practitioner or other health professionals licensed by the State or credentialed by the appropriate professional organization.

Monthly gross income means the monthly sum of income received from sources identified by the U.S. Census Bureau in computing median income. (See 228.66.)

Other public agencies means State and local public agencies other than the State agency, and Indian Tribes.

Room means shelter only: and *board* means 3 meals a day or any other full nutritional regimen.

Secretary means the Secretary of the U.S. Department of Health, Education, and Welfare.

Services plan means the State Comprehensive Annual Services Program Plan under section 2004 of the Act.

SSI (Supplemental Security Income) means monthly cash payments made by the Social Security Administration to an aged, blind or disabled individual who meets the requirements for such aid under title XVI of the Act, and also includes State supplementary payments made by a State on a regular basis to an individual receiving SSI, or who would, but for his income, be eligible to receive such benefits, as assistance based on need in supplementation of such benefits.

State means the 50 States and the District of Columbia.

State agency means the appropriate State agency, designated by the chief executive officer of the State or as otherwise provided by the laws of the State, to administer or supervise the administration of the State's program, and except where the context otherwise requires, includes local agencies administering the program under the supervision of the State agency.

State plan means the State plan under section 2003 of the Act.

Title XX means title XX of the Social Security Act.

The following excerpts from Subpart C, "Comprehensive Annual Services Program Plan" describe the way in which states must plan their Comprehensive Annual Service Programs to meet federal guidelines and obtain funding.

§ 228.22 SERVICES PLAN

(a) The Chief Executive Officer of the State, or such other official as the laws of the State shall provide, shall publish in both proposed and final form the Comprehensive Annual Services Plan (hereinafter in this part referred to as the services plan) prepared by the State agency prior to the beginning of each services program year. The proposed and final services plans shall meet all requirements of this Subpart.

(b) The final services plan shall also include: (1) A summary of the public comments, including the State's response to the comments; and

(2) An explanation of differences between the proposed and final services plan, if any and the reasons therefor.

§ 228.23 PROGRAM GOALS AND OBJECTIVES

(a) The services plan shall provide that services offered are directed at the goals of:

(1) Achieving or maintaining economic self-support to prevent, reduce, or eliminate dependency;

(2) Achieving or maintaining self-sufficiency, including reduction or prevention of dependency;

(3) Preventing or remedying neglect, abuse, or exploitation of children and adults unable to protect their own interests, or preserving, rehabilitating, or reuniting families;

(4) Preventing or reducing inappropriate institutional care by providing for community-based care, home-based care, or other forms of less intensive care; or

(5) Securing referral or admission for institutional care when other forms of care are not appropriate, or providing services to individuals in institutions.

(b) The objectives to be achieved under the program shall be directed to the goals in paragraph (a) of this section, and shall be stated in the services plan in measurable terms so that an assessment may be made of the extent to which they are achieved.

§ 228.24   INDIVIDUALS TO BE SERVED.

The proposed and final services plans shall:

(a) Specify which of the categories of individuals described in §, 228.60 will be provided services in the forthcoming program year; describe the income levels for eligibility, and include the Statewide definition of family in accordance with § 228.1:

(b) If the State limits services to individuals with certain characteristics, describe the limitations imposed for each category in sufficient detail to enable individuals to know if they are likely to meet the eligibility requirements, e.g., one parent families whose income is not more than 80 percent of the median income; mentally retarded SSI recipients, or alcohol abusers whose income does not exceed 50 percent of the median income;

(c) Specify which of the categories to be served will be charged a fee;

(d) Include the fee schedule, specifying any variations by service or by geographic area, as permitted under § 288.62; and

(e) Specify whether family planning services, information and referral services, and services to prevent or remedy neglect, abuse or exploitation will be provided without regard to income.

(f) If the State is determining eligibility on a group basis in accordance with § 228.61, the services plan shall so state and describe any specific conditions or characteristics (other than income), that must be met or that individuals must have so that they will know if they might qualify to receive a particular service for which eligibility is determined on a group basis. Conditions or characteristics that may be used by the State as a basis for determining that a service is to be offered on a group eligibility basis may include one or more of the following: the nature of the service, characteristics of persons to receive the service (such as age, physical or mental conditon, place of residence, single parenthood, common problems, etc.), location of the service site(s), nature of the community where the service will be provided, or other factors which lead the State to reasonably conclude that substantially all the persons to whom the services will be offered are members of families which have a monthly gross income of no more than 90 percent of the State's median income, adjusted for family size.

§ 228.25   AVAILABILITY OF SERVICES BY GEOGRAPHIC AREA

For the purpose of delivering services described in the service plan, the State agency may divide the State into geographic areas, but only if such geographic areas encompass the entire State, including Indian reservations. The State shall consider, in defining geographic areas, the boundaries of planning areas of other human services programs. If the State chooses to establish such geographic areas, the services plan shall:

(a) Describe those geographic areas;

(b) Provide that the services described in § 228.26(f) will be available to eligible individuals in every geographic area; and

(c) Where different services are made available to a category of individuals in different geographic areas, provide that the services furnished in a geographic area will be available to all eligible individuals in that category who reside in that area.

§ 228.26 SERVICES

The services plan shall: (a) Describe each discrete service, including the service(s) which is (are) available to individuals on the basis of group determination of eligibility, in as much detail as necessary to enable a reasonable prudent person to understand what is included in the service. For purposes of this paragraph, services such as "child welfare services" "services to alcoholics" or "protective services" are not discrete services but rather clusters of services, each of which shall be separately described. If medical or remedial care or room or board as described in §§ 228.40 and 228.41 are part of a service, the plan shall so specify in describing that service.

(b) Specify the effective date when each discrete service is available if the effective date is other than the beginning of the program year. For each discrete service that is to be offered in a prescribed time frame, specify the effective date on which that service is available and the effective date on which that service is to be discontinued. (See § 228.50 (a)(2).)

(c) Specify the method of delivery for each service, i.e., directly by the State agency, by a provider (public or private), or both;

(d) Indicate the relationship of each service to one or more of the program goals and one or more of the program objectives specified in § 228.23;

(e) Specify the categories of individuals in each geographic area to whom each service will be provided, including any services provided on a group basis;

(f) Include among the services to be provided in each geographic area:

(1) At least three services for SSI recipients;

(2) At least one service directed at each of the program goals specified in § 228.23.

(g) Describe the foster care services required under section 408 of the Act to be provided to all recipients of AFDC-FC, if such services are available under title XX;

(h) Describe any family planning services that will be provided pursuant to section 402 (a) (15) of the Act. Failure to include such family planning services will not constitute a deficiency in the services plan. However failure to provide family planning services pursuant to section 402 (a) (15) of the Act may result in a loss of FFP to the State under its AFDC program.

(i) The State agency shall identify in its services plan the point in its organizational structure or the level of staff where it has placed authority:

(1) To make the decision for the State that it is not feasible to furnish child day care in a day care center or group day care home which complies with Federal staffing standards; and

(2) To furnish child day care by granting a waiver of otherwise applicable Federal staffing standards in a day care center or group day care home which serves few title XX funded children (see § 228.42 (c) (2)) and meets applicable State staffing standards.

§ 228.27 ESTIMATES OF INDIVIDUALS TO BE SERVED AND EXPENDITURES

In order to provide residents of the State with information on the scope of the services program, the services plan shall include estimates of State and Federal expenditures applicable to the title XX program as follows:

(a) For each discrete service, a list of estimated expenditures and estimated numbers of individuals to be served, by each category of eligible individuals and by each geographic area;

(b) Estimated expenditure for the forthcoming program year; and

(c) A comparison of estimated aggregate non-Federal expenditures for the forthcoming program year with those of the preceding completed program year.

§ 228.28   PROGRAM RESOURCES

(a) The services plan shall indicate how the State intends to finance its title XX program by providing an estimate of the funds to be used from the State's title XX allotment, and by separately identifying and estimating State and local appropriated funds, and the aggregate of donated and other funds to be used to meet the expenditures under the program. ("Other funds" include any State or local funds used in the title XX program that are in excess of the State's allotment ceiling so long as such funds are administered in accordance with all requirements of this Part.)

(b) Where a State program year is the same as the Federal fiscal year, States shall include in the services plan the full amount of the federal allotment. Where a State program year extends through more than one Federal fiscal year, States shall include in the services plan the full amount of the federal allotment for both fiscal years. The services plan shall also indicate the proportion of each Federal fiscal year encompassed by the State's program year.

§ 228.29   PROGRAM COORDINATION AND UTILIZATION

The services plan shall describe:

(a) How the planning and the provision of services under the program will be coordinated with and utilize the following programs:

(1) Under the Social Security Act:

(i) title IV-A, AFDC (including WIN);

(ii) title IV-B, Child Welfare Services;

(iii) title XVI, SSI; and

(iv) title XIX, Medical Assistance (Medicaid); and

(2) Other appropriate programs for the provision of related human services within the State—for example, programs for the aging, children, develop mentally disabled, alcohol and drug abusers; programs in corrections, public education, vocational rehabilitation, mental health, housing, medical and public health, employment and manpower.

(b) A general description of the steps taken to assure maximum feasible utilization of services under these programs to meet the needs of the low income population; and

(c) A general description of the steps taken to assure public participation in the development of the services program, including contacts with public and private organizations, officials of county and local general purpose government units, and citizen groups and individuals, including recipients of services.

(d) The description shall also include the extent to which the title XX agency utilizes grants and otherwise encourages child day care providers under contract to employ AFDC recipients.

§ 228.30   ORGANIZATIONAL STRUCTURE

The services plan shall describe the organizational structure of the State agency through which the program will be administered including where individuals may apply for services and have their eligibility determined, and the estimatded number of volunteers or a brief description of volunteer activities.

§ 228.31   NEEDS ASSESSMENT

The services plan shall describe the steps taken to assure that the needs of all residents of, and all geographic areas in, the State are taken into account in the development of the services plan. The description shall include the data sources used (or to be used).

§ 228.32 PLANNING, EVALUATION AND REPORTING

The services plan shall describe the planning, evaluation, and reporting procedures and activities the State has carried out or plans to carry out in connection with its services program. Examples of these procedures and activities which may be described include the following:

(a) *Planning.* Relationship with the State budget process and the legislature; input from other State, regional and local planning units and from local general purpose governmental units; citizen organizations and individuals; relationship of needs assessment and service resources inventory to setting of program priorities and allocation of resources.

(b) *Evaluation.* Purpose, scope and timing of current and proposed evaluations, and the schedule for dissemination of evaluation results.

(c) *Reporting.* Description of planned formal reports, such as reports to elected officials or to the public (but excluding reports furnished to SRS), and the schedule for issuance.

§ 228.33 THE PUBLIC REVIEW PROCESS

A State's services plan does not become effective for its services program year until the public review process is completed in accordance with §228.33, § 228.34, and § 228.35 (if applicable).

(a) *Purpose.* The purpose of the public review process is to enable the residents of each State to participate meaningfully in the State decision making processes with respect to the States services plan. The public review process is intended to assure that each State has provided opportunity for prior public participation of title XX clients, title XX advisory groups, public and private organizations, public officials and the general public in needs assessment, identification of priorities and allocation of resources throughout the development of the services plan. (See § 228.29(c))

(b) *Scope.* The public review process shall include at least:

(1) Publication of the proposed services plan and a display advertisement describing that plan, and a summary of the plan, if any, at least 90 days before the beginning of the program year, with a 45-day period for public comment;

(2) Consideration of, and public access to, comments received;

(3) Publication of any corrections required to bring the proposed services plan into compliance with the requirements of §§ 228.21 through 228.33;

(4) Publication of the final services plan and a display advertisement announcing its publication no earlier than 45 days after publicaton of the proposed services plan;

(5) Publication of any necessary corrections to the final plan;

(6) Publication of any proposed amendments to the final plan with a 30-day period for comments;

(7) Publication of any corrections required to bring the proposed amendment into compliance with the requirements of § 228.21 through § 228.33;

(8) Publication of the final amendments; and

(9) Publication of any necessary corrections to the final amendment;

(10) Public access to copies of the proposed and final services plans.

(c) *Approval prior to publication.* Prior to publication, the proposed and final services plans shall each be approved by the Governor or such other official as the laws of the State provide.

(d) *Retention of published services plans.* Copies of the proposed and final services plans shall be retained for at least three years in specified local public offices and made available for public and Federal inspection throughout the program year.

(e) *Handling of public comments.* (1) Written comments on the proposed services plan shall be considered by the State agency if received within 45 days after publication of the display advertisement announcing publication and availability of the proposed services plan; and

(2) Such comments shall be retained for at least 3 years for inspection by the public and by Federal officials.

(f) *Display advertisement; general requirements.* (1) A display advertisement is one prepared for and published within the main news section of a newspaper; advertisements placed in the legal or classified sections of a newspaper do not meet this requirement.

(2) Such advertisement must be published in the newspaper of widest circulation (and in foreign languages or foreign language newspapers where appropriate) in each geographic area described in the proposed and final services plans.

(g) *Display advertisement for the proposed plan.* A display advertisement shall at least:

(1) Specify the beginning and ending dates of the program year;

(2) Include a brief description of the services to be offered under the services plan;

(3) Describe the categories of individuals to be served:

(i) Identify those whose eligibility is based on income maintenance status (AFDC or SSI); and

(ii) Specify the maximum dollar amount of income that a family of four can have and still be eligible on the basis of income status; and

(iii) Indicate that such dollar amount is adjusted by family size.

(4) If the State has different income levels for different services, or different income levels for different geographic areas, specify that those different income levels are described in the proposed plan and in the plan summary (if the State has published a summary);

(5) Indicate beginning and ending dates of the 45-day period for public review and comment.

(6) Specify a toll-free telephone number that can be called to obtain without charge either a copy of the proposed plan or a summary thereof; or state that such copies can be obtained by calling a specified local public agency in each county, such as the local social services agency.

(7) Identify a local public agency in each county such as the social services agency where copies of the proposed services plan are available for public review; available for distribution to the public either free (if no summary is provided) or at a reasonable cost; or where copies of the proposed service plan may be ordered, if distributed from another source; and

(8) Specify the address where written comments may be sent and, if there are to be public hearings on the proposed plan, the location, date, and time for such hearings; or state that information concerning the hearings can be obtained by calling a specified toll-free number or by telephoning specified local agencies after a given date.

(h) *Summary of proposed services plan.* If the State publishes a services plan summary (to be provided free in lieu of a free copy of the entire services plan), it shall contain at least the following information:

(1) The beginning and ending dates of the program year;

(2) The categories of individuals including any limitations, who are eligible for services;

(3) The categories of individuals to whom a fee will be charged if they wish to be provided services under the services plan;

(4) Fee schedules, including any variations by service or by geographic area;

(5) A description of each discrete service to be provided under the plan;

(6) The services that will be made available to each category of individuals in each geographic area under the services plan;

(7) For each service, estimated expenditures, and estimated numbers to be served by each category of eligible individuals and by each geographic area; and

(8) Amount of the Federal allotment to the State and the amounts of State and local appropriated funds and of other funds to finance the services program; and

(9) A toll-free telephone number that can be called to obtain information on where to apply for services or the name of a local public agency in each county where applications for services will be accepted.

(i) *Display advertisement of the final services plan.* The display advertisement of the final services plan shall contain at least:

(1) A statement that the final services plan has been published and is available for review by the public;

(2) An explanation of any differences between the proposed and final services plans and the reasons therefore;

(3) A toll-free telephone number that can be called to obtain information about the services plan and where to apply for services; or the name of a local public agency in each county, where information regarding the services plan will be made available and where applications for services will be accepted;

(4) The name of a local public agency in each county where copies of the final services plan are available for public review and distribution to the public either free or at a reasonable cost; and

(5) The location where public comments on the proposed services plan are available for review.

Sections 228.34, 228.35, and 228.36, which are not included, show how regional reviews of state programs are to be carried out and how corrections and amendments to the proposed plans are to be made.

Subparts D, E, and F outline various limitations to services.

Subpart G on purchase-of-service agreements outlines standards to be applied to private agencies offering services and the allowed rates of payment.

Subpart H discusses provisions for training and retraining of the various categories of the *providers* of services.

Subpart I, entitled "General Provisions," discusses which administrative costs may be federally funded and which may not.

Subpart J discusses the federal funding available to pay welfare recipients who are employed by certain day care centers.

The document ends as follows:

Effective date: These regulations shall be effective 90 days after publication or earlier at State option with the following exceptions: (1) Section 228.70(d) is made retroactive to October 1, 1975, at State option; (2) Sections of Part 228 (as listed below), that were issued as interim final regulations implementing Pub. L. 94–401 (1976 Amendments to Title XX of the Social Security Act) published in the FEDERAL

REGISTER (41 FR 55668) on December 21, 1976, are effective October 1, 1975, at State option, with the following exceptions: Additional allotments to States (§ 228.52) are available from 7–1–76 through 9–30–77; State grants to child day care providers (Subpart J) may be made on or after September 7, 1976 for use through September 30, 1977; and the option to waive Federal staffing standards in out-of-home facilities with few title XX children (§ 228.42 (c) (2)) is effective no earlier than September 7, 1976.

The list of sections effective October 1, 1975, at State option, is as follows:

SUBPART C

§ **228.24** (**c**) and (**f**)
§ **228.26** (**a**)
§ **228.29** (**d**)
§ **228.36** (**d**)

SUBPART D

§ **228.40** (**c**) (1) and (2)
§ **228.41** (**e**) (1) and (2)
§ **228.42** (**c**) (1) and (**d**)
§ **228.44** (**e**) (1) and (2)
§ **228.48**

SUBPART E

§ **228.51** (**c**)
§ **228.56** (**b**)

SUBPART F

§ **228.60** (**b**) (3)
§ **228.60** (**f**)(2)(ii)
§ **228.60** (**f**) (1) (iii)
§ **228.60** (**f**) (2) (iv) (**A**) and (**B**)
§ **228.61**(**a**) (3)
§ **228.61**(**c**) (2)
§ **228.61**(**d**)

(Catalog of Federal Domestic Assistance Program No. 13754 Public Assistance Social Services.)

NOTE.—The Social and Rehabilitation Service has determined that this document does not require preparation of an Inflationary Impact Statement under Executive Order 11821 and OMB Circular A-107.

DATED: January 6, 1977.

ROBERT FULTON,
*Administrator, Social and
Rehabilitation Service.*

Approved: January 18, 1977.
MARJORIE LYNCH.
Acting Secretary.
[FR Doc.77-2656 Filed 1-28-77;8:45 am]

Document 9.3 shows how one State complied with the federal requirements for the Comprehensive Annual Services Program Plan referred to in Document 9.2.

The numbers in parentheses opposite the sub-headings in Document 9.3, e.g., (228.33), refer to the sections of Part 228, Chapter II, Title 45 of the Code of Federal Regulations, as revised. Part 228 is excerpted with section headings in Document 9.2. By referring back and forth between Documents 9.2 and 9.3 you will be able to see the relationship between the federal government and State welfare programs.

Document 9.3 / Excerpts from *State Plan for Social Services, 1977–1979,* Program Period 1: October 1975 to June 1977, Summary of Public Comment (228.33), (228.34)

PROCESS

A display advertisement briefly describing the proposed Title XX Comprehensive Social Services Plan for Wisconsin was published in eight newspapers throughout the state on July 1, 2, and 3, 1975. The eight newspapers were *The Superior Evening Telegram, Rhinelander Daily News, Eau Claire Leader-Telegram, Wausau Record Herald, Green Bay Press Gazette, La Crosse Tribune, Madison Wisconsin State Journal,* and *Milwaukee Journal.*

In addition public hearings were held in Milwaukee, Madison, Wausau, Green Bay, and Eau Claire during the month of July 1975.

Approximately 3,000 proposed plans were distributed.

Comments were received from approximately 250 individuals or agencies. Those represented were federal, state, and local public agencies, including board members, members of the state legislature, the general citizenry, and members of voluntary agencies and organizations, especially the Big Brother organization, who were concerned about funding for their program.

Following is a summary of the comments about various parts of the plan and changes made in response to those comments.

PROGRAM YEAR

Less than five comments were received about the program year. In all but one, the concern was that a review and evaluation of the comprehensive service plan should take place at a midpoint in the proposed program period of twenty-one months. This will be done in order to begin the planning phase for the second program period. A suggestion that the initial program period be nine months was not accepted because of the complexities involved in developing a second plan so soon and the fact that such a short period would not enable any increased synchronization with other planning–budgeting processes followed by agencies utilizing Title XX funding.

GEOGRAPHIC AREA

Several comments were made about the failure in the plan to take advantage of the concept of having geographic areas smaller in size than the state, i.e., counties or

From *Final Comprehensive Social Services Plan* for *State of Wisconsin.* Program Period October 1, 1975 to June 30, 1977. Madison, WI.: Department of Health and Social Services, 1977. p. 1–23.

regions. This was exhaustively explored as a possibility, and at least three basic factors prevented the plan from being written to accomplish this. First, a review of the state statutes related to social services does not appear to give subdivisions of the state an option to limit or expand the availability of needed social services. Second, the limitation on both federal and state dollars would also prevent agencies from adding to the basic services discussed above. Third, it was the belief of the plan writers, which included county social service department personnel, that county agencies did not have the necessary data to make valid estimates of people to be served or dollars to be spent. This is a specific requirement which must be included in the plan for each designated geographic area. Almost all comments questioning the state as the geographic area came from other than county social service department staff or board members.

INCOME LEVEL FOR ELIGIBILITY

Suggestions were made that the eligibility ceiling would be too high if 115% of the state's median income were used to determine the cut-off level based upon family gross income. Some respondents were under the impression that money would be supplied to families and individuals to bring their income up to the level cited as the eligibility ceiling. Others felt that services would be provided free to all income levels.

This section was revised in order to clearly identify the eligibility ceiling for various size families and to identify the income level at which charges for services would begin for various size families. The income was lowered to 100% of the state's median income.

FEES FOR SERVICES

Mixed suggestions were received on the question of whether charges for services should be made for actual recipients of income maintenance. Although testimony and reaction were equally divided on this issue, the proposed plan was retained on the principle that ability to pay should not hinge on particular sources of income. Such charges for AFDC and SSI will probably only occur when the recipient has income in addition to an assistance grant.

Suggestions were received that fees should start at levels below 80% of the median income. In light of these recommendations and the clarification received on the final Federal Regulations that starting gross income levels could vary by family size, the monthly charge schedule already in use by the Department of Health and Social Services will be used for Title XX purposes. This schedule starts at points lower than the 80% income level. Since the current schedule will be in use only until October 31, the new charge schedule which will be in effect November 1, 1975 is also included. In order to more adequately convey information concerning what the monthly charge for services will be, the entire monthly charge schedule for various size families and income levels has been included.

PROGRAM COORDINATION

Fifteen comments were made about program coordination which ranged from concern about apparent lack of coordination to the need for a directory of children's agencies. The comments were studied to determine their applicability to plan modification. Comments were general and did not become specific as to how program coordination could or should be incorporated. As a result of the comments received, the section was expanded to clarify the distinction between coordination that was carried out as a part of the Title XX planning process and that coordination which exists through the Department and other agencies on an ongoing basis.

NEEDS ASSESSMENT
Several comments expressed concern that the proposed Title XX plan and the final Title XX plan were developed without a needs assessment. As is indicated in the plan, a waiver of this requirement was permitted for the first plan only. Wording has been added to the plan to indicate the intent to initiate needs assessment which is a federal requirement for all subsequent plans. Because of the uncertainty about the makeup of a unit and its location in the department to do this, the methodology for its accomplishment cannot be spelled out.

PLANNING, EVALUATION, AND REPORTING
Concern was expressed about the lack of specifics in this section of the plan. Additions have been made to indicate what the beginning efforts of the department will be in these areas.

AMENDMENTS
A few comments suggested that the process for amending the plan should be spelled out in more detail. Therefore, it is being explained in somewhat more detail.

FEDERAL FINANCIAL PARTICIPATION
This section was expanded somewhat for purposes of clarification.

GLOSSARY OF SERVICE TERMS
The public comments process produced approximately forty responses directed toward service definitions in the Title XX Plan. The concerns expressed in the majority of responses were directed toward clarification of some service definitions to achieve better public understanding. These suggestions for clarification were adopted to the extent possible, since many of the service definitions must be utilized by several delivery agencies.

SERVICES
In reviewing the correspondence and the comments presented at the public hearings, few specific recommendations were made regarding the addition or elimination of any services. The comments about services were mainly related to the impact of providing particular services to specific target groups and adequate funding of certain services.

In only two instances were recommendations made regarding the elimination of services. Concern was expressed regarding the service of "Leisure Time Activities." However, because the concept of recreation is included specifically in Wis. Stats. 46.03 (17) (c) as a service which "shall" be included, the concept was retained in the plan and the title of the service was changed to "Recreation." It was not possible to accept the recommendation to eliminate "Sheltered Employment" as a service due to the participation of the Division of Vocational Rehabilitation in Title XX funding.

The major change in the plan in relation to services was the addition of "Special Living Arrangements" to Goals III and IV. In reviewing the services, it was found that this service had not originally been attached to these goals due to an oversight.

"Adoption Services" have been eliminated from Goal IIIA because this service was not deemed appropriate to this goal.

TARGET GROUPS—EXPENDITURES

In general, funds were reallocated among target groups to reflect more consistency in the estimated expenditures for a specific service. In response to a number of comments from several agencies regarding insufficient funding, some redistribution of funds was made within the allocations available.

The estimated number of people to be served was readjusted to reflect a more consistent cost of service among target groups and goals.

In most instances, *total funds* allocated to specific services within particular goals were not affected; however, in several cases, significant reallocations did take place.

Existing funds for "Special Living Arrangements" were reallocated to allow for the provision of this service under Goals IIIA and IV.

Dollar amounts were redistributed to all identified target groups.

"Adoption Services" appeared unrealistic for Goal IIIA and was eliminated for that Goal.

The wording of the "Objectives" was changed to better define target groups, i.e., "clients" for "children."

Purchased Services are identified by asterisks.

The term "No Eligibility" was eliminated from the plan in Goal IIIA. In those instances where funds had been allocated to this group, people and dollars were shifted to the remaining target groups within that service area, and services to be delivered without regard to income were identified in the plan.

AVAILABILITY OF PLAN AND PUBLIC COMMENTS

A copy of the final services plan will be retained in each county welfare department and at the Division of Family Services Central, Regional, and District Offices throughout the program period. It may be reviewed during regular working hours.

All public comments including tapes of the public hearings will be retained in the Central Office of the Division of Family Services for a three-year period.

DEPARTMENT OF HEALTH AND SOCIAL SERVICES COMPREHENSIVE SERVICES PROGRAM PLAN (PART 228, SUBPART C)

The State of Wisconsin Department of Health and Social Services is submitting its Comprehensive Services Program Plan in compliance with P.L. 93-647 and Sec. 228, Chapter II, Title 45 of the Code of Federal Regulations.

PROGRAM YEAR (228.21)

The first program period will begin on October 1, 1975 and will end on June 30, 1977. This will enable the second program planning period to be simultaneous with the state's planning for its next biennial budget, which will cover the period July 1, 1977 through June 30, 1979. Because of the length of the first program period, the implementation of the plan will periodically be evaluated, reviewed, and amended if necessary.

PROGRAM GOALS (228.23)

The Wisconsin Comprehensive Services Program Plan provides that the services offered will be directed at the federal goals of:

(1) achieving or maintaining economic self-support to prevent, reduce, or eliminate dependency;

(**2**) achieving or maintaining self-sufficiency including reduction or prevention of dependency;

(**3**) preventing or remedying neglect, abuse, or exploitation of children and adults unable to protect their own interests or preserving, rehabilitating, or reuniting families;

(**4**) preventing or reducing inappropriate institutional care by providing for community-based care, home-based care, or other forms of less intensive care;

(**5**) securing referral or admission for institutional care when other forms of care are not appropriate or providing services to individuals in institutions.

The objectives to be achieved under the program shall be directed to the goals in the preceding paragraph of this section and are identified later in the plan.

INDIVIDUALS TO BE SERVED—SERVICES TO BE PROVIDED (228.24-228.26)

The services enumerated in this plan will be available to (1) recipients of Aid to Families with Dependent Children, (2) those persons whose needs were taken into account in determining the needs of Aid to Families with Dependent Children recipients, (3) recipients of Supplemental Security Income or state supplementary benefits, and (4) Income Eligible persons (including recipients of services provided without regard to income).

Eligibility for services will be determined at the time an application for services is made.

Services will be available to individuals and families whose monthly *GROSS* income does not exceed 100% of Wisconsin's median income. However, *CHARGES* for services other than adoption services will be made between the income levels as indicated in the following chart:

MONTHLY CHARGE SCHEDULE (228.62)
Effective 10-1-75 through 10-31-75

Family Size	% of State's Median Income	Charges for Services Begin After These Monthly Gross Income Levels	Maximum Eligibility Ceiling
1	66%	$ 400	$ 608
2	60%	475	795
3	56%	550	982
4	56%	650	1169
5	55%	750	1350
6	55%	850	1543
7	60%	950	1578
8	65%	1050	1613
9	70%	1150	1648
10	74%	1250	1683

Charges for non-exempt services will be made for all individuals and families whose income falls within the levels indicated above. This will include charges for services to income maintenance assistance recipients whose gross income is within the levels indicated.

Monthly charges will not be made and services will be provided without regard to income for the following services to Goal IIIA—preventing or remedying neglect, abuse, or exploitation of children and adults unable to protect their own interests:

- Counseling
- Court Services
- Diagnosis and Evaluation
- Education and Training
- Health Related
- Legal Services
- Planning, Placement, and Supervision
- Protective Payment Services

In addition, Information and Referral services will be provided without regard to eligibility and without charge.

Adoption rates are established utilizing the following fee schedule:

a. The fee for a first adoption is based upon the family gross annual income, less a $1,000 deduction for each dependent child and is 5% of the adjusted income. The maximum fee is $1,000.
b. The fee for a second and all subsequent adoptions is computed at 3% of the family's annual income after deducting $1,000 from income for each dependent child. The maximum fee is $1,000.
c. Applicants will be billed at the time of legal adoption.
d. The fee may be adjusted for subsidized adoptions and difficult-to-place children.

The services to be offered by the Department of Health and Social Services are defined in the Glossary of Terms, included as Attachment I. If the services enumerated in this plan are unavailable without cost, funding will be provided under P.L. 93-647, as the need arises and resources become available.

The services may be provided or purchased by the state agency or by local public agencies from private and/or public providers. Attachment II describes the services to meet the individual program goals, the objectives of each service, and the categories of eligible individuals to whom the service is to be offered. These pages also estimate the number of individuals to whom service will be made available and the estimated expenditures for the services.

Family Planning services will be provided upon request to all Aid to Families with Dependent Children recipients (including minors who can be considered sexually active) and to all other families who are within the income levels established in this plan.

Information and Referral services will be provided to an estimated 340,363 individuals at a projected cost of $1,224,000.

PROGRAM RESOURCES AND ESTIMATED EXPENDITURES 228.27 and 228.28

Program Resources to carry out the Title XX Plan are identified below and provide a comparison between estimated aggregate non-federal expenditures for the proposed program period and those of the preceding program year. The dollar amount identified as federal funds represents the total federal funds available for the plan period.

| | Expenditures FY 1974-75 | Estimated Expenditures | |
		Annual Rate 10/1/75-9/30/76	Plan Period 10/1/75-6/30/77
Federal	$54,500,000	$54,500,000	$ 95,375,000
State	23,230,000	23,230,000	40,651,000
Total	$77,730,000	$77,730,000	$136,026,000

GEOGRAPHIC AREA (228.25)

The State of Wisconsin is to be considered as a single geographic area for the provision of the Social Services listed and directed to the goals described in the plan. The services specified in the plan will be available as need arises and resources are available.

PROGRAM COORDINATION AND UTILIZATION (228.29)

The Department of Health and Social Services has the responsibility for the administration of Title IV-A, AFDC; Title IV-B, Child Welfare Services; Title IV-C, WIN; Title IV-D, Child Support and Establishment of Paternity; and Title XIX, Medical Assistance, as well as Title VI, Services to Aged, Blind, or Disabled. The Department has a close working relationship with other agencies and departments who have responsibilities for administering the balance of the Social Security Act programs within the State of Wisconsin.

In order to assure as much coordination as possible a committee made up of representatives from a wide range of human services agencies was assembled to assist in the development of the Title XX Comprehensive Services Program Plan. The committee consists of representative(s) from

- Division of Family Services
- Division of Mental Hygiene
- Division on Aging
- Division of Corrections
- Division of Health
- Division of Vocational Rehabilitation
- Bureau of Planning and Analysis, in the executive services of the Department of Health and Social Services
- County Welfare Departments
- Voluntary Agencies
- The Wisconsin Board on Aging
- The Developmental Disabilities Council

The Title XX planning process included two separate reviews by the Department of Health and Social Services Advisory Committee on Social Services. This committee currently numbers fourteen and has citizen members, agency representatives—both public and private. It includes Whites, Blacks, and Native Americans.

The proposed Comprehensive Service Program Plan was approved for public hearings by the former State Health and Social Services Board. This nine-person board was appointed by the Governor and confirmed by the State Senate. Its members represented a variety of cultural and citizen groups. With the passage of the current biennial budget, the board was abolished effective July 1, 1975. A Human Resources Coordinating Council has been created by the Legislature to advise the Governor and Legislature in the broad area of social services.

In addition, there have been individual consultations with a wide variety of non-profit and proprietary service organizations.

As part of its ongoing coordination efforts to reduce service duplication and improve the quality of services, the Department of Health and Social Services has or will establish ongoing interagency planning with

- Department of Public Instruction
- Department of Industry, Labor, and Human Relations
- Department of Local Affairs and Development
- Department of Transportation
- Wisconsin County Boards Association
- The University of Wisconsin
- The State Board of Vocational, Technical and Adult Education
- The Association of Wisconsin Child Caring Agencies
- The Wisconsin Public Welfare Association
- The Wisconsin Council on Human Concerns
- The Wisconsin Board of Juvenile Court Judges
- The Wisconsin Medical Society
- The Wisconsin Bar Association
- The County Sheriffs and Police Chiefs Association
- Wisconsin Area Agencies on Aging
- Wisconsin CAP Directors Association
- National Association of Social Workers
- The People's Rights Organization

- Plus other organizations and agencies.

The agencies listed plus others share a common concern about the quality of life in Wisconsin and the preservation of human resources.

In the future there will be a maximum utilization of and coordination with other public and voluntary agencies including proprietary who provide related or similar services to those services provided under this plan. The Department of Health and Social Services is assisting in the development of human services systems to maximize the integration and coordination of services at the local level.

ORGANIZATIONAL STRUCTURE (228.30)

Within the single (statewide) geographical area, there are seventy-two County Departments of Social Services created by statute. Covering the same geographical area are 51.42 Boards whose responsibility by statute is community mental health, mental retardation, alcoholism, and drug abuse services. Additionally, the statutes establish 51.437 Boards whose responsibilities are to assure a full range of services to the developmentally disabled. These local agencies will carry responsibility for the delivery of Title XX services.

Through a network of regional and district offices, the staffs of the Divisons of Family Services, Mental Hygiene, Corrections, Vocational Rehabilitation, and Health and Aging will also be responsible for the delivery of some Title XX services.

Requests for services may be made either at the local agency described above or at the field offices of the state agencies. Eligibility determination occurs at the delivery level and is provided by local agencies, state agencies, and by provider agencies under contract.

The Department of Health and Social Services provides for the use of non-paid or partially paid volunteers to assist in providing services. Volunteers are trained by the agency to assure they appropriately handle the tasks assigned.

NEEDS ASSESSMENT (228.31)

The state's biennial budget has been finalized and funds for social services have been allocated for the 1975-77 biennium. Since services mandated by state statutes and/or federal regulations consume Wisconsin's entire federal allocation, a needs assessment was not undertaken prior to the first program period.

Factors influencing the decision were (1) the short planning time permitted before the proposed plan must be published and (2) legislative mandate for the primary local agencies providing social services to file a coordinated plan and budget for 1976. The time frame for this activity is later than that required for Title XX and would be duplicative of Title XX efforts.

The coordinated plan will be the beginning of activity leading to a needs assessment throughout the state. A major emphasis will be placed upon developing a statewide needs assessment as soon as possible. This may involve contracting with an outside firm.

Planning continues for the installation of a computerized social services information system. This data base which will reflect trends will be the beginning point for a needs assessment as an integral part of the next Comprehensive Services Program Plan. Also in the planning stage is the development of a new bureau whose responsibility among others will be planning for the second Title XX Plan.

PLANNING, EVALUATION, AND REPORTING (228.32)

The Department is in the process of developing an evaluation and reporting system. A unit within the department to plan and coordinate such activities is being considered. With the creation of such a unit, activities and staff resources will be directed toward meeting these requirements in coordination and synchronization with the needs assessment which has been previously described. Such procedures will be further developed for the next comprehensive services program plan submitted by the State of Wisconsin.

On the effective date of the plan, the department will initiate a federally approved cost allocation study which will provide information about utilization of services, target groups being served, and service costs.

AMENDMENTS

The Comprehensive Services Program Plan may be amended whenever necessary to reflect substantive changes relating to services offered, eligibility levels, categories of people to be served, as well as changes in federal or state law. Amendments requested by local public delivery agencies must have, at least, approval of the County Board of Supervisors. Such amendments shall be recommended by the Secretary and approved by the Governor pursuant to s.16.54, Wisconsin statutes.

FEDERAL FINANCIAL PARTICIPATION (228.90)

Through Title XX the federal government is able to participate financially in up to 75% (90% in Family Planning) of the costs associated with carrying out Wisconsin's Title XX program. These costs are included in Attachments II and III.

Federal Financial Participation will be claimed for expenditures which are identified and allocated in accordance with an approved cost allocation plan.

Such expenditures include but are not limited to

- salary, fringe benefits, and travel costs of staff engaged in carrying out service work or service related work;
- costs of related expenses, such as communications and office space and depreciation of equipment, furniture, and supplies.
- costs of state advisory committee on services, including expenses of members in attending meetings, supportive staff, and other technical assistance;
- costs of agency staff attendance at meetings pertinent to the development or implementation of federal and state service policies and programs;
- cost to agency for the use of volunteers in the program;
- costs of operation of agency facilities used for the provision of services, except that appropriate distribution of costs is necessary when other agencies also use such facilities in carrying out their functions;
- costs of administrative support activities furnished by other public agencies or other units within the single state agency which are properly cost allocated;
- costs of technical assistance, data collection, surveys, and studies performed by other public agencies, private organizations, or individuals to assist the agency in developing, planning, monitoring, and evaluating the services program;
- costs of public liability and other insurance protection for staff as well as foster parents and volunteers;
- medical or remedial care when an integral but subordinate part of a service, as described in the service plan;
- room and board when an integral but subordinate part of a service described in the service plan;
- services to individuals living in hospitals, skilled nursing facilities, intermediate care facilities or prisons;
- educational services if unavailable through state or local educational agencies without cost and without regard to their income;
- emergency shelter care provided as a part of protective service to any child including runaways when the child is in clear and present danger of abuse, neglect or exploitation, the need is documented by personnel authorized by state law to place children, and is provided for not more than 30 consecutive days in a 12-month period;
- services provided by foster care institutions when those services are identified in the service plan and included in the contract with such foster care institutions;
- child care licensed or certified under rules of the State Department of Health and Social Services and will meet the standards as set forth in the federal regulations as well as the federal interagency day care requirements;

- public information program and outreach services to carry out the purposes of Title XX;
- community planning and development activities directed toward the goals of Title XX;
- activities directed toward the development of community-based facilities including licensing under th rules and regulations of the State Department of Health and Social Services;
- the cost of foster parents' and homemakers' physical examinations, and
- the cost of damage caused by foster children to foster homes.

TITLE XX: GLOSSARY OF TERMS USED IN DOCUMENT 9.3

ADOPTION SERVICES

All the activities involved in providing adoptive services. This includes study services, placements, and supervision.

CHORE SERVICES

The performance of household tasks, essential shopping, and unskilled or semiskilled home maintenance tasks usually done by family members to enable individuals to remain in their own homes when unable to perform such tasks themselves. Activities include but are not limited to installing weather stripping, repairing furniture, minor painting, cutting grass, and clearing walkways of snow and leaves.

COUNSELING

The utilization of special skills to assist individuals, families, or groups in achieving objectives through exploration of a problem and its ramifications, examination of attitudes and feelings, consideration of alternative solutions, and decision-making.

COURT SERVICES

Assisting the courts when requested or required in investigations, studies, recommendations, and supervision (excludes adoptions).

DAY CARE SERVICES

The provision of care for any portion of the 24-hour day in a setting licensed or approved by the appropriate agency for purposes of personal care and/or for promotion of social, health, and emotional well-being through opportunities for companionship, self-education, and other developmental activities. Settings include licensed day care centers as well as certified in-home and family day care and may include provision of a noon meal. Medical if not covered under Title XVIII or XIX may also be included as an integral but subordinate part of the service.

DAY SERVICES PROGRAM

Non-residential comprehensive coordinated care, services, and/or treatment (including medical if integral but subordinate and not covered by Title XVIII or XIX) to enhance motivation and social development and to alleviate disabilities when present. Day services shall provide a continuous delivery of services for a scheduled portion of a 24-hour day and may include the cost of a noon meal. Examples are licensed or approved day treatment facilities, day care for the mentally handicapped, etc.

DIAGNOSIS AND EVALUATION
Activities (including medical if integral but subordinate and not covered under Titles XVIII or XIX) leading to identification of the nature and/or extent of the presenting problems; the services necessary to remove, ameliorate, or manage the problem; and the development of measurable client objectives.

EDUCATION AND TRAINING
Those activities which assist persons in obtaining education and/or training in accordance with their capacities and/or vocational needs. This service can include payment for educational expenses as well as the actual provision of a broad and varied curriculum of practical and/or academic subjects primarily designed to develop the ability to learn, acquire useful knowledge and basic learning skills to improve his economic well-being, and/or to improve the ability to apply them to everyday living. Payment for educational services may only be made if the services are unavailable without cost and are not the responsibility of a state or local educational agency.

FAMILY PLANNING
Counseling, educational, referral, and medical services (including diagnosis, treatment, drugs, supplies, devices, and related counseling when furnished, prescribed by, or under the supervision of a physician) to enable individuals of either sex (including minors) to voluntarily determine the number of or to plan the spacing of their children.

HEALTH RELATED
Identifying needs for preventive and prompt remedial medical services and dental services, locating qualified providers of those services, and helping solve any problems which may prevent persons from obtaining and making optimum use of services available. (This includes activities involved in the Early and Periodic Screening Diagnosis and Treatment (EPSDT.)

HOME AND FINANCIAL MANAGEMENT
Assisting in or providing for management of household budgets, maintenance and care of the home, child rearing, nutrition, preparation of food, and consumer education.

HOME-DELIVERED MEALS OR CONGREGATE MEALS
Assisting individuals to utilize a nutritional program. This can include payment for the cost of food, preparation, and/or delivery of meals to an individual in his or her home or a central dining facility.

HOUSING SERVICES
Services directed toward working with landlords and others to upgrade substandard rental housing, to obtain repairs to homes if substandard or unsuitable, and to find other housing suitable and adequate at affordable prices. Includes payments made for the performance of skilled home maintenance tasks not usually done by family members. Activities include but are not limited to construction of ramps if an occupant is wheel-chair bound, modifying living facilities, and providing specialized equipment so a handicapped person may function more independently; or other minor modifications. (This service includes payment of moving expenses.)

INFORMATION AND REFERRAL

Provision of factual information to individuals and organizations concerning human problems and available services and resources. The referral process includes a follow-up responsibility.

LEGAL SERVICES

The services provided by a professionally trained attorney. (For DFS and County Departments of Social Services, this service consists of referral and follow-up.)

PERSONAL CARE SERVICES

The services (including integral but subordinate medical services as part of a plan not covered by Title XVIII or Title XIX) performed for an individual to improve or maintain well-being, including but not limited to feeding, bathing, dressing, and the cost of home care.

PLANNING, PLACEMENT, AND SUPERVISION

Activities of the agency staff leading to placement of children and/or adults in an approved or licensed setting which is suitable to the needs of the individual and ongoing activities assuring the appropriateness of and need for that placement through periodic review.

PROTECTIVE PAYMENT SERVICES

Services may include fees for guardians and conservators and related costs of bonds and filing fees. The decision as to who is to have a protective payee and the actual selection of the payee are the responsibilities of the income maintenance unit or agency.

RECREATION

Recreational services provided for planned and supervised activities designed to (1) help meet specific individual therapeutic needs in self-expression and social interaction and (2) develop skills and interests leading to enjoyable and constructive use of leisure time (includes but is not limited to camping, Big Brother, YWCA, YMCA, 4-H, etc.).

SHELTERED EMPLOYMENT

Non-competitive employment in a workshop, at home, or in a regular work environment. Sheltered employment may occupy up to a full working day and may include the cost of a noon meal. (Sheltered employment may be one of a number of components included in a sheltered workshop program.)

SPECIAL LIVING ARRANGEMENTS

Provision of living quarters, board and room, (if integral but subordinate), and basic services in foster family homes, foster care institutions, and other special living arrangements. This includes emergency shelter.

TRANSPORTATION

Provision of transportation and related costs to make it possible for individual or families to travel to and from facilities and resources. Services may include but need not be limited to the cost of transportation and attendants or escorts when necessary.

References

1. Reich, C. *The Greening of America.* New York: Random House, 1970.
2. Ryan, W. *Blaming the Victim.* New York: Vintage, 1971.
3. De Lone, R. *Small Futures.* New York: Harcourt, 1979, pp. 65–73.
4. Schiller, B. *The Economics of Poverty and Discrimination.* Englewood Cliffs, N.J.: Prentice-Hall, 1976, p. 44.
5. Friedlander, W. *Introduction to Social Welfare.* Englewood Cliffs, N.J.: Prentice-Hall, 1974, pp. 82, 83.
6. Ibid., pp. 128, 129.
7. Richmond, M. *Social Diagnosis,* New York: Russell Sage, 1917.
8. Axinn, J., and Levin, H. *Social Welfare: A History of the American Response to Need.* New York: Dodd, 1975, p. 241.
9. Ibid., p. 245.
10. De Lone, R. Op. cit., ch. 1, 3.
11. Yinger, M. *A Minority Group in American Society.* New York: McGraw-Hill, 1965.
12. De Lone, R. Op. cit.
13. Schiller, B. Op. cit., p. 151.
14. Lawrence, W., and Leeds, S. *An Inventory of Federal Income Transfer Programs, Fiscal Year 1977.* White Plains, N.Y.: The Institute for Socioeconomic Studies, 1978, pp. 185–188.
15. "When the Untrained Woman Must Find a Job," *Woman's Day,* August 7, 1978, p. 14.
16. Fink, A. et al. *The Field of Social Work,* 5th ed. New York: Holt Rinehart and Winston, 1968, pp. 132, 133.
17. Schiller, B. Op. cit., p. 90.
18. Ibid., pp. 94, 95.
19. National Conference on Social Welfare. *The Future for Social Services in the United States. Final Report of the Task Force, 1977,* pp. 12–16.
20. Goodwin, L. *Can Social Science Help Resolve Social Problems.* New York: Free Press, 1975.
21. Kadushin, A., and Schenk, Q. "An Experiment in Teaching an Integrated Methods Course," in C. Kasius, ed., *Social Case Work in the Fifties.* New York: Family Service Assn. of America, 1962, pp. 334–345.

chapter 10

Programs to Mitigate Economic and Social Differences

Programs to mitigate economic and social differences are based on the assumption that poverty and underprivilege come not from individual deficiencies but, rather, from societal differences. This implies that the recipients of services are normal and that they face deprivation only because of the way in which the groups to which they belong are defined by the larger society. Therefore, the primary objective of these programs is to lessen the differences that exist between the poor and the groupings in the society that have greater access to material and social resources.

Three major program goals are instrumental to the achievement of the primary objective:

1. modification of the internal characteristics of the groups to which the poor belong
2. modification of the external relationships of the groups to which the poor belong
3. dispersal of the poor.

Note that these program goals do not aim to modify the society. Instead they aim to modify the characteristics of impoverished groups, mainly to enable those segments to move into the "middle-class" rankings of the society. We will briefly describe the important aspects of each of these program goals.

Modification of Internal Group Characteristics

The great waves of immigration in the latter part of the nineteenth and the early part of the twentieth centuries resulted in large groups of poor immigrants crowded together in the cities. These newcomers had cultural and social characteristics quite different from those of the earlier immigrants who had previously lived in the cities. For the new immigrants to become "Americans," it was necessary that they learn "American" ways. They had to learn a new language, develop skills to obtain employment, and acquire social characteristics that would make them seem less like "foreigners." When this was accomplished, it was assumed by society that the immigrants would also be able to avoid or escape from poverty. The first organizations formed to help accomplish these tasks were the settlement houses. Altruistic persons, usually women from prosperous American families, went to live in the poor neighborhoods that were populated by immigrants. They "settled" in these neighborhoods to assist the newly arrived to become Americans. The buildings from which they fielded their services were "settlements" in the ghettos. The "settlement" workers were the forerunners of contemporary social workers.[1]

Settlement houses offered a variety of services to modify the cultural and social characteristics of the immigrant groups. There were language classes, homemaking classes, instruction in job skills, citizenship classes, and informal activities that stressed the social skills needed to function in the community. Many of the programs that the early settlement pioneers developed have now been taken over by public organizations, particularly the public schools. Education is still regarded as a primary means of eliminating the differences between the poor and the more affluent groups in society, a legacy coming directly from the programs first developed in settlement houses.

For instance, integrated schools combined with busing of inner-city children to school in the affluent suburbs is one of the recent major public services developed to overcome social and cultural differences. The efforts of ethnic and racial minorities to expand their educational opportunities in public schools and in colleges also attest to the importance that these groups place on education to mitigate the cultural and social differnces that prevent them from improving their social and economic position relative to other groupings in society. The Headstart program would also fit into this category. Women too feel that education is important for overcoming differences. Federal statistics show that women currently represent 49% of the overall college enrollment in the United States, and projections indicate that women students will soon outnumber their male counterparts.[2]

In recent years social services have also expanded under the auspices of the public school systems. Nurses, counselors, psychologists, and social workers are now commonly employed by the schools. Lunch and breakfast programs, either free or at reduced cost, are provided by the federal government. The expansion of these services, it is thought, will enable the poor and underprivileged to make the best possible use of their educational opportunities so that their differences from other more privileged social groupings will be minimized.

Modification of External Group Relationships

Along with the strong commitment to the value of work apparent in this country, there is a commitment to the formal value of political equality as was originally spelled out in the federal constitution. Nonetheless, this value has remained mainly an ideal rather than a practical reality. The poor and their advocates recognized that those who have greater access to political power also have a commensurately larger share of social and material resources. However, it was not until the late nineteenth century that organized efforts to obtain political power for the disadvantaged began to emerge. An early example of this effort came about when the city of Chicago refused to provide sanitation services for the poor who lived around Hull House. In response, Jane Addams used her influence to get herself appointed sanitation inspector for the city. She used the position to obtain sewer, water, and garbage services for the area.[3]

The labor movement owes much of its present-day eminence to the classes for workers that were part of the efforts of early settlement pioneers. Workers were shown how government operated and how to organize to achieve their aims and were taught skills such as reading and writing. This was done so that they could form themselves into groups wherein they could develop political power.

The civil rights movement, the women's movement, the American Indian movement, and the efforts of members of the Latin American minority groups are all contemporary manifestations of the activities of disadvantaged groups to modify their socioeconomic relationship to the more privileged groups in society by increasing their political power. Cesar Chavez, head of the United Farm Workers in the American Southwest, is, in many ways, the direct descendant of Jane Addams, having been the pupil of Saul Alinsky who developed his organization techniques in the area of Chicago where Hull House first began its work.[4]

The goal of the use of political power to modify the social position of the disadvantaged underlies a number of recent welfare programs. We will describe some of these in a later section of this chapter and show how the power concept operates in these programs.

Dispersal of the Disadvantaged Groups

Geographical location furnishes a well-defined label of the socioeconomic status of the residents of an area. For this reason similar houses will carry different price tags depending on the geographical area in which they are located. As soon as it is possible for persons to do so, they move from the geographic area of the community in which they have lived as members of disadvantaged groups to a house in the suburbs, or better yet, in the country. A new home in a "better" neighborhood is a powerful motivating symbol for the upwardly mobile, even though the high-priced home is not necessarily a better home than the one left behind. Indeed many houses in the suburbs are small and poorly constructed. The move is made not so much to acquire better housing as it is to acquire "better" neighbors. The reasoning is somewhat circular. One displays the improvement in one's economic position by moving to a "better" neighborhood where it is hoped that new social contacts,"better" schools, and so on will help to further improve one's economic condition or at least the socioeconomic condition of one's children.

This same general social concept lies behind governmental programs for dispersal of poor and disadvantaged throughout the community as an effort to mitigate social and economic differences. In the urban renewal programs of the 1950s and 1960s, whole neighborhoods were condemned and razed. The residents were sometimes assisted to find other housing, sometimes left to their own devices. Ethnic groups were broken up and scattered throughout the community.[5] More current attempts at dispersal include efforts to place small group homes for the mentally or physically handicapped in affluent neighborhoods and to encourage or force neighborhoods to build public housing for the poor and elderly.

Specific Programs to Mitigate Economic and Social Differences

We have noted a number of times that welfare programs are organized in a patchwork fashion with overlapping objectives. Programs to mitigate economic and social differences are even more hodgepodge, with even more overlapping objectives. They often attempt to implement all three instrumental program goals at the same time. Because they are virtually impossible to categorize, we will not try to do so. Instead we will proceed to the description of some of the services offered by the major programs, together with the aims and concepts underlying these programs.

Neighborhood Centers

Settlement houses were important organizations in the provision of welfare services during the latter part of the nineteenth century and the first third of the present century. Neighborhood centers are their present-day counterparts.

Neighborhood centers are multifunction agencies, both in the services that they offer and in the sources of their funding. Located in the geographical areas in which disadvantaged groups live, they offer many of the services that the old settlement houses offered. They hold a variety of classes, provide leisure activities for all ages, and serve as gathering places for groups that wish to deal with matters pertaining to the well-being of the community. In addition, neighborhood centers often furnish facilities in which some of the services described in the previous two chapters can be delivered to the recipients.

The earlier settlement house programs were voluntary in every sense of the word. They were supported by private donations and were staffed by unpaid volunteers. Even though volunteer workers and nongovernmental sources of financial support such as religious organizations, foundations, and United Funds are still important to neighborhood centers, the trend is toward a paid staff and support from public funds. This trend has resulted in a gradual shift toward a concentration on the modification of internal group characteristics. Within this framework, the emphasis is often upon individual personal improvement rather than upon social change.

Housing

There are few marks of social distinction more telling than the home in which a person lives and the location of that home in a community. That "a man's home is his castle" is a time-honored value, one that was defined long before the American Revolution. This value accounts for the drive on the part of Americans to own their own homes. Nearly 70 per cent do so, and, despite the dramatic inflation in the cost of both new and older housing, young adults try to purchase homes as soon as possible.[6]

The social significance of housing is reflected in real estate advertising. There are "starter homes" for those just entering the market. These are usually modest, older homes in less affluent sections of the community. "Executive" homes can be found in "exclusive" or "prestige" areas. This is most likely to be in one of the suburbs that surrounds the larger cities. In the United States, less desirable housing is generally in the central city. This pattern is not the same in all societies. In many of the cities of South America, the poor live in "favellos" located on the outskirts of the city; the more desirable housing is in the residential ring that surrounds the central business district.

Regardless of the pattern, it is generally the rule in modern societies to segregate individuals in housing according to their ranking in the socioeconomic hierarchy. Because providing for housing is generally seen as the individual's responsibility, and because the poor have limited funds, the quality of their housing is generally poor. For this reason, human services professionals have been concerned about housing for the poor and have advocated the establishment of programs to improve the circumstances in which the poor live. Because housing programs are among the most important to mitigate the economic and social differences of the poor, we will discuss the development of housing programs at some length.

In the nineteenth century, those who migrated to the cities, whether from abroad or from rural areas of the United States, clustered in whatever shelter they could find in the city centers. Shoddy apartment buildings with almost no plumbing and less fire protection were sometimes thrown up to accommodate them. Former single-family residences were converted into multifamily dwellings with whole families crowded into a single room.[7]

As the newly arrived were able to improve their financial circumstances, they moved to outlying areas, taking their place as middle-class citizens. They were happy to get out of the tenements and expected those that were left behind to do likewise. For a time it was thought that the process would continue and that the slums would eventually disappear. After all, America was the land of opportunity, so in theory it was possible for everyone who desired to do so to overcome the hardships and enjoy the benefits of adequate housing and a better class of neighbors in other areas. The discovery that this did not happen *automatically* was one of the reasons for the establishment of public housing programs for the poor.

In the United States, legislation concerning housing was first passed in 1867 in New York City. The purpose, however, was not to assist the poor but to prevent the spread of epidemics.[8] Other cities enacted similar legislation, setting minimum standards for light, space, and water supplies. In most cases the laws affected only new housing and had little impact on housing already in existence.

The federal government entered the housing arena in the 1930s, at first to prevent the unemployed middle class from losing their homes and then to build lowcost housing for persons who had lost their homes as a result of the Depression.

During World War II, the federal government made financial assistance available for the construction of housing. Again the purpose was not to aid the poor but to provide living quarters for civilians who worked in defense plants and for servicemen and their families. The same kinds of programs continued after the war, to help in the resettlement of veterans and defense workers.

The Federal Housing Act of 1949 was a landmark. This was the beginning of the attack on areas in the cities that were designated as unsightly, blighted, or deteriorated. The so-called slum housing often abutted the central business district. Commuters from the suburbs who passed through these ugly sections did not like what they saw. Furthermore, the business districts in the centers of the cities were expanding, and there was a need for more space for roads, parking, office buildings, and stores. The only available space nearby was taken up by the decrepit homes of the poor. The Federal Housing Act provided for the construction of public housing units in other areas that were supposed to take care of the residents of homes that were razed. The razed houses were replaced by the expanding business district, roads, and, in some cases, high-cost housing for the well-to-do.[9, 10]

All this was rationalized in two ways. It was thought that dispersing the poor into other areas of the cities and breaking up the ethnic ghettos would help to eliminate poverty and would give the poor an opportunity to learn new ways from their new neighbors. This would help them to overcome the characteristics of their group that had hitherto prevented them from self-improvement. Settlement house staffs participated in these relocation efforts. Sometimes the settlement house itself was "redeveloped" in the hope that its disappearance would attest to the elimination of poverty.

The second rationale was in some ways contradictory to the first. The Federal Housing Act provided for the building of public housing units on the grounds that, if the poor were taken out of their substandard housing and put into clean new apartments, their other problems would disappear. In many cases, however, the poor could not afford the rents in the new buildings. In other cases, the new units were so shoddy and poorly planned that they quickly became little more than vertical slums.

The Pruitt-Igoe public housing project built in the 1950s in St. Louis is an example of the latter. Peter Blake says in his book, *Form Follows Fiasco,* that, although this project was "hailed as a truly enlightened scheme, it had to be dynamited, at least in part, less than twenty years later. Reason: It had proved to be totally destructive of human life and a menace to the few remaining survivors."[11]

It was soon observed that in most cases the poor were merely displaced into other areas of the city where the deteriorating housing was so minimally maintained that the landlords could could still obtain a profit by renting to the underprivileged. In other words the poor were pushed deeper into the already overcrowded slums. This observation sparked a modification of the program from urban development to urban renewal. Emphasis was placed on preventing areas from becoming blighted in the first place, or, if they were already partially blighted, on restoring them. Truly deteriorated buildings were still razed, however.

This is not to say that the programs were completely unsuccessful. Although many endured great hardship, relocation programs did enable substantial numbers of white slum dwellers to better their housing conditions. During the 1950s, the social planners concentrated on enabling white slum dwellers to adapt to the areas in which they were relocated. For these fortunate ones, the process of modifying their relationships with other groups in the community with whom they came into contact was completed. The 1960 census shows that, as a result of the programs of the 1950s, the percentage of white families living in substandard housing dropped from 32 per cent to 13 per cent in that ten-year period.

But alas, for many, poverty was still a fact of life. When white poor persons are dispersed and take on the social and economic characteristics of those about them, their identity with poverty disappears. This is not so easy for black people; their color betrays them to the white majority who tend to define blacks and other minorities of color as being poor and underprivileged. The programs of the 1950s did nothing to solve the problems of the blacks and other ethnic minorities. While the number of whites living in substandard housing dropped to 13 per cent in 1960, the number of black Americans in substandard housing remained at 44 per cent. This discrepancy was aggravated by the migration of black Americans from the rural south to the urban northern cities that accelerated after World War II. In the substandard housing that escaped the wrecker's ball, the whites were immediately replaced by blacks from the south and to a lesser extent by Hispanic minorities.[12]

Public housing programs were modified in the 1960s to include more social planning and social services. A key concept in increased social services was the involvement of the poor in the planning and execution of programs for their housing. This was encouraged by the 1960 amendments to the Housing Act. It was assumed that, if the poor became involved, their relationship to the more powerful groups would be altered with the poor obtaining more power. The local government and business persons who had been in control of the housing programs did not welcome this idea with much enthusiasm. All went reasonably well, however, as long as the poor were only on advisory boards, but, when the social planners were able to place the poor on boards that had real control over the operation of the housing programs, the local government and business officials saw that they would have to share their power with local neighborhood blocs. Considerable conflict ensued and local officials generated enough resistance so that the politicians at the federal level modified the housing acts in 1970 and returned the control of the programs to the local city officials and their appointees.

Currently, human services workers assist tenants in housing projects for low-income groups to form tenant groups that have an advisory role to the local housing authorities. They also assist in relocation of families displaced by the razing of substandard housing so that the effects of displacement may be minimized. And, finally, human services housing specialists work to coordinate the services of the many agencies who serve the poor so that if housing is a concern, the agencies can better assist individuals to solve their housing problems.

Since the 1960s the housing situation of the poor has not been modified materially.[13] About the same percentage of black Americans live in substandard housing now as did then. The effort to eliminate poverty by physical and social planning, which started out with optimism and a "can do" attitude, has now become a holding action. The programs have helped to prevent the housing situation from further deterioration, but for the past twenty years they have failed to work any substantial improvement.

Community Action Programs

A very different approach for the mitigation of economic and social differences was the Community Action Program (CAP). The young planners that President J. F. Kennedy recruited into the poverty programs in the early 1960s decided that the state and local governments were the focal points of resistance to change in regard to welfare services to the poor. They saw the federal government as the political unit in American society that could bring about reform in social services, and, yes, they too dared to dream that their work would eliminate poverty. President Johnson carried on the dream and declared that his War on Poverty would usher in the Great Society. Under the Economic Opportunity Act of 1964, which created the Office of Economic Opportunity (OEO), CAP was to be the cornerstone of this great effort.

Bypassing the state and local governmental authorities, CAP was organized at the local level as an independent agency that received funds directly from the federal government. The governing bodies of CAP were composed of representatives from churches, schools, neighborhood centers, small businesses, and activist groups from the poor areas of the cities. They hired their own staff and dispensed monies to programs that were thought to be carrying out the aims of CAP.

The Community Action Program hoped (1) to modify the internal characteristics of the groups to which the poor belong and (2) to modify the relationships of these groups to other social groupings. Human services professionals attempted to reach the first objective through various job training, literacy and "basic" education programs. Their approach was similar to that pioneered in the settlement houses many years before. To reach the second objective, workers encouraged participation of the underprivileged on CAP boards.

The slogan of CAP, "maximum feasible participation," caught the imagination of the poor. The black community especially saw CAP as a means by which they could take action on their own to improve their circumstances. In 1965, the year after the passage of the Economic Opportunity Act, 415 local communities had organized themselves and applied for and received grants to create local community action agencies. This burst of energy resulted in the establishment of Job Corps centers, VISTA projects, Neighborhood Youth Corps programs, work study programs, work experience projects, and adult basic education projects in forty of the fifty states in the first year of CAP's existence. The speed at which these programs were established is explained by the fact that CAP agencies developed mainly into an administrative framework through which federal monies were funneled into the already existing agencies that then designed and administered the service programs. Most of the excitement was confined to the first year of implementation, because by the second year members of the CAP boards were beginning to bicker among themselves as to how programs should be run, who should staff them, and what the nature of the programs should be. Some of the representatives of the groups from the poor community wanted their own people to run the programs; others felt that the traditional social agencies and the usual human services personnel should do the job. "Maximum feasible participation" developed into a struggle to see which groups could exert the most control.[14]

The Community Action Program was not without effect, however. Among other things, CAP assisted the activities of the civil rights groups by giving them some financial support. It also allocated funds to local organizations such as churches and local schools for self-help services, neighborhood clean-up activities, the youth corps, and so on.

Officials of state and local government soon became aware that the involvement of the poor posed a threat to their control of welfare programs. If the poor became more powerful, the relationships among the interest groupings (the state government, the local government, and the urban poor) would be altered. They reacted in the same way that they did when control of urban renewal became a threat. In 1965, Congress capitulated and decreed that one third of the members of the local CAP board must be appointed by the mayor or his designate. Furthermore, a particular CAP board had to be officially designated by the state and local officials as the proper one to receive funds under the Economic Opportunity Act. In 1966, funds for CAP were cut back by Congress. This thwarted the federal planners' efforts to help the poor to modify their relationships with other groups in the community.[15]

Human services professionals involved with CAP and with other programs operating under OEO were often surprised at the vehemence of the opposition that arose as soon as their efforts began to pay off in increased activity on the part of the poverty programs. Opposition came not only from the political sector (which was expected) but from the community as well (which was not expected). If the staffs of these programs had understood the operation of representative law and compromise law as discussed in Chapter 6, both planners and human services professionals might have been better able to anticipate the resistance that developed and perhaps have even established programs that would have taken the potential resistance into account.

Formal organizations, particularly those that are publicly supported, have no choice but to function to enforce the values of the overall society whether or not their stated goals so indicate. The goal of OEO was to bypass state and local political and economic institutions, a violation of representative and compromise laws of long standing. Nonetheless, OEO tried to implement its goal by programs that promoted the major societal values of commitment to work and to political equality.

Work groups, such as those that exist in factories, government, education, and even among human services workers, saw the actions of CAP as a threat, because if CAP were successful job opportunities for their own members could be limited. When individuals in these groups became aware of this possible threat to their financial security, they increased their activity to guarantee job security for their members.

At the same time, civil rights activities were going on. These included marches of various kinds and some civil disturbances. Members of residential neighborhoods saw these attempts to gain political equality as threats to the value of their homes and to the safety of their families. A cry for law and order was raised. Most of the civil rights activities were *not* at all related to CAP programs, but these programs were said to have caused the unrest because of their avowed goals of equal opportunity through political equality.

Through the operation of compromise law and representative law, equilibrium was reestablished. One wonders what the result of OEO and the rest of the war on poverty might have been if the federal planners had been more aware of the operation of representative and compromise law and had guided their promotional efforts accordingly.

At present, some remnants of the community action agencies exist, but they act mainly as arms of the local government, dispensing funds to conventional programs that are oriented primarily toward carrying out services aimed at economic maintenance or individual improvement as described in Chapters 8 and 9. For instance, these agencies are presently charged with the distribution of fuel subsidies for the poor. This is an economic maintenance service rather than a service to mitigate social differences.

Strategies for Provision of Services to Mitigate Social Differences

When human services professionals are employed in programs that endeavor to mitigate social and economic differences, they are often called community organization workers. They also use interview and group techniques, as discussed in Chapter 9, but they use these techniques quite differently. Instead of attempting to modify the self-concepts of the clients or assisting them to acquire skills to enhance their personal functioning, community organization professionals generally consider the people they work with to be competent, capable individuals who are hampered only by the society that surrounds them. The community organization professional uses his or her skills in interviewing and in group leadership to get individuals and groups to engage in the following strategies:

1. training
2. negotiation
3. compromise
4. arbitration
5. confrontation

Table 10.1 presents definitions and uses of these strategies in reference to the objective that is to be attained.

Training is not usually described as a strategy, but in this case it is; it is an important one, too, because it underlies the rest. Training can begin with simple literacy programs, but the goal is not necessarily to help the individual get a better job (although this may be a side effect); the major goal of all training is to encourage clients to learn more about their surroundings, to be able to read the newspapers, to learn how to get publicity that might be beneficial to them, to be able to read the laws that govern welfare programs, and to be able to read rental agreements and other contracts that have an effect on them. The training that the community organization professional

Table 10.1 / Range of Strategies Utilized to Mitigate Economic and Social Differences

Persuasion ⟶ Force

Training	Negotiation	Compromise*	Arbitration	Confrontation
Training and developing knowledge, skills, attitudes and leadership to:	Bargaining, conferring and discussing to reach agreement to	Adjusting, settling and mutually agreeing over differences, with concessions on both sides to	Settling of a dispute by outside party to:	Forcing boldly, defying, being antagonistic, engaging in hostile acts and opposing to
1. find and hold a job	1. develop jobs	1. develop "make work" programs when economy cannot guarantee jobs	1. force equal opportunity for all groups to employment—through use of courts if necessary	1. strike for more and better jobs
2. cooperate with others	2. run local programs	2. settle on some control over local programs	2. use federal or state agency to enforce representation on local boards	2. refuse to cooperate with local program; forcefully close the agency
3. know the local community	3. establish cooperation among local groups	3. establish a working relationship among local groups	3. utilize arbitrator to monitor wage demands, power struggles for control, accessibility to resources of community	3. battle local groups; demonstrations and counter demonstrations

4. understand power	4. obtain and improve educational services	4. get the best education available under the circumstances	4. use courts to guarantee integration and equality of school services;	4. vandalize schools; boycott schools; disrupt educational activities; take over the facilities
5. understand politics	5. develop and improve neighborhood services	5. accept neighborhood services not quite as good as those in other parts of the city, but improved from before	5. get one arm of government to force another arm to provide primary services to local neighborhood	5. riot; destroy property; harrass police and local businesses
6. understand the value of individual effort and how to direct it	6. make other welfare services more responsive to needs of poor	6. continue welfare programs, but not at a level to correct poverty	6. bring pressure from alderman to force housing authority to step up services	6. refuse to let welfare workers in neighborhood; demonstrate in streets; march to welfare offices, city hall, state capitol
7. disseminate to powerful community groups information on the nature of poverty and the reasons why its mitigation is for the welfare of all	7. develop housing programs of value to poor	7. work toward improved housing but realize that moving out is only way to get better housing	7. use bank examiners to get banks to stop redlining.	7. arson, destruction, vandalism; terrorize the defenseless; forays into well-to-do neighborhoods

* Note the equivocal nature of the term. It can also mean to endanger an individual's or group's interests.

† Adapted from R. LaPiere, *A Theory of Social Control*. New York: McGraw-Hill, 1954, Part III.

tries to promote is designed to provide clients with knowledge and skills that will increase the power of the groups to which they belong.

Human services professionals engaged in community organization are required to operate in the political arena more than do most other human services professionals. It is in the political setting that societal resources are allocated. For this reason, political procedures must be utilized when any group wants to assert a claim on an increased portion of those societal resources. Training in the political process is thus an important strategy for the community organization worker to impart to his or her clients. Only when this is accomplished can the other strategies be put to use.

The community organizational professional teaches the persons with whom he or she works how to use all five strategies. The worker's aim is not to lead the struggle, but to teach the clients to carry out the strategies on their own. The worker trys to move out of the picture entirely, even though this is sometimes difficult to do.

The strategies described in Table 10.1 are in order of their progression from emphasis on persuasion to the emphasis on force. The progression also reflects the way in which strategies move from emphasis on common interests to the emphasis on divisive or exploitative interests.

At present the first three strategies are the ones most used by community organization professionals. This reflects the current social condition wherein most community groups perceive that there are common interests that they share with other groups in the society. These include the value of work, individual reward for individual effort, opportunities for all citizens to better their circumstances, and protection from the harshest effects of events over which individuals have no control. The commitment to the social order is reflected by reliance on the first three strategies. Order is maintained through the function of representative and compromise law. This shows that at present most of the poor feel that their interests are more effectively protected by the preservation of the social order than by the disturbance of it that can occur when confrontation is used.

Confrontation still takes place, however. Cesar Chavez's drive for greater social and economic equality for the Mexican–American farm laborers in California is an example, but even his use of confrontation is sporadic. Confrontation is the least used of all the strategies of community organization. The fear of the use of coercive strategies forces contending groups to rely heavily on those strategies that emphasize the elements of persuasion. This is in marked contrast to strategies of other societies such as Italy, Spain, Ireland, Iran, or Lebanon, where the enforcement of the social order through the operation of representative and compromise law is weak and where groups relate to each other more extensively through the strategies that emphasize coercion and force.

It is important for human services professionals in community organization to understand the structures and processes that exist in the communities in which they carry out their activities. They can then adapt their techniques and strategies to achieve results that are in accord with the perceptions of the groups that contend for the available material and social resources of the society.

Summary

This chapter concentrated on programs that stemmed from the recognition that poverty has some societal causes and that it is not just the individual responsibility of the poor. These programs are based on two perceptions: (1) that the poor are poor because their cultural and social patterns are different from those groups who have higher rankings in the American stratification hierarchy and (2) that the poor are poor because they lack the power to grasp material and social resources for themselves. With these perceptions in mind, programs were developed to enable the poor themselves to obtain the desired goods and social standing that were available to more advantaged Americans. The programs to mitigate economic and social differences did not aim to work major changes in the American society but, rather, to make possible the "maximum feasible participation" of the poor in mainstream America and thus give the poor a fairer share of the benefits of society.

The strategies utilized range from training the poor in participatory social skills to the use of confrontation with the groups who control societal resources. The most used strategies emphasize training and cooperation rather than confrontation. Nonetheless, when differences run high, confrontation has been utilized.

The American society is so strongly oriented toward economic and social stability that the recent governmental (i.e., publicly supported) efforts to promote "maximum feasible participation" have largely disappeared. Most of the present programs to mitigate economic and social differences are sponsored by the affected groups themselves. Examples are the United Farm Workers under Cesar Chavez, the NAACP, the Urban League, the SCLC, and the National Organization for Women. Indeed, most of the progress in the mitigation of economic and social differences has been achieved by the organized efforts of the affected groups. Only the future will reveal whether governmental programs will be able to lend effective support to these efforts.

Chapter 11 will describe the ways in which the programs described in Chapters 8, 9, and 10 are translated into welfare services.

References

1. Clarke, H. *Principles and Practice of Social Work.* New York: Appleton, 1947, p. 94.
2. *The Wall Street Journal,* July 25, 1978, p. 1.
3. Clarke, H. *Op. cit.,* p. 34.
4. Alinsky, S. *Reveille for Radicals.* Chicago: Univ. of Chicago, 1964, ch. 1.
5. Fried, M. *The World of the Urban Working Class.* Cambridge, Mass.: Harvard U. P. 1973.

6. *The Wall Street Journal*, July 27, 1978, p. 1.

7. Bettmann, O. *The Good Old Days—They Were Terrible*. New York: Random House, 1974, p. 314.

8. Friedlander, W. *Introduction to Social Welfare*. Englewood Cliffs, N.J.: Prentice-Hall, 1974, p. 314.

9. Blake, P. *Form Follows Fiasco*. Boston: Little, Brown, 1974.

10. Sheppard, H., ed. *Poverty and Wealth in America*. Chicago: Quadrangle, 1970, p. 123.

11. Blake, P. *Op. cit.*, p. 154.

12 Friedlander, W. *Op. cit.*, p. 318.

13. Grosser, C. *New Directions in Community Organization*. New York: Praeger, 1976, pp. 96–100.

14. Magill, R. *Community Decision Making for Social Welfare*. New York: Academic Press, 1979, ch. 4.

15. *Ibid.*, ch. 4

part /three
The Work Place

chapter/11
Organization
of the
Work Setting

In the previous chapters we described the characteristics of society and of individuals, and we noted some of the ways in which society and individuals relate to each other. We discussed the local community, the human services professional, the manner in which poverty is perceived in America, the programs that are developed to deal with poverty, and the services that are provided under the auspices of these programs. However, we have not discussed the manner in which these values, definitions, groups, individuals, programs, and services operate so that when they are observed they can be identified as being a part of the American welfare enterprise.

Somehow all these seemingly vaguely related but disconnected ideas, patterns, and activities must be brought together so that they make sense to the parties concerned, be they politicians, human services professionals, other officials, taxpayers and other members of the general public, or the recipients themselves. This involves considerable work on the part of a large number of people. To make sense and to be useful, the work must be coordinated so that what one person does relates to what other people do, and so that the total work produced contributes to the achievement of an anticipated objective.

In other words, the work must be organized. This organized work takes place in a setting called an organization. This chapter describes the characteristics of the organizations that translate welfare programs into welfare services. It concentrates on the description of organizations that deal directly with recipients, even though the welfare enterprise also operates at state and federal levels. State and federal governments deal more with program development, resource generation, and political policy than they do with direct services. These levels of organization are as important as the local level, but it is at the local level where the human services professional meets the recipient.

This focal point of the whole welfare enterprise is the subject of this chapter. We will describe the local level of welfare organizations mainly from a structural perspective. We will show how structure is mandatory to welfare services and will point out the benefits realized from structure. We will also illustrate how the use of structure is a complex process that can yield results sometimes not intended by human services professionals.

Structure in Society

When dealing with the activities of humans, one must deal in abstractions. Stable relationships nevertheless exist. The relationships that exist among the various parts of a recognized activity are called structure. It is structure that makes it possible for people to act toward themselves and others in an orderly fashion. Structure exists on many levels. It exists between two persons (e.g., a married couple) as well as among the large numbers of people that may be engaged in the operation of a factory. Structure serves to furnish the means of dividing up the work that needs to be done. Structure makes it possible to distribute goods and services according to the preferences established by the values of the society. Structure makes it possible for humans to obtain predictability in their lives and thereby feel that they exert some control over what they do during the course of their existence.

The structure of human relationships is induced from noting the regularity of relationships that exist among people. Let us see how the concept of structure applies to the family. The nuclear family has a series of structural elements, such as parents and children. Within these elements there are subelements, such as husband and wife, oldest child and youngest child. These elements are also stratified, which makes it possible to assign statuses to them. In a patriarchal family, the husband would have the highest status, and the youngest child the lowest. In a matriarchal family, the mother would have the highest status. These statuses are often called *offices* because they are positions that are recognized by all members of the group. These offices command some degree of control over the activities of the group. The office of husband signifies some control to the wife, and vice versa. Father signifies a certain control to the children. The oldest child is expected to exercise some control over the younger children. So, with office comes responsibilities and, therefore, certain rights as well. Father is given a kind of respect that is different from the respect given to mother. In the patriarchal family, father is expected to reward and punish the children, but the punishment is meted out according to the respective place of the children in the family. Structure makes it possible for persons to see themselves in relation to others and to understand how to behave in relation to these others. Structure makes it possible to understand what one can or cannot do in specific situations and thereby to be able to operate as a social being. The more highly structured the situation wherein humans interact, the more highly controlled the situation, and the smaller the possibility for individualistic behavior that might be triggered by the isolated desires of a single person. Structure, then, also results from commonly accepted definitions of the elements of the situations and, if participated in by the members of the group according to these commonly held definitions, results in further development of structure that places even further constraints on the individualistic bent of the members of the group. Structure is therefore the means whereby social control is exercised.*

To understand the structure of human relationships, try to see them from the perspective of a kaleidoscope as opposed to a photograph. The arrangement of the elements in a photograph is fixed; they stay the same even if held upside down. In a kaleidoscope, the arrangement of the elements changes depending upon how the viewer holds the instrument. If turned or given a shake, some of the pieces will disappear and others will emerge. The viewer gets a different impression of the nature of the kaleidoscope even though it is the same instrument containing the same bits of colored material.

Social behavior should be considered from the vantage point of a kaleidoscope rather than a photograph. One can describe the family as an institution in which the young are indoctrinated with the values, rules, and specific practices that will enable them when grown to behave in a manner in keeping with the expectations that society has for its members. When all families are seen as preparing the young to participate in other social institutions, such as the economic institution, the institution of religion, the institution of marriage, and so on, the families are performing an institutional function.

From another perspective, the family can be seen as a group. In this case, one can describe the organization of the family according to its internal characteristics and describe the specific patterns of relationships among the members. One sees the existence of father, mother, and children and describes the ways in which these persons interact with each other in terms of the roles that they take in different situations.

Another perspective is the intergroup or community setting of the family. The family is then seen as one of a number of social situations in which individuals participate during the course of daily activities. One can

* For further elaboration of structure, see LaPiere.¹

describe the father as a husband in the family, a worker in the employment setting, a worshipper in a religious setting, or a bowler in a recreational setting.

In each case, the family is being described from a different perspective. The structure of welfare services can also be seen from these three perspectives: (1) institutional, (2) group or intraorganizational, and (3) community or interorganizational.

The next sections of the chapter will deal with these organizational perspectives.

Welfare as Institutional

American institutions can be divided into two categories: primary and secondary. Primary institutions are those that exist to achieve the major objectives of society. Secondary institutions assist primary institutions in the achievement of their objectives.

In American society the *primary* institutions are economic, political, and military.[2] Welfare is in the category of a *secondary* institution. It operates in conjunction with economic institutions to provide for transfer of resources from the haves to the have nots to concentrate upon the enforcement of the value of work to the poor, to provide services to enable individuals to adjust to their socioeconomic circumstances, and to provide services that mitigate the differences that exist among the various socioeconomic groupings. In all these examples, welfare services support the economic institution in American society.

Because welfare services are in the main publicly funded, they are subject to the control of the political institution of the society. We described in Chapter 10 how, when welfare services such as the Community Action Program became a perceived threat to their power, local officials moved to limit the power of CAP. Welfare services that do not support the operation of the political structure will in time be modified so that they do so. Therefore, public welfare programs and services reinforce the local political institutional structure, not the other way around. The welfare institution in America is value enforcing, norm enforcing, stability enforcing; it is *not* value generating, rule creating, or change facilitating.[3]

Welfare as Intraorganizational

By moving the kaleidoscope so that another structural perspective emerges, one can observe welfare organizations according to their intraorganizational or internal characteristics. There are two important structural categories of internal organizational characteristics: informal and formal. Informal organizations exist primarily for the support of their members. Formal organizations exist to accomplish a stated task. Families are called informal organizations because they exist to sustain the individuals that comprise them; welfare agencies are called *formal organizations* because they exist to provide services to a clientele that is external (though certainly related) to the organizations.

Some of the internal structural characteristics of formal organizations are:

1. role divisions, authority
2. role divisions, labor
3. stratification within role divisions by rank and office
4. formally stated objectives
5. published rules
6. delineation of membership
7. recruitment procedures
8. indoctrination procedures
9. rule enforcement procedures
10. informal structure in formal organizations

Formal organizational structure can be either personal or bureaucratic.* The personal form of formal organization is possible when members of the organization are able to perform their duties directly, on a face-to-face basis. When an organization becomes too large for this, impersonal methods of operation become necessary, and the organization takes on bureaucratic characteristics. Welfare organizations began as personal ones. While some still operate on this basis, most welfare organizations today have bureaucratic characteristics.**

There are two types of formal welfare organizations: public and private. Private organizations are currently overshadowed by the immensity of public welfare organizations. Ornati notes that in 1960, private giving amounted to 17 per cent of the overall financial outlay for welfare services in the United States.[5] The structure of both private and public welfare agencies is similar. Private agencies are usually smaller, and the work setting is more personal than at most public agencies.

We turn now to a discussion of the nine characteristics of internal structure of private and public welfare agencies, noting some of the similarities and differences.

* For a detailed analysis of the differences between personal and bureaucratic structure, see LaPiere[4]

** A recent type of private agency is the *proprietary* agency. This is a personal form of organization incorporated by either a single individual or by a group of individuals to perform a service such as counseling, medical care, group home care, day care, legal services, and so on. These agencies exist to make a profit for their owners. They contract with public agencies and provide services for a fee. Many of the scandals that have occurred recently around welfare services involve the fees paid to the proprietary agencies for the services that they are supposed to have performed.

The emergence of the proprietary agency, in spite of the anomaly of appropriating public funds to support a profit-making agency, is related to the high value ascribed to private, profit-related activity as opposed to the low value and suspicion that is often ascribed to public services.

Role Division, Authority

All organizations have substructures that exist to control the resources and activities of the organization and to facilitate the work. In the private welfare agency, control is usually exercised by a board of directors. In the public agency, responsibility for control lies with a public board to which the administrators of the organization are responsible.

The board of directors of the *private* agency is composed of individuals who represent the interests of the sponsoring unit. If this is a religious denomination, there will be members from that group on the board. If the private organization is nonsectarian, as for instance are most family service agencies, the board members will be chosen from among prominent individuals in the local business community. In addition, most of these boards have members that sit on one or more of the committees of the fund-raising arm of private welfare, the local United Fund, or United Way organization.

The United Fund of a community is where the ultimate control of private welfare resides. The head of the United Fund board is usually a part of the local economic elite, perhaps a senior officer in a bank or an executive in a prominent business. Each year funds for private welfare are solicited from the metropolitan area, with business enterprises contributing the major share. Funds are allocated to the private agencies according to the requests that are submitted. Most of the time care is taken that requests do not run counter to local business interests. If they do, it is unlikely that that portion of the request will be honored. For instance, if a private welfare agency were to ask for funds to strengthen an antiredlining program that it had developed to oppose the policy of lending agencies who have refused to lend money to persons desiring to purchase homes in blighted areas, the agency would probably find the funds stricken from the request. United Fund boards tend to steer away from community organization services. They concentrate on programs to assist persons to adapt to circumstances with which they must cope in the local community. These might be family problems, emotional difficulties, lack of leisure skills, and issues of adaptation of ethnic and racial groups in the local community. Most of the funds are for services that are frequently offered to the middle class or the temporarily poor who wish to avoid the stigma of being associated with public welfare agencies. Funds are rarely used for income transfer.

When one looks at the composition of the boards of the private welfare agencies, one finds individuals who serve on more than one agency board and also on the United Fund board. This "interlocking directorate" tends to guarantee the maintenance of authority from the United Fund to the welfare organizations that use United Fund resources. It also helps to guarantee that any administrators appointed will have characteristics that will inhibit them from advocating programs that run counter to local economic interests.

United Fund leaders often use the annual fund-raising activity to determine the potentialities of younger business persons. The following newspaper article illustrates how this is done and how the authority structure of the business leadership is merged into the authority structure of private welfare organizations.

United Way Gets "Loan"

BY THOMAS HEINEN OF THE JOURNAL STAFF

Meet the LE.

For those of you who don't have your doctorates yet in 20th century acronyms, the letters stand for "loaned executive."

No, an LE is not a person who sits in judgment on your applications for home and auto loans. That's someone else.

What the LEs really are is a key part of stepped up efforts by the United Way of Greater Milwaukee to increase contributions and outrace inflation.

Although the 1978 United Way campaign won't officially tap you on the shoulder until Sept. 18, the 32 LEs who will help form the backbone of the fund drive started their training this week.

For the most part, loaned executives are just that—management level people who are loaned to United Way. They help coordinate the 20,000 volunteers who work on the fund drive, and they perform numerous tasks that ease solicitation efforts at area companies.

Most of the executives were described by United Way officials as rising young managers who have been tabbed by their companies for bigger and better things. The volunteer work helps the community while broadening the executives' experience and skills.

From United Way's perspective, the beauty of the program is that the firms providing LEs pay the LEs salaries while they work full time for United Way for three months.

Donald K. Mundt, executive vice president of Northwestern Mutual Life Insurance Co., persuaded the companies to participate in the program.

"AN EYE OPENER"

Although LEs have been used in Milwaukee since 1961, when six executives participated, their number had increased to only 24 as of 1977. "It was kind of an eye opener to see what cities relatively our size were doing," Mundt said.

He toured several cities earlier this year with 1978 campaign Chairman Willard Davidson and other United Way officials.

For example, Minneapolis used 90 LEs last year, and Cleveland had 80. Chicago had 60 for six months each, Mundt said, and some companies in those cities supplied as many as five executives.

As a result, Mundt came back and started knocking on the doors of the chief executives of companies large enough to spare an executive. He got LEs from 29 companies, four of which had never loaned an executive before.

Mundt also got three of those firms to loan two executives each. That's the first time that has happened in Milwaukee. Not surprisingly, one of those firms was his own.

LAWYERS, TOO

Mundt also homed in on law firms, getting quality if not quantity.

In Cincinnati, the five principal law firms in town each give a loaned executive, he said.

In Milwaukee, Mundt got one firm, Foley & Lardner, to participate. What surprised him was that Joseph E. Rapkin, a senior partner, wanted to volunteer himself.

Although Rapkin's name wasn't included in the list of 32 LEs undergoing training this week, he is scheduled to work part time and lead of a group of LEs who will help volunteers solicit from employees of the Milwaukee Public School System.

After a luncheon and orientation session Tuesday at the Visiting Nurse Association of Milwaukee, 759 N. Van Buren St., the 9 women and 23 men who will be LEs visited other agencies and groups that receive United Way funding.

LE's IMPRESSIONS

Afterward, they shared some of their impressions.

"It's kind of exciting because it's completely different," said Hugh Tollack, 26, a senior tax specialist with Peat, Marwick, Mitchell and Co. "It doesn't really relate to income tax."

C.T. Joupp, 53, a coordinator of special services for Blue Cross-Blue Shield, echoed the views of some of the executives after touring a Latin community center on the South Side.

"They're doing a heck of a tremendous amount of good in this neck of the woods," he said, "and that's something a number of people out there don't know about. We're going to tell them."[6]

In most cases, the authority for *public* welfare organizations rests in a local board that operates at the county level. Members of this board are appointed by the political leader of the county (the county executive if there is one) with the approval of the elected representatives on the county board. Sometimes the county board appoints the welfare board directly. Interestingly, there is usually little overlap between membership of the county boards of public welfare and the boards of the United Funds or private agencies. Whereas the membership of these boards is recruited from the business community, boards of public welfare are usually recruited from the ranks of labor leadership, political allies, or friends. The local public welfare board appoints the administrators of the public agencies, usually from the ranks of the personnel of the agencies who have civil service certification. This ensures that the administrators have had long experience with the routine operation of the organization and also tends to keep programs going according to long-established procedures.

Local public welfare boards have many constraints on their authority. Much of the funding for services comes from the state or federal level, and there are guidelines attached to each expenditure, usually in the form of federal and state statutes and rules and regulations. Many times the boards are merely pass-through bodies having only the accounting function for expenditures that are made according to the dictates of the federal or state authorities. Often the local public welfare boards are held responsible by critics for programs that they have neither planned nor approved.

Each private agency has its own individual board that defines the policy or character of the services given and oversees its operation. Individual public welfare agencies have no comparable boards. The welfare department that dispenses funds and provides services for dependent children, the aged, or the handicapped; the mental health agency that provides services to persons with emotional difficulties; the public hospital that serves the medically indigent— all operate under the authority of some type of board of public welfare. There are many variations in the way in which these boards are constituted. Some states have only one statewide board. Others have boards in every county. Some may even have a city board, although this is now rare. In many cases, the location of the board may be at some distance from the place where the agency is itself located.

The important point to keep in mind in regard to authority, however, is that private welfare agencies are controlled by the economic leadership of the local community, whereas public welfare agencies are controlled by political leadership.[7] In both cases, programs, policies, and goals are determined by persons who are external to the agency actually providing the service.

Role Divisions, Labor

The personnel of the *private* welfare organization who actually do the work of providing services to the clientele usually have a professional degree or its equivalent. They tend to specialize according to both the category of service and the category of clientele. For example, a worker might specialize on issues within families but concentrate on the children in the families. Or one might specialize on issues of emotional difficulties but concentrate on adults, perhaps even limiting activities to the adult male or to the adult female. Workers in private organizations usually belong to professional groups such as the National Association of Social Workers, the American Psychological Association, or the Family Service Association of America. Rarely do they belong to unions or similar groups that deal directly with working conditions. They tend to identify with their professions first and their work organizations second. They are oriented toward providing services to individuals or groups with "problems," and they concentrate on adapting their clients to society rather than on providing income assistance, funds for housing, or medical care or on assisting members of poor neighborhoods to organize to eliminate the conditions that keep them poor and underprivileged. Workers in private organizations negotiate directly and independently with their employers in regard to their employment and working conditions. Workers in private welfare organizations see themselves as a homogenous group of independent professional entepreneurs.

Workers in *public* agencies perform a wider variety of tasks than do those in private welfare organizations. These range from certifying financial eligibility of prospective recipients through managing the financial assistance once it is given, visiting the home and neighborhood of the recipients, appearing in court with recipients when necessary, to providing services similar to those provided by workers in private agencies.

Workers in public welfare organizations also have a wider variety of qualifications. Some hold professional degrees; others have not completed high school. At all levels, federal, state, and local, workers are classified fairly rigidly according to civil service categories. The commission assigns them classifications such as case aide, welfare worker, social worker, or nurse, which defines the salary and the type of work that the worker will be permitted to do. Salary and working conditions are rarely negotiated individually. The case aid is usually the lowest classification; senior social worker, teacher, nurse, psychologist, physician, and so on are usually the highest.

Those in lower civil service categories tend to identify with the organization that employs them; those in the higher categories are more likely to identify with other professionals. Many workers in lower classifications belong to employee unions such as the Association of Federal, State, and County Municipal Employees (AFSCME) or a counterpart thereof. Higher-level workers tend to limit themselves to membership in the various professional associations.

Stratification Within Role Divisions by Rank and Office

Rank and office are characteristics of positions that members of all groups hold. These are strictly defined in highly structured groups such as welfare organizations, particularly in the public welfare setting.

Rank is the authority that an individual holds that permits the individual to do one task rather than another. Rank determines position and relationships relative to other members of the organization; it does *not* authorize the person to determine the actions of other members of the organization. Seniority, age, sex, and achievement are the usual criteria for determining rank.

Office is the position that bears responsibility for some aspect of the operation of the group. Office provides the holder with power over others and demands consequent respect because of this. Persons are usually appointed to a certain office by those in greater authority. This might be done because of their rank, their ability, or their management skills or simply because they follow orders and present no threat to the appointers.

Rank and office may be combined in the same person, but this is not necessarily the case. It is possible for a person with high rank to be under the authority of a person with lower rank and higher office. The clearest example of the difference between rank and office can be found in the military. Let us consider two persons both holding the rank of commander in the U.S. Navy. They are both in the same subunit, a squadron. One has been in the service longer than the other and receives more pay because of this seniority. However, it is possible for the person with less seniority to hold the office of skipper of the squadron and for the person with more seniority to be third in the line of authority, perhaps holding the lesser office of engineering officer. From the standpoint of rank, each claims the same privileges in the facilities provided and is relieved from certain odious tasks. Both can claim seats of privileged locations in the wardroom, the movies, or in transportation vehicles. Neither will have to stand in line for pay, meals, and so on. The list of privileges that rank confers is long, especially when contrasted to those held by someone with rank of seaman recruit. Still each commander holds a different office. The commander with the higher office of skipper has authority and power over the engineering officer and also has greater responsibility. The numerous, possible combinations of rank and office in an organization are part of the structure by which organizational members relate to each other.[8]

Rank and office are encountered in welfare organizations even though they may not be as easy to recognize as they are in the military. For instance, we stated that one determinant of rank is sex. That men have a higher rank in the marketplace than do women is reflected both in the higher pay that men receive for equal work and in the concentration of men in occupations with highest status and remuneration.[9, 10] (This is one of the reasons for women's rights organizations.) In the early days when welfare organizations were first formed, women occupied the top offices. Men were in a minority; they served as employees with both low rank and low office. However, as the human services professions achieved higher status and higher pay scales, men have been attracted in greater numbers. In recent years, men have replaced women in the highest offices of welfare organizations. The influence of rank according to sex in this case takes precedence over rank according to seniority.It has deeply affected the ratio of men to women in the offices held in welfare enterprises.

The office of supervisor is, in many ways, peculiar to welfare agencies. There is no counterpart in the organizations that control the work of professions such as medicine, theology, law, or higher education. In welfare agencies, however, the workers, even those with graduate degrees, are subject to some form of direct organizational control. Their work is overseen by the person who holds the office of supervisor. The person may actually be called supervisor, but in some agencies other names exist for this office. The supervisor may be younger, less experienced, and newer to the organization and thus of inferior rank than the workers being supervised.

The following excerpt from a staff manual of a family service agency illustrates some of the ways in which workers are stratified in a private welfare agency. In this case, employees are classified by two criteria: the amount of time actually spent on the job each week and the rank and/or office held. Note that the office of supervisor is not listed. This does not mean that no supervision takes place; it means only that the office of supervisor is not assigned to a particular classification.

Document 11.1 / Staff Manual Family Service Association

Introduction

The personnel policies and practices of the Family Service Association are based on the agency's aim to provide the best possible service to clients and the community. Sound personnel practices are conducive to a high quality of professional service since employment conditions have a direct bearing on staff performance and morale.

In the formulation of personnel practices, the Board, Executive Director, and staff have both unique and shared responsibilities deriving from their respective functions and competence. The major functions of these three groups are, respectively, policy making, administration, and practice. The agency's Board has responsibility for consideration of and approval of personnel policies. The Executive Director offers leadership in both the development and implementation of these policies in relation to Agency program. The staff has responsibility for contributing to these policies as they relate to professional practice and individual professional development. No one of these groups can discharge its primary responsibilities without collaborating with the others.

The Board of Directors has delegated to the Executive Director authority over the employment and administration of personnel and charged him with the responsibility of implementing the Agency's personnel policies. In doing so, the Executive Director may exercise discretion flexibly to facilitate the Agency's functioning, all consistent with the intent of the Board of Directors as evidenced in the Personnel Policies.

DEFINITIONS

Employee classifications, for policy purposes, are defined as follows:

A. *Employee*—any person who receives a salary or wage from Family Service.
   1. Full-time—an employee whose work averages at least 40 hours per week.
   2. Part-time—an employee whose work averages at least 20 hours per week but less than full-time.
   3. Hourly—an employee whose average hours worked are fewer than 20 hours per week.
   4. Temporary full-time—an employee whose work averages at least 40 hours per week and who is employed to complete only a specific project (or projects).
   5. Temporary part-time—an employee whose work averages fewer than 40 hours per week and who is employed to complete only a specific project (or projects)
B. *Classifications*
   1. Case Aide—a direct service employee holding less than a Bachelor's Degree or its equivalent—UCS Classification 7 or 8.
   2. Case Worker—a direct service employee possessing a Bachelor's Degree or its equivalent, but not a Master's Degree or its equivalent— UCS Classification 9.
   3. Extern (Family Counselor I)—a direct service employee holding at least a Master's Degree or its equivalent in social work or a related field, UCS Classification 10.
   4. Senior Staff (Family Counselor II, III)—a direct service employee holding at

Excerpted from *Staff Manual* Family Service Association. Milwaukee, WI: 1973.

least a Master's Degree or its equivalent in social work or a related field and who meets the requirements of UCS Classification 11 or 12.

5. Program Director—direct service personnel designated as such by the Administration and who meet the requirements of UCS Classification 13.
6. Associate Director—personnel designated as such by the Executive Director and who meet the requirements of UCS Classification 14.
7. Executive Director— the Agency's principal administrative officer, designated by the Board of Directors pursuant to the requirements of FSAA and unclassified by UCS.

The alliteration of rank and office is similar in public and private welfare organizations except that in public agencies rank and office are even more highly structured than in private agencies. The public agencies are larger and more impersonal, and they need more formal stratification of the authority substructure within the major role divisions than do private agencies. In a public agency there will probably be a chief administrator and a variety of subadministrative offices. There might be deputy administrators for personnel, for budget, for the physical plant, for children's services, for services to the aging, and so on. The chief welfare administrator often reports to another administrator who is employed by the local public welfare board to oversee the operation of all the agencies in the area under its control, such as hospitals, detention homes, nursing homes, mental institutions, and so on. Often the administrator of an agency will have more education, greater seniority, and the like and thus will outrank the administrator employed by the public board. One has the rank, but the other has the office.

Within the public agency, strict supervision is maintained. Each division will have its coterie of supervisors who direct the operation of the workers who deliver the programs to recipients. The authority structure of welfare organizations is necessary to ensure that resources match the services and are available when needed and that services carry out the aims of the dominant publics. Once the authority structure is established, it is difficult to modify the nature of the services offered, because the structure of authority enforces stability of intraorganizational relationships.

Formally Stated Objectives

All formal organizations have some sort of written statement that spells out the reasons for their existence, what they purport to do, and how the objectives may be achieved.

In private agencies, these come from variety of sources. The most general come from associations of the agencies, for instance, the Family Association of America or the United Way of America. But each agency employs professionals who probably belong to a professional association such as NASW (National Association of Social Workers), which also has stated objectives. If the agency is affiliated with a religious denomination such as Catholic Charities or the Lutheran Social Services, the stated objectives will be influenced by the denomination that provides the financial support. But these agencies also receive some of their funding from the United Fund, which also has its own stated objectives. To put it another way, the stated objectives of private welfare agencies often contribute to the hodgepodge of services; they do not clear them up.

The following excerpts illustrate some national and local objectives that govern the operation of a family service agency. Note the general nature of the stated objectives at the national level and the specific nature of the stated objectives at the local level.

Document 11.2 / National Objectives: Optimal Social Functioning

THIS BROAD SOCIAL GOAL IS TO ENABLE INDIVIDUALS TO FUNCTION IN SOCIETY AT THE OPTIMAL LEVEL OF THEIR CAPACITIES AND POTENTIAL. THIS INVOLVES PROVISION OF OPPORTUNITIES FOR PERSONAL DEVELOPMENT OF THE INDIVIDUAL, OPPORTUNITIES FOR SELF-FULFILLMENT AND HIS OR HER SOCIAL FUNCTIONING AT HOME, AMONG FRIENDS AND ACQUAINTANCES, AT WORK, AT PLAY, AND IN THE LARGER COMMUNITY IN GENERAL. THE SERVICES SYSTEMS ARE THUS GEARED TO PRESERVING AND STRENGTHENING INDIVIDUAL AND FAMILY LIFE AND TO CREATING AND PROMOTING CONDITIONS CONDUCIVE TO PERSONAL GROWTH, ENABLING INDIVIDUALS TO LEAD A PERSONALLY SATISFYING AND ENRICHING AND SOCIALLY USEFUL LIFE, IN HARMONY WITH FAMILY, FRIENDS, COLLEAGUES, AND IN PEACEFUL CO-EXISTENCE WITH FELLOW HUMAN BEINGS.

INDIVIDUAL AND FAMILY LIFE SERVICES SYSTEM
System consists of services aimed at the preservation, strengthening, and restoration of families; provision of family substitute and family supplementary services; and a variety of individual and family auxiliary services to assist them in their normal social functioning.

FAMILY PRESERVATION AND STRENGTHENING SERVICE
The Family Preservation and Strengthening Service encompasses programs designed to assist families and individual members of a family unit whose social functioning has been or might be impaired, for one or more reasons such as marital conflict, disturbed parent–child relationships, boyfriend–girlfriend relationships and who, because of societal conditions, personality, or relationship problems, experience or may experience some stress. The primary objective of the programs offered under this service is to preserve, strengthen, and, where possible, restore the family unit.

COUNSELING
Counseling (Casework, or Casework Counseling) is a program which uses the casework method (i.e., a professional relating to a client via interview, talking, discussion,

Excerpted from *UWASIS II*. Alexandria, Va: United Way of America, 1973.

and lending a sympathetic ear) to advise and to enable families and individuals within a family unit or individuals not living as part of a family to come to grips with and to resolve emotional problems or temporary stresses encountered by them. Under this program, a counselor helps his or her client with an experience or opportunity in which the client can express his or her attitudes and feelings about a problem of social functioning and can gain a new perspective through discussion of possible means of handling it. Counseling may be on a one-to-one basis or on a group basis and may be conducted by volunteers under the supervision of professional staff. Program elements include some or all of the following: counseling children; counseling families; counseling out-of-wedlock pregnant girls; counseling unwed parents and couples; counseling adoptive parents; counseling divorced couples.

Document 11.3 / Local Objectives: Family Service Association

1. What is the agency's overall purpose?
   The principal goal of the agency is to facilitate optimal family and personal development through the provision of direct services to families and individuals, the development of new knowledge about the provision of those services, and the training and education of others serving families.
2. What are the Board approved agency operational goals for the current fiscal year?
   22,100 hours—Family Counseling
   2,000 hours—Family Life Education and Service Consultation
   2,500 hours—Vocational Counseling and Job Placement
   2,000 hours—Budget Counseling
   34,200 hours—Family Homemaking
   28,800 hours—Adult Homemaking
   4,050 hours—Protective Services for Handicapped Adults
3. Give address and name of person in charge for all locations of agency programs:
   John Smith, Executive Director
   Family Service Association
   Newtown, U.S.A.
4. What intake or admission policies will be used to determine who will be served?
   Applicants for agency service from Family Service will not be denied service for reasons of race, sex, color, creed, age, national origin, mental or physical disability, inability to pay or because of their previous treatment history.
5. How will volunteers contribute to the agency during this year? Number   420   hrs.
   Service/Month _____. Job Responsibilities and Qualifications:
   At least 40 volunteers manning Parents Helpline trained by the Hotline Council and supervised by a Family Counselor.
6. Will emergency services by available? If so, when and how?
   Emotional Crises—Family Counseling Dept., M-F
                    Parents Helpline, M-Sat., 9AM-11PM
   Survival Needs: Travelers Aid Dept., M-F
   Overindebtedness: Consumer Budget Counseling, M-F
   Children and Handicapped Adults needing in-home services, M-F

Adapted from *1977 Proposed Program Support* Milwaukee, WI: United Way of Greater Milwaukee, Inc, 1977.

7. Will facilities be fully utilized during the next year—if not, why not?
   Yes.
8. What fund raising activities is the agency planning for this coming year?
   None outside of annual dues of $5 for corporation members.
9. Explain restrictions on use of funds from other sources, estimate when final allocation from other sources will be made:
   Endowment Fund Earnings—No restriction
   Purchase of Service—SSI recipients, Dec. 1976
   51.42—Mental Health clients, Spring 1977
10. Attach copy of fee schedule and policy for agency and/or each program.

In the case of public agencies, the most general statement of objectives is contained in the statutes establishing the program at the federal level. Implementing objectives are developed by the executive department responsible for the program especially when the legislation is vague. The federal government has regional centers through which the funds for programs pass on their way to the states and local communities. These regions have subobjectives that apply to the region served.

States, counties, and cities all pass laws and ordinances to govern the establishment and operation of local agencies. From these laws and ordinances, further statements of objectives of the programs are drawn. The Comprehensve Employment and Training Act of 1973 (CETA) has this statement of overall purpose:

> It is the purpose of this Act to provide job training and employment opportunities for economically disadvantaged, unemployed, and underemployed persons, and to assure that training and other services lead to maximum employment opportunities and enhance self-sufficiency by establishing a flexible and decentralized system of Federal, State, and Local programs.[11]

There are eight sections of the act that spell out the rules for the operation of CETA programs. In federal terminology, these sections are called "titles." Seven titles describe the different programs and one covers the administrative regulations. Title I covers a long list of potential manpower services. Section 101 of Title I reprinted here, illustrates how specific objectives are written into the statutes as part of the design of the program.

Document 11.4 / Title I—Comprehensive Manpower Services

DESCRIPTION OF PROGRAM
   Sec. 101. It is the purpose of this title to establish a program to provide comprehensive manpower services throughout the Nation. Such program shall include the develop-

From *Laws of the 93rd Congress* 1st session. Washington, D.C.: G.P.O., 1973. P. 927,928.

ment and creation of job opportunities and the training, education, and other services needed to enable individuals to secure and retain employment at their maximum capacity. Comprehensive manpower services may include, but shall not be limited to, programs and activities designed to carry out the purpose of this title, such as—

(1) outreach to make persons aware of the availability of manpower services and persuade them to use such services,
(2) assessment of the individual's needs, interests, and potential in the labor market and referral to appropriate employment, training, or other opportunities,
(3) orientation, counseling, education, and institutional skill training to prepare the individual to enter the labor market or to qualify for more productive job opportunities,
(4) training on the job,
(5) payments or other inducements to public or private employers to expand job opportunities, but payments to employers organized for profit shall not exceed the difference between the costs of recruiting, training, and providing supportive services for low-income persons and those regularly employed,
(6) services to individuals to enable them to retain employment,
(7) payment of allowances to persons in training for which they receive no remuneration and payment of such allowances for transportation, subsistence, or other expenses incurred in participating in manpower services or employment as are necessary to enable the individual to participate therein,
(8) supportive services to enable individuals to take advantage of employment opportunities, including necessary health care and medical services, child care, residential support, assistance in securing bonds, or any other necessary assistance incident to employment, and any other service needed to participate in employment or manpower services,
(9) development of information concerning the labor market and activities, such as job restructuring, to make it more responsive to objectives of the manpower services program,
(10) manpower training, employment opportunities, and related services conducted by community-based organizations,
(11) transitional public service employment programs, and
(12) any programs authorized by part A of title III and by title IV of this Act.

The complete CETA law that describes all eight titles, the amount of money to be appropriated, and the many ways that the money will be channeled to recipients take some fifty pages in the *Laws of the 93rd Congress* as printed by the government printing office.

Published Rules

Formal organizations have manuals of rules that govern the activities of those who work in the organization. Welfare organizations do this when it is felt that it is necessary to state specifically what workers are supposed to do in the variety of work circumstances to which they are exposed. The more controversial the program or the more open it is to public scrutiny, the more likely there is to be a written manual that states the procedures that workers are supposed to follow. This is done more to protect the agency from harm than to protect the clients or even the workers.

The following excerpt from the manual of a family service agency shows the detail that can exist. Note that the rules are not limited to contact with clients but that they cover such internal matters as use of kitchen facilities and funds for expressions of sympathy.

Document 11.5 / Staff Manual Family Service Association

REVIEW PROCEDURE

For the proper operation of the Agency, all staff members must articulate problems they perceive within the Agency. To accomplish this effectively, staff members must use regular Agency channels for the description of problems. To insure the effective and beneficial review of your suggestions or objections, follow the following procedure:

A. Case aides, Case workers and Externs must first discuss problems with their immediate supervisor.

B. Senior Staff members must (1) discuss their problems with any supervisor, staff consultant, Program Director, Associate Director or the Executive Director; (2) present a problem for discussion at any Agency subgroup; or (3) request that Agency administration call a voluntary meeting of all staff members concerned with the problem.

C. If a staff member is dissatisfied with the resolution of the problem recommended or effected by either of the prior steps, and if he has not done so already, he must discuss the problem with the Executive Director.

D. If any staff member is dissatisfied with the resolution of the problem recommended or effected by any of the prior steps, he may present a written description of the problem to the President of the Board of Directors, with a copy to the Executive Director. At his discretion, the President of the Board of Directors may submit the problem to the Board of Directors, with or without review by any committee designated by the President or the Board, or may accept the resolution of the problem reached at a previous step in the above procedure and shall advise the staff member accordingly.

For any problem submitted for review to the Executive Director or Board of Directors, the Agency will provide a written decision and an explanation of the reasons therefor to the employee submitting the problem.

ADMINISTRATION
A. HOURS
The Agency is open from 8:00 a.m. to 9:00 p.m.—Mondays and Wednesdays
                          8:00 a.m. to 7:00 p.m.—Tuesdays and Thursdays
                          8:00 a.m. to 5:00 p.m.—Fridays

Adapted from *Staff Manual*, Family Service Association. Milwaukee WI: 1973

B. COFFEE BREAKS

1. Material cost must be borne by the consumers and should be as equitably distributed as possible. Price is $.05 per cup. This can be paid on a per cup basis daily or weekly in keeping with the consumer's estimate.
2. Two 60-cup urns of coffee will be prepared daily, if required, starting at 9:00 a.m. A smaller urn of hot water will be available for other beverages.
3. The use of the paper cups will be confined to the Staff Lounge.
4. Staff must exercise care regarding the appearance and cleanliness of the building if coffee is carried outside of the Staff Lounge or meeting rooms.
   a. For meetings held elsewhere, coffee should be served in the thermos jugs. Thermos jugs, priced at $.50 each, may be drawn from the urn and paid for on a cash basis.
   b. Those wishing to drink coffee in their offices must provide their own coffee mugs.
   c. Coffee for client groups will be paid for from the Agency's "petty cash." In this case, paper cups will be used in meeting rooms.

C. AGENCY'S KITCHEN

The Kitchen was not intended for the regular use of staff and should be used sparingly. The kitchen *may not* be used by staff on days of luncheon meetings being held at the Agency.

D. COURTESY FUND

In accord with staff desire, the committee responsible for handling the fund will observe the following principles:

1. The fund will be used for expression of staff sympathy at time of illness, death, or best wishes at termination of employment.
2. The funds will be maintained by annual staff contributions of $3.00 per member, subject to additional levies as needed. New staff members may contribute on a pro-rated basis.
3. A member of the committee will be responsible for collecting and maintaining the fund.
4. A plant or flowers ranging from $5 to $10 will be sent to a hospitalized staff member.
5. A plant, flowers, or memorial in like amount, depending upon designation of the individual concerned, will be sent in connection with death of immediate staff, spouse, or children or parents of single staff member or person in lieu of parents.
6. Best wishes will be extended upon termination of employment with dessert and coffee during lunch hour. After three years, a gift of $5-25, proportionate to tenure (including retirement) will also be given.
7. Staff recognizes that the committee must exercise discretion in handling the fund and that individuals are free to express sympathy or best wishes in their own way if they desire.

E. PERSONAL CONTACT WITH CLIENTS

Normally, support personnel with the exception of the switchboard/reception area and case aides in dealing with their own clients, will have very little opportunity to have personal contact with clients coming to the Agency for counseling. For the most part, the only personal relationship which exists in terms of clients will be between the client's counselor and the client, himself.

If the occasion should arise for you to have personal contact with a client who is not in counseling with you, please keep in mind the following:

1. Be pleasant and courteous at all times.
2. Give information regarding Agency facilities, hours, etc., when requested.
3. Do not carry on conversations with clients. Keep any contact you have with clients short and impersonal.
4. Do not discuss counselors or case records with any client or anyone outside the Agency.
5. Except in a learning situation, do not request information from counselors regarding their clients.
6. Do not discuss case records you may be typing with staff or with others outside the Agency. If you get in the habit of casually discussing client's cases, it becomes too easy to divulge confidential information to those who ethically should not have access to such information.
7. Keep conversation regarding clients out of the Staff Lounge.
8. Do not discuss clients in the hallways.
9. Do not socialize with fellow staff members in the hallways.
10. Keep your personal conduct on a professional level in the hallways or other areas where clients may, or could, be present.

Manuals of public agencies are similar to private agency manuals, except that they are more extensive and more detailed.

Delineation of Membership

Formal organizations distinguish their members from nonmembers. In the military this is done by uniforms with their many bars, patches, medals, and so on. A member of a mental health or medical organization might wear a white coat. In a religious organization, the cassock, habit, or clerical collar signifies membership. Waitresses, bus drivers, the police, employees in all kinds of organizations wear uniforms or articles of clothing like a jacket so that their membership in the organization may be instantly recognized both by the public and by other members of the organization. Some organizations spend large sums of money to promote the public's trust in a particular mark of membership. ("You can trust your car to the man who wears the star," for example.)

Members of welfare organizations rarely wear uniforms of any sort unless they are also members of occupational categories such as the medical or religious ones. This does not mean, however, that members of welfare organizations go unrecognized. Membership in an organization can also be delineated by the development of a vocabulary that is intelligible only to the members. Physicians separate themselves from patients by describing ailments and treatments in terms that few patients can understand. Human services professionals also develop a specialized language with such terms as "eligibility," "oral dependency needs," "transference," and "ego." Arrangements of letters take on meaning in this language: HEW, DHHS, AFDC, SDS, TA. Some program names look like words but are really acronyms: VISTA, BECOME, ACTION. Members know what these mean. They know the grant numbers under which they work and talk of a "J-6-11" as familiarly as if it were a member of the family. Members of welfare organizations also sprinkle their conversation with references to Title XIX or Title XX or other titles in the public laws and are confident that members will know what they are talking about but that few outside the organization will. Even though they wear no conspicuous badges or uniforms, a knowledgeable person can soon discover to which welfare organization particular workers belong just by listening to them talk.

Regardless of uniform or argot, delineation of membership in most organizations is actually accomplished by the setting of exacting standards that the prospective member must meet. To become a member, one must hold a certain certificate or degree, pass certain tests, or have spent a specified amount of time in training. This is done to guarantee that the new member will be able to perform according to the expectations of the organization. At present, much of this preparation for membership is carried out in educational institutions.

Recruitment Procedures

Formal organizations do not have a means of guaranteeing perpetual membership as do families or communities, so they must commit some of their resources to replenish their membership. Recruitment procedures are carefully formalized to make sure that the new recruit will contribute to the enhancement of the organization and not to its detriment. Each level in the organization has requirements for membership, such as age, education, sex, experience, previous accomplishments, and good references from members of other organizations. Private welfare organizations usually hold a series of interviews to assess the recruit's suitability. Public organizations usually combine a written examination with a panel interview under the auspices of the civil service commission. The commission certifies two or three qualified candidates to the hiring official who then chooses which one he or she thinks will be best for the job.

Two examples of position announcements follow. The first example includes the entire announcement, even though it deals with positional vacancies other than "social service." It illustrates the detail with which the requirements for applicants are spelled out. The first section deals with qualifications and application procedures pertaining to all applicants. It concludes with a section containing additional requirements pertaining only to social service positions.

The second position announcement describes a vacancy in a county agency.

Document 11.6 / State Career Candidate Vacancy Bulletin

The State Career Candidate Bulletin is a biweekly listing of entry-level professional positions that have recently become vacant. Each listing outlines job duties, location, starting pay, qualification requirements, contact deadline date and various background and personal factors preferred by the employing department. *Approximately 800 positions will be filled through these listings during the next twelve months.* The qualifications for entry-level professional positions filled through this bulletin are graduation from a four-year college or university accredited by a regional accrediting association recognized by the Council on Postsecondary Accreditation or an equivalent combination of education and relevant experience. A college degree is mandatory for positions requiring licensure or registration by law and college graduation is required to obtain the license or registration. Candidates completing their degree or equivalent within the next six months will also be considered. Read carefully each position vacancy description that is of interest. The listing will describe the procedures required of you to be considered for the position. These may vary by position. *You will be considered for employment only if you meet the qualifications as described in this biweekly bulletin.* Candidates who possess an accredited four year degree but not the stated major for non-technical vacancies may be considered if they possess a minimum of 12 months full-time professional work experience in the vocational area of the vacancy. Types of vacancies will differ with each bulletin. There are approximately 85 job classifications under the program, including the following major areas: *General Administration; Social Services; Engineering; Accounting and Finance; Information Services; Laboratory, Medical and Therapy; Natural Resources; and Teaching.* Listings in all these areas will be published as vacancies occur. Mailing list service is available to candidates wishing to receive biweekly bulletins at their residence. Mailing list cards and general information brochures are available at State Job Service offices, most college placement offices or at our office. *Candidates utilizing our mailing list cards must continue to return their cards to receive future bulletins.* The list of eligible candidates established through the attached vacancy descriptions may also be used to fill similar vacancies with that and other departments in the near future. It is possible that any vacancy listed in this bulletin may be filled with a person from within the Civil Service. All candidates hired through the program will serve a probationary period of from six to twenty-four months and most will receive a pay increase upon the successful completion of the first six months. *The State is committed to an Affirmative Action policy.* State residence may be required for some positions. For the purpose of participating in civil service examinations, a State resident is a person who: (a) Is eligible to register to vote; or (b) Has resided within the state at least one year out of the immediately preceding three years; or (c) Has resided within the state for a total of five years; or (d) is the spouse of a person meeting the requirements of (a), (b), or (c). Monthly and annual pay rates quoted in this publication are approximate. Civil Service pay is determined on an hourly basis.

RESEARCH ANALYST 3
LOCATION: First vacancy—Department of Health and Social Services, Division of Community Services, Bureau of Alcohol and Other Drug Abuse. This register will

Adapted from *Career Candidate Vacancy* Bulletins, State of Wisconsin. Madison, WI: Bureau of Personnel.

be used to fill other similar positions that become vacant during the next six months in the area. *JOB DESCRIPTION: Tasks and Knowledge Required Upon Appointment*: Under limited supervision, prepare charts, tables and graphs from information received from formula projects and the State Interim Information System for dissemination to the State Advisory Council on Alcoholism and for inclusion in the State Alcohol and Other Drug Abuse Plans. Conduct on-site visits to formula grant projects to review evaluation systems and provide technical assistance in deficient areas. Provide verbal and written feedback to formula projects regarding their evaluation reports. *Knowledge of*: variety of alcohol and drug abuse programs and services; statistical techniques; management by objectives/results; writing specific objectives. *Additional Tasks and Knowledge at Full Performance Level*; Disseminate new research related to alcohol and drugs to community programs. *Knowledge of*: research design; Management Information System design; Hughes Formula Grant legislation; relevant Alcohol and Other Drug Abuse journals. *QUALIFICATIONS*: Such education, training or experience which would provide reasonable assurance that the skills and knowledge required upon appointment have been acquired. An example of how the skills and knowledge could be acquired is by completion of coursework leading to a master's degree in the social or behavioral sciences; or a bachelor's degree and two years of statistical work experience. *State residence is required. Apply by April 21.*

SOCIAL WORKER 1—County
SOCIAL WORKER 4—County
The State Career Candidate program recruits professional Social Workers for all County Social Services Departments, and for some juvenile courts. Although the duties of all vacant positions will vary to some degree, the vast majority will involve the following: Under supervision the Social Worker 1 makes social studies of persons and families in need of social service; determines through interviews, home visits and collateral investigations the range of services needed by individuals and families; and makes recommendations for administrative decisions. The Social Worker 4-County responsibilities are similar; however, they are expected to carry a more complicated or specialized caseload. Candidates should be able to demonstrate how they could help clients formulate and vocalize opinions so as to aid the Social Worker in determining a course of action to take in helping the client overcome problems; monitor client progress toward goals and the current status of client problems through interviews, observation, and reading of case records; discuss client's immediate situation to assess their ability for self help; counsel client to build self esteem. *QUALIFICATIONS: Such education, training, work or other life experience which would provide reasonable assurance that the skills required to perform the tasks and knowledge required upon appointment have been acquired. Normally the skills and knowledge for Social Worker 1—County would be acquired by a bachelor's degree in social work or sociology. Normally the skills and knowledge for Social Worker 4—County would be acquired by a master's degree in social work.* Monthly starting salaries are shown below and to the right of the county with the vacancy. An asterisk (*) is used where salaries are either pending the outcome of negotiations or pending formal action in establishing a minimum entrance salary for the classification. Employe benefits such as vacation, sick leave, health insurance, county retirement contribution, life insurance, mileage allowance, etc., vary by county, but are in most instances excellent. Candidates wishing to be considered for vacancies must submit a resume outlining their education, work and life experiences, with a statement as to why the candidate wishes to be a social worker for that particular county. Candidates must state their county of

residence in the resume. These materials must be submitted to Department of Health and Social Services, *no later than April 24*. The materials received by that date will be reviewed and qualified candidates will be invited to participate further in· the selection process. *Each county has the option of considering only their own residents.*

Document 11.7 / County Child Abuse Project—Position Vacancy
Child Abuse Coordinator

PROJECT GOAL
Stimulate, support, coordinate and allow to mature the multidisciplinary and multi-agency approach to the prevention and treatment of child abuse victims.

DUTIES & RESPONSIBILITIES
Stimulate, support, coordinate and institutionalize the development of the multidisciplinary child protection team in the hospitals and the community; develop effective and sufficient treatment options; develop regular treatment advisory committee meetings which coordinate treatment; develop workshops/seminars for professionals and concerned citizens.

Relate to multi-agency personnel and volunteers to enlist and maintain their participation.

Mediate and uncover interagency and interdisciplinary conflicts and duplication of services.

Devise methods and procedures which implement the project.

Initiate and coordinate efforts aimed at child abuse prevention.

Research, utilize and involve community resources.

Develop fund raising strategy.

Evaluate project.

QUALIFICATION REQUIREMENTS
Such education, training, work or life experiences which would provide reasonable assurance that the necessary skills and knowledge required to perform the job duties have been acquired. MSW preferred.

Thorough knowledge of laws, regulations and practices pertaining to federal/state child welfare programs; human growth and behavior, casework principles and methods; community organization principles and methods; causal factors underlying family breakdown and community disorganization; identify and utilize assistance and health resources; skill in setting and measuring goals and objectives, resolving conflict, and developing supporters.

Indoctrination Procedures

Formal organizations indoctrinate new members to engender loyalty to and dependence upon the organization. This is done so that the recruit will

Adapted from *Position Vacancy* Notices, Kenosha County, WI.

perceive little conflict between the demands of the organization and the demands of other aspects of the society, or, if conflict is perceived, the conflict will be resolved in favor of the organization.

Much of this is done even before the recruit is employed through the many internship or field work schemes that professional education requires. As students, potential social workers, psychologists, nurses, educators, and physicians spend at least half their time working in job settings for educational credit. They receive grades for the work performed. This field education socializes recruits so that upon graduation they will fit into their work organizations. It also weeds out those who exhibit inability to perform as the organizations demand. Upon employment, organizations require periods of in-service training, periodic seminars, staff meetings, retreats, and conferences with experienced workers, thus continuing the process of indoctrination.

Loyalty and dependence are furthered by the prestige membership grants to its holder, by the possibilities for promotion that are held out, and by the guarantees of economic and social security that are made possible by evidencing one's commitment to the values and rules of the organization. It is difficult to behave contrary to the organizational expectations when rewards are given for satisfactory performance and are withheld if the worker exhibits nonconforming behavior.

Rule Enforcement Procedures

All formal organizations have procedures that contribute toward proper performance. Failure to observe the performance requirements of the particular position can lead to some form of punishment. These include discussions with the supervisor, conferences with an administrator, letters of admonishment, withholding of salary increments and promotions, transfer to another less prestigious position, negative comments by peers, suspension, and finally dismissal. Conversely, conscientious adherence to the rules will result in praise from the supervisor, commendations from the administrator, salary increase and promotions, peer esteem, and a secure position in the organization that protects one from economic and social adversity.

Not all rule enforcement is from "the top down," however. There are times when workers attempt to force their superiors to follow the rules. This is known as "whistle blowing" and can result in sanctions directed toward the "whistle blowers" by those with greater authority. Whistle blowers are often looked upon as organizational deviants, whereas supervisors are seen as integral to the functioning of the organization. In fact, both whistle blowers and supervisors are necessary to ensure that rules are followed by all members and the objectives of the organizations are met.

Informal Structure in Formal Organizations

Up to this point we have been describing the *apparent* characteristics of structure of formal organizations, which are a matter of record and can readily be observed. These characteristics of structure are supposed to make it possible for organizations to obtain maximum return from the material and human resources that are invested. For instance, because the qualifications of personnel are carefully examined and because each position has specific requirements that are carefully spelled out, it should follow that if six social workers are qualified to fill a certain position, it will matter little which one is picked because, it is presumed, the same performance will result. Organizational members carry out their activities by the objectives and rules and are given the desired rewards of pay and security. According to the "overt," or apparent, structural perspective, formal organizations can concentrate on the achievement of the stated goals and waste little effort or resources on extraneous activities.

Even common sense on the basis of limited experience indicates that this is not really the way in which organizations perform. Almost everybody has come into contact with organizations that do not carry out their functions according to the expectations one would have by examining their overt structure. Clerks can be surly, government officials uninterested, workers unproductive, a product unsafe; all are the result of the functioning of large organizations. To understand the operation of formal organizations, it is necessary to look beyond the overt structure to what scholars term the *covert* structure—that part of the organization that operates on the basis of personal, informal relationships among the members of the organization.[12, 13]

Here we find something similar to compromise law at work. Members of formal organizations develop friendships with other members; they want to be liked by their fellow workers, to be respected, to be defined as persons as well as officials. They want to relate to others on the basis of intimacy as well as on the basis of rules. Members of formal organizations have strong ties into the rest of the community and desire to perform their official duties so that they do not weaken these extraorganizational affiliations. In spite of indoctrination, members of formal organizations have their own personal values and patterns of behavior that often conflict with the formal objectives and rules that the organizations state should be their guide for behavior.

This gives rise to an informal, unwritten structure that must be understood if one is to comprehend the operation and performance of formal organizations. This can be seen quite clearly in reference to certain organizational rules. The rules may state that employees may take forty-five minutes for lunch, but in fact they may take an hour or more. Those who return according to the rule may be censured by fellow workers by being told, "If you only take forty-five minutes, you make the rest of us look bad." The rules might state that $5.00 is the maximum to be given for flowers for someone in the hospital or an engagement present or whatever, but informally the workers know that $6.00 to $10.00 is what is expected.

Another element of informal structure is the existence of informal objectives. For instance, stated objectives may call for equal treatment for all minorities, but in a particular agency a worker might find that one minority is favored over another.

Peirce, in his article "A Functional Perspective of Social Welfare," presents an excellent analysis of the consequences of the co-existence of formal and informal objectives for social welfare organizations.[14] He states that formal objectives commit welfare organizations to initiate changes in society to eliminate poverty, illness, and underprivilege. Informal objectives, however, prevent the formal objectives from being achieved because they take precedence and commit the organization to the functional maintenance of the status quo. Even though the stated intent of welfare programs is to distribute income from the upper to the lower classes, the net result of the programs is to redistribute income more within the lower classes than from the upper to the lower class.

Peirce goes on to say that this all could be changed if workers in these organizations realized that they were saying one thing and doing another. Realistic knowledge about the internal character of the organizations by its members would enable them to change the character of the organizations so that they are oriented toward change functions rather than toward maintenance functions.

An example of this is given in the welfare experiments conducted in Denver and Seattle. Several thousand poor families have taken part in the experiment that began in 1971. Some were guaranteed incomes at various levels at about and below the poverty line. Families in the control group continued receiving the usual types of welfare aid. Those in the experimental group who received a guaranteed income surprised the planners by working less and by experiencing more family breakup.

Bradley Schiller discusses the results in the following article.

When Welfare Families Know Their Rights
By Bradley R. Schiller

In offering his welfare reform proposals last year, President Carter noted that "the welfare system is antiwork and antifamily." It is antiwork because it provides income guarantees to those who don't work, and imposes high taxes on the wages of those who do. It is antifamily because in most cases it disqualifies poor families that remain intact with an unemployed or low-wage father.

There has never been any serious disagreement about the *theoretical* impact of the welfare system on the employment or family stability of poor families: The system is indeed both antiwork and antifamily. What has kept the welfare debate alive for so long is that the *actual* antiwork and antifamily effects of the welfare system have not been that large.

For example, one out of four welfare mothers holds a job at least part of the year, despite the fact that the welfare system may take away as much as 67 cents out of each dollar she earns. Even more remarkable is the fact that one out of 10 welfare mothers works full time, despite the very high tax (as much as 67%) imposed on her very low wages (around $3 an hour).

Such evidence suggests that welfare mothers have a much stronger work ethic than most Americans (as Leonard Goodwin documented in some fascinating Brookings Institution studies) or that they respond "irrationally" to market incentives. The irrationality argument is based on the premise that welfare mothers are not completely informed about the loss of welfare benefits implied by a decision to work, either before or after they take a job.

The same kind of discrepancy between theory and practice is evident with respect to the antifamily provisions of the Aid to Families with Dependent Children (AFDC) program. There is a very strong financial incentive for poor fathers to desert their families, as desertion of the father (in fact or in appearance) makes the mother and children eligible for welfare (AFDC) benefits.

In view of this incentive, it is truly amazing that nearly three million poor families—including over 11 million individuals—continue to be headed by a male, despite the fact that nearly all of these families would be better off financially if they split up. What should one conclude? Do poor people have stronger family ties than the rest of us? Or don't they understand the complexities of the welfare system?

Recent evidence from the continuing welfare experiments in Seattle and Denver provides some answers. The basic intent of the experiments is to test the impact of different welfare-benefit provisions (especially higher guarantees and lower tax rates) on poor families. However, the most "startling" finding reported to Congress by the Stanford Research Institute economists conducting the study is that the experimental families are splitting up faster than anyone expected. Indeed, the rate of family break-up increased by 61% among black families and by 58% among white families after they began participating in the experiment.

The initial reaction to this extraordinary increase in the rate of family break-up has been greeted with dismay by welfare officials. HEW has been quick to point out that the Seattle-Denver experiments do not provide the jobs promised by President Carter's welfare reform proposal, and that such jobs might foster greater family stability. But such responses not only obscure the fact that President Carter's proposals also contain antifamily incentives, but miss a more fundamental point: What really distinguishes the welfare experiments from the regular welfare system is the amount of information provided to welfare recipients.

Families in the Seattle-Denver experiments are completely informed about their welfare rights and the consequences of employment and family break-up for their welfare benefits. By contrast, most welfare families are uninformed about welfare regulations and must go to extraordinary lengths to obtain clear, succinct answers about their welfare rights.

In other words, the distinguishing feature of the welfare experiments is that they encourage "rational" behavior. In so doing, they quickly are closing the gap that has long existed between welfare theory and welfare fact.

The current welfare system is in fact both antiwork and antifamily, and we have not yet witnessed the full implications of its perverse incentives; the Seattle-Denver experiments have provided a preview of what lies ahead. The question now is whether Congress will be sufficiently impressed by this glimpse of the future to undertake serious welfare reform before the full burden of the present system is evident.[15]

Note that Schiller states that "what really distinguishes the welfare experiments from the regular welfare system is the amount of information provided to the welfare recipients."

And yet one of the oft-stated formal objectives in most welfare programs is that recipients should be completely informed about various aspects of the programs so that they may make their own decisions about what they want to do. Informally, this objective is usually ignored, because the consequences for welfare programs in this country would be drastic if all recipients received the same kind of information as those participating in the Denver-Seattle experiments received.

Welfare Organizations and the Community

Informal objectives have a tendency to take precedence over formal objectives because no single entity in a society can function independently of the other entities to which it is related. Welfare organizations are no exception. If the larger society that supports welfare services holds values such as the value of work and the family that are not furthered by the objectives of the welfare orga..ization, the organization, being dependent on the larger society for its existence, will establish informal objectives that enable it to perform in accordance with the operational values enforced by that portion of society to which it is accountable. The poor have little power. As long as those with power do not share the expectations of the poor and the reformers, there will be divergence between formal and informal objectives. In formal organizations, the greater this divergence, the less likelihood there is of achievement of the stated goals.

We stated in Chapter 7 that welfare services have a number of publics that attempt to influence the character of the services. These publics are the critics, the advocates, the supporters, the providers, and the recipients. The strength of these publics depends on the power that they command over the production and distribution of the material and social resources of the society. It is to be expected then that, if advocates articulate a formal goal for welfare such as the more equitable distribution of goods and services to all sectors of society, and that, if providers hold the same goal and if recipients agree, the organization would operate to achieve this goal. However, critics do not desire a reordering of the economic structure of American society because, if this happened, they would lose some of their command over resources currently available to them. In addition, the supporters such as economic and political leaders do not wish to redistribute the continuing surplus any more than is presently being done because they, too, would lose in the process. The formal goal of redistribution is talked about, but serious plans for its accomplishment are left for some indeterminate future.

The power of the persons in the publics, not the numbers, is the crucial factor in the structure developed by welfare organizations. The relative power of the publics determines whether or not organizations are oriented toward the achievement of formal objectives or toward informal ones.

The Stability of Organizations

Before leaving the subject of structure, it is necessary to discuss the stability-producing characteristics of formal organizations.

When an organization evolves a well-articulated structure, the organization itself begins to have a life of its own. The inertia that develops within formal organizations can make them nearly immune to influence even from those publics that initially had power to control their performance.

Nonetheless, structure is necessary; if the work of a large number of persons is to be coordinated, no member of the organization can be allowed to do only what he or she feels like doing. By reducing the work to rules and routines, structure prevents chaos, but in so doing, it also stifles imagination and enforces sameness and repetition. Structure also tends to emphasize the efficiency of operation more than the effectiveness. When procedures have been refined so that a task is accomplished in an efficient (but not necessarily effective) manner, it does not matter if the task can be done better or even if the task is no longer necessary. It is difficult to change any of the elements of a task once the process has been declared efficient. For instance, means tests may not be the most effective way to determine need because they are often unable to take into account individual circumstances of applicants.* However, since they are an efficient procedure, they remain part of the operation.

The formal organization with sufficient structure to have a life of its own also seeks to enhance its stability by controlling nonmembers. Welfare organizations exert considerable control over the behavior of the recipients of welfare services because, if they are to continue to receive services, they must also observe the rules. This discourages initiative on the part of the recipients and enforces their conformity.

As a formal organization moves toward a condition of internal stability, it tends to isolate itself more and more from the rest of society. As this occurs, the efforts of the organization become more directed toward maintenance of its structure and function and less to achieve the objectives for which it was originally developed. Etzioni calls this phenomenon "goal displacement."[16]

Goal displacement occurs because the economic security and social well-being of every member of the organization is dependent upon that member's being able to remain employed. Because any change in the organization would threaten the position and therefore the livelihood of one or more of the members, and because it is not predictable exactly which person or persons might be displaced, all members tend to work toward the maintenance of all positions. It has been said that, if the poor were ever moved out of

* See chapter 8, pp. 119, 120.

poverty or if crime were ever eliminated, welfare organizations would have to reinvent both so that their jobs would not be jeopardized.

Self-validation is another process that organizations utilize to enhance their stability. They do this by taking advice and criticism only from members of similar organizations. When an organization is to be evaluated, it is often done by persons in occupations similar to those of the members of the organizations being evaluated. Hospitals are evaluated by physicians, schools by educators, and welfare organizations by social workers, psychologists, or administrators of other welfare organizations. Members of organizations usually read only materials written by fellow workers. They try to ignore criticism from other parts of society. In these ways, members tend to hear only that which validates their opinion of everything's being as it should be.

Organizations encourage group decisions. This promotes the division of responsibility and denies individual responsibility. If a committee makes a decision or if the decision is made in department "x," the individual member of the committee or the department is protected from being held accountable for his or her acts. When the responsibility for making a decision is assigned to a group rather than to an individual, it becomes difficult for the various interested publics to understand who really is responsible. Anything new that turns up that is not covered by the present rules can be referred from office to office until either the person seeking the service becomes discouraged and goes away or the problem gets lost in some organizational file.

This is not to say that organizational stability is all bad. Indeed, it has as much to recommend it as it has to arouse concern. Without stability, recipients of services could never be guaranteed the continuance of service. Without stability, the larger society could not guarantee continuing order. Without stability, no projections could be made for the future. Without stability, the work of society could not be done. In the short run, stability offers less risk than change.

But the resistance to change produced by this stability can be frightening. When the maintenance of stability becomes the primary objective and issues in the society are neglected in its favor, society loses its viability. Stagnation is the result. In the long run, this can be the greatest risk of all.

Summary

In this chapter we have described the characteristics of the structure of welfare organizations as well as the ways in which welfare organizations perform the tasks that they are required to perform by the society that created and supports them. We also discussed the importance of the organization to human services professionals, both as a vehicle by which their work is accomplished and as a significant factor in their sense of personal well-being and achievement. We pointed out that welfare organizations are not unique among organizations in society. Welfare organizations function in much the same fashion as do other organizations, because they are subject to the same forces of control as other organizations. Private welfare agencies are subject primarily to the control of economic institutional leadership, whereas public welfare agencies are subject primarily to the control of political institutional leadership.

Human services professionals find themselves caught between two forces; (1) their ideological commitment to services for their clientele and (2) their personal necessity to respond to the performance expectations of the organization that employs them. It is the organization that rewards their efforts with promotions and salary increases, not the clients whom they serve. When the rules of the organization conflict with the needs of the clientele, human services professionals are faced with a serious dilemma. Sometimes the choice is stark: abide by the rules of the organization to the detriment of the client, or suffer the consequences, such as loss of promotion, salary increase, or, at the extreme, loss of the job. Fortunately, this is not the usual situation. Most of the time there is a relationship between the rules of the organization and the welfare of clients.

Human services professionals should understand the general characteristics of organizations in American society and the particular characteristics of welfare organizatons in which they work. This understanding enables human services professionals to use the resources of the organization to best advantage for the clients and for their own personal success as well. This will also make it possible for workers in welfare organizations to recognize where organizational changes are necessary and to devise effective menas for making the changes that encourage goal attainment rather than goal displacement.

Presently, organizational stability as well as stability in the distribution of economic and social resources is the pattern in the United States. However, what will happen in the future is not easily predictable, because there are identifiable trends that can lead to either continued stability on the one hand or to substantial change on the other. In chapter 13 we will identify these trends, state their possible results, and describe some of the implications for welfare programs and services.

Before we do this, however, in Chapter 12 we will describe the variety of services offered by human services professionals. The examples will describe the services from the perspective of the contribution of social work. Nonetheless, the inventory is comprehensive; social work is a human services profession that participates not only in the services fielded by welfare organizations, but in all settings where people come to seek help.

References

1. LaPiere, R. *A Theory of Social Control*. New York: McGraw-Hill, 1954, pp. 160–182.

2. Reynolds, L., Henslin, J., eds. *American Society*. Part 1. New York: David McKay, 1974.

3. Ibid. pp. xi, xii.

4. La Piere, R. *Social Change.* New York: McGraw-Hill, 1965, pp. 401–441.

5. Ornati, O. *Poverty Amid Affluence.* New York: Twentieth Century Fund, 1966, p. 111.

6. *Milwaukee Journal*, August 9, 1978, p. 2.1.

7. Presthus, R. *Men at the Top.* New York: Oxford U.P., 1964, pp. 201, 282–320.

8. LaPiere, R. *A Theory of Social Control* pp. 162–167.

9. de Lone, R. *Small Futures.* New York: Harcourt, 1979, p. 18.

10. Fanshel, D. "Status Differentials: Men and Women in Social Work," *Social Work* (November 1976): 451–453.

11. *Laws of the 93rd Congress,* 1st sess. Washington, D.C.: G.P.O.,

12. LaPiere, R. Social Change. pp. 405, 406.

13. Blau, P. *Bureaucracy in Modern Society* New York: Random House, 1956, pp. 45–61.

14. Peirce, F. "A Functional Perspective of Social Welfare," *Social Work Education Reporter* (March 1970): 48–50, 61.

15. Schiller, B., "When Welfare Families Know Their Rights," *The Wall Street Journal,* July 11, 1978, editorial page. Reprinted by permission of *The Wall Street Journal,* © Dow Jones & Company, Inc. 1978. All Rights Reserved.

16. Etzioni, A. *Modern Organizations* Englewood Cliffs, N.J.: Prentice-Hall, 1964, pp. 10, 11.

chapter /12

Helping Others: The Good That Social Workers Do

Throughout this book we have used the phrase "human services professional" to designate the many types of occupational categories that are involved in helping others through public and private welfare programs. Of all human services professionals, the greatest numbers are in social work. In fact, social workers provide the widest variety of services to the widest variety of clients in the widest variety of settings, many of which are not related to welfare concerns. This chapter concentrates on what social workers do to assist people who want and need help.

Social workers are concerned individuals who have a sincere desire to help people. And help people they do, people who often have no one else to whom they can turn for assistance when the problems they face are so overwhelming that they cannot cope with them alone. The concern and interest that social workers show can be a significant factor in enabling people to persevere until some of their problems are resolved. The efforts of social workers do make a difference in human lives, and this difference is often a crucial one. The satisfaction that social workers receive from helping others makes this choice of profession very worth while.

The kinds of problems that people bring to social workers are presented here in alphabetical order. These are not all the types of problems that social workers encounter and help to solve, but those listed do represent most of the important ones. The alphabetical arrangement is for convenience only and does not imply any order of importance of people's needs. As you read about the ways in which social workers help others, you will see that many of the problems that people bring are related and that many different services can be furnished by a single agency. Nevertheless, wherever and however it may be done, social workers give personal, useful, fundamental assistance of the kinds to be described.

Adoption

Adoption is the provision of children to childless parents and the provision of parents to parentless children. This service is possibly one of the most interesting and varied that social workers provide, because it involves taking care of the rights and expectations of parents who want children, parents who are giving up their children, and the children who are being adopted.

Most of the children who are available for adoption come from unmarried mothers. Until recently, unmarried mothers were under considerable social pressure to give up their children, so there was a continuous supply of children for parents who wanted to adopt. Now, however, attitudes have relaxed, and more single mothers are keeping their children; the result is a decreased demand for social workers in adoptive services. The decreased demand is also related to the development of medical techniques to increase fertility among heretofore sterile couples so that they can look forward to having their own children rather than having to adopt them. Nevertheless, hundreds of thousands of children are still being placed for adoption annually.

Social workers carry the major responsibility in the adoptive process. They gather information about the prospective parents to ensure that the child they receive will have a good home and be compatible with the parents, and vice versa. Social workers manage the adoption through the courts, assist the mother giving up the child with the problems she may have during this period, and prepare the adopting parents for the arrival of the child. In fact, in many ways, social workers are the temporary parents that the state provides while children are moving away from the parent of origin to the parents of adoption. In adoption social workers play a number of roles, acting for the society to protect the rights of the child, supporting the parent of origin so that she can lead a productive life after she gives up the child, and teaching the adoptive parents how to do a good job with a child that has been placed in their care as one of their own but without the natural processes of conception, pregnancy, and birth.

Adoptive services are performed by private agencies such as children's service societies, church-related agencies such as Lutheran Social Services and Catholic Charities, and child welfare divisions of public welfare agencies. A master's degree is required for employment in agencies that provide adoptive services.

Child Abuse and Neglect

Child abuse is mistreatment of children by their parents. It can involve physical punishment, beating, shouting and screaming, and, in extreme situations, torture. Child neglect is lack of proper care for children by their parents and includes proper feeding and sanitation and a lack of medical care.

Until recently children were considered the exclusive property of their parents, who could pretty much do with their children as they wished. But there is a growing realization that children have rights too, among which are the rights to be cared for properly by their parents. Social workers have been among the leaders to secure recognition of the rights of children. Cases of child abuse and neglect usually come to the attention of social workers as a result of a telephone call by a neighbor or relative but sometimes by nurses, physicians, or other human services professionals. Social workers try to work out the problems so that if at all possible the child can remain in the home. If this is not possible, the social worker can take the parents to court and, in extreme cases, terminate parental rights and remove the child from the home. Most of the cases, however, are settled without resort to the judicial system.

A master's degree is usually required for social workers who work with abused or neglected children. Services to abused or neglected children are given through private agencies such as children's service societies or church-related agencies. They are also provided by child welfare divisions of public welfare agencies.

Crime

Crime is usually viewed as behavior that is committed by adults against persons or property that brings the adult offender to the attention of law enforcement authorities. Social workers provide important services to those involved in crime. Social workers can be employed by the court, in which case they might gather background information on the offender that will assist the judge in knowing what kind of sentence to give. The social worker is the person that keeps the well-being of the offender in mind while knowing that the offender's victims must also be protected.

Social workers also work in prisons, reformatories, detention centers, and other places in which offenders may be incarcerated. Here they assist the offenders to adjust to life in the institution and keep in touch with the offenders' families, help the families with problems associated with having one of their members in prison, and prepare the offender to return to society.

Sometimes the court will not sentence the offender to prison but will place him or her on probation instead. In this situation, the offender is under the immediate supervision of the probation officer, who is often a social worker. The social worker sees that the offender does not violate the terms of parole, finds and keeps a job, stays in touch with the family, and lives properly in the community.

When released from prison, the offender is often placed on parole for a period of time. This is done to enable the parolee to readjust to the community after being away. The person who looks after the offender while on parole is also often the social worker. The social worker-parole officer who works with a parolee has the same responsibilities for the parolee as does the probation officer.

Social workers who work with offenders are usually employed in public agencies, such as the courts, divisions of corrections, the various institutions where offenders are kept, and in the larger local police and sheriff departments.

Delinquency

Delinquency includes the types of behavior described under the section on crime except that the offenses are committed by persons who are not legally adult. Delinquency also includes behavior such as truancy, uncontrollability in the home, vandalism, teenage prostitution, running, and so on. Juvenile offenders are usually dealt with by separate courts called juvenile courts, which utilize the services of social workers as do the adult courts. The primary emphasis, however, is on trying to get the behavior under control, keeping the delinquent in the home and working with the family. When this fails, the young person can be sent to a juvenile institution. Social workers work here in the same fashion as they do in adult institutions. However, because the emphasis is on keeping the offenders in the community, only as a last resort are juveniles sent to institutions. With this in mind, social workers dealing with delinquents work with schools, churches, police departments, community centers, neighborhood houses, and families to try to help the young offender to fit into normal community life.

Social workers who work with delinquents are employed as juvenile officers in local police and sheriff departments, in the courts, in child welfare divisions of public welfare departments, in some instances in school systems, as well as in state divisions of correction, private organizations such as Pathfinders, and so on.

Discrimination

Discrimination is unequal treatment that is given by the members of a society to groups that are singled out because of some special characteristic shared by the members of those groups. This can include racial or ethnic characteristics as in the case of blacks, hispanics, or native Americans; sexual characteristics as in the case of women; or physical characteristics as in the case of the physically handicapped.

There are opportunities for social workers to work in agencies that have special programs to combat the unequal treatment that results from discrimination. These services range from programs of education designed to remove the discriminatory practices of the general public toward these groups to direct services to members of these groups designed to enable them to cope with the discrimination they have experienced and fight the existence of discrimination itself. Examples of these agencies are the federal Bureau of Indian Affairs; federal, state, and local civil rights commissions; housing authorities, neighborhood and community centers; and schools and colleges. Some private business organizations also have programs to combat discrimination in hiring and work practices.

Drugs

Until the last several decades, use of drugs such as alcohol, heroin, barbituates, marijuana, and so on was thought to be a crime, and users were treated as criminals. At present this behavior is generally defined as an illness, especially in the case of legal drug use, such as alcohol. In the case of illegal drug use, such as heroin, the behavior is often dually defined as a crime and as an illness. At any rate, social workers are involved with other human services professionals in working intensively with drug users to help them to stop using the drugs that hamper their ability to live productively in society. Social workers perform therapy with drug users, work with their families, try to get the addicts into special groups such as Alcoholics Anonymous, do public education work to get the public to realize what the problems are and how they can be handled, and cooperate with law enforcement agencies in trying to dry up the supply of drugs in the case of illegal sources.

Social workers dealing with drug addiction are employed in drug rehabilitation centers, correctional institutions, and hospitals as well as in some private agencies that have drug treatment programs. A master's degree is usually required for persons who work in the area of drug addiction and abuse.

Emotional Problems

Emotional problems range from a mild disturbance of an individual's affective states to the severe derangement of psychoses. Social workers often deal with the mild disturbances in which individuals are for the most part able to continue their daily routines. These are anxiety, depression, feelings of guilt, listlessness, and so on. Emotional disturbances may also arise from stressful job situations, problems with friends or loved ones, and so on. Social workers deal with these types of problems in a variety of agencies that provide services to emotionally distressed individuals, from family service agencies, church-related agencies, mental health centers, and other public agencies, to small privately owned agencies. Social workers also develop private practices to serve individuals with emotional problems.

Family Financial Management

It is not only the poor who have difficulty making their financial resources stretch to meet their everyday demands. Rising expectations, easy credit, and inflation all make it difficult for some individuals and families to budget available resources to cover obligations incurred. When people find their financial situation hopeless, they may come to a family service agency or, if they are receiving welfare, to the public agency for assistance. Social workers are often called upon to assist families to straighten out their financial affairs. This is an important service, because, if they are not resolved, financial problems can result in emotional problems, crime, delinquency, alcoholism, and so on. There are also financial counseling programs in private business organizations in which social workers are employed to assist persons with their problems of financial management.

Family Planning

Family planning is the determination of the number and time of birth of the children a couple wishes to have. Family planning is a fairly recent service made possible by the development of reliable birth control technologies. Social workers work with medical personnel to assist couples in planning their families. The major task of the social worker is to get the couple to see the advantages of family planning, to direct them to the resources in the community that can assist them in this process, to discuss the financial implications of their planning, to help them understand any negative attitudes toward planning and birth control that they might encounter, and so on. Social workers are employed in family planning clinics, either publicly or privately supported, Planned Parenthood Associations, and certain church-related agencies that operate family planning services.

Financial Assistance

This is one of the most controversial, yet perhaps most basic, of the services that social workers provide. When people are poor, it is often presumed that they have some personal difficulty that makes it impossible for them to earn and budget money. In some cases this may be true, but often people need money because, in spite of what they may do, they cannot acquire it by their own efforts. Without financial assistance of some sort these persons would suffer privation and perhaps even die. Social workers, welfare workers, and case aids (or whatever the official designation of those who furnish financial assistance) do a job that often is not appreciated by those whom they serve and are criticized by those whose taxes support their work. Yet through their efforts those who need financial assistance are helped and the taxpayers are spared the wretched conditions that would exist if those in financial need were not cared for. Furnishing financial assistance to those who have no resources of their own is as basic a service as are the health and safety services furnished by firefighters and the police, even though the rewards may be fewer and recognition less. Those in financial assistance work must have compassion and a sense of social responsibility—a concern for the welfare of others. Their reward derives partly from the satisfaction of seeing that those in need receive resources that sustain them, even though not as well as the workers might like.

Practically all financial assistance is furnished today through the public welfare agencies. There are many opportunities for employment at the various levels of occupational qualification, because every county in every state in the Union has a public welfare agency.

Homemaker

On occasion a parent or spouse, usually the wife and mother, is unable to continue her function in the home, a function that may be crucial to the well-being of the children or the husband. In this circumstance a skilled homemaker will come into the home each day for a specified period of time and keep the family responsibilities intact. Persons who do this are usually employed as case aides or are given the title "homemaker." They are employed by public welfare agencies, family service agencies, private child welfare agencies, and church-related agencies. They may also be employed by hospitals. These "homemakers" are often supervised by professionally trained social workers who themselves are familiar with the responsibilities of a person who provides homemaker services to families who need this type of assistance.

Housing

Many people are forced to live in substandard housing or have difficulty finding housing that will take care of the needs of themselves and their families. Certain neighborhoods are often denied the financial services that are available to other neighborhoods, for example, city services. People who live close together in public housing projects often have a variety of problems associated with their housing that need attention. Many times the solution to these problems is the responsibility of social workers. Social workers may be employed by local housing authorities or neighborhood improvement associations, they may be on the staffs of housing projects, or they may be employed by state and federal housing agencies. They will work with the people with the housing problems, work with financial institutions to make funding available to the neighborhood, lobby with legislative bodies and other politicians to obtain needed services, and speak to interested and concerned groups to explain the issues involved in the provision of adequate housing to everyone in the community. This service not only assists individuals with difficult problems of living, but it can prevent many other problems from arising when citizens' housing needs are not adequately met.

Illegitimacy

When unmarried teenagers and adult women become pregnant, they must decide whether or not to carry the baby to term. It is often not desirable for a prospective mother to abort the fetus because of religious, familial, or cultural proscriptions. On the other hand, there is still stigma attached to giving birth out of wedlock. Even if this is not a serious problem for the mother, there are often other problems: adequate medical care, financial resources during pregnancy and following birth, and the relationship of the father to the child if his whereabouts are known. The decision to keep the child or to give it up for adoption must be made by the mother, but the social worker will help her to understand the decision she is making.

In all this, social workers often play crucial roles. Social workers are often the first specialists to become involved and the persons who often follow the events to their conclusion, assisting the mother with the problems that arise along the way; from helping her through her pregnancy to providing her with birth control information in order for her to avoid such a difficult situation in the future. These services are usually provided by private and church-related child-serving agencies, as well as by child welfare divisions of public welfare agencies.

Illnesses and Handicaps

Whether from birth, accident, or disease, illness and physical or mental handicaps are frightening to the sufferer and to the family. Worse, illnesses and handicaps are financially very expensive to treat. Social workers have long known that the financial expense, worry over job loss, concern for family, and fear of what might happen in the future are of as much concern as the illness or handicap itself. Social workers also know that, if these concerns are not dealt with positively, the afflicted person may not be able to become independent in any way. Social workers have demonstrated the effectiveness of assisting with these personal problems in the promotion of recovery and health. For this reason the medical specialty in social work is recognized as an important portion of health care.

Medical social services are offered by most hospitals, out-patient clinics, nursing homes, schools for the handicapped, organizations such as the National Foundation, Crippled Children's Society, Arthritis Foundation, and so on. The master's degree is usually required for employment in medical social work services.

Immigration and Refugees

This is a time of international unrest and turmoil. Large numbers of people migrate not only within countries but from country to country as well. Our country has had substantial migrations from Korea, Vietnam, Mexico, and Cuba, for example. There are many problems of adjustment to the new land by immigrants and refugees. Often these people cannot make the adjustment independently and so need the services of specially trained personnel to assist them. The community in which they will live must be prepared to receive them also. Social workers are an important source of service to the newly arrived persons, assisting them to find a community in

which to live, housing, clothing, food, employment, and other basic requirements. Sometimes social workers even try to find members of the family
whom the family has been unable to locate.

Social workers who provide this kind of service are employed by the Red
Cross and other private agencies, federal agencies who administer refugee
programs, or churches who offer services to people newly arrived in the
United States.

Jobs and Job Training

Since the major circumstance related to poverty in the United States is
lack of adequate employment, job training and job finding is a major service
offered by public welfare agencies. Social workers, welfare workers, and case
aides, among others, are intimately involved with those who receive financial
assistance. They are also closely involved in seeing that the recipients receive
training for jobs if necessary and helping them to find a job when the training
is completed. A variety of job training and job placement programs are in
effect, and social workers play an important part in these programs, among
them Work Assistance Programs, Work Incentive Programs, Comprehensive
Employment Training Act Programs, sheltered workshops, and rehabilitation
services. This is a major service that social workers give and a major source
of assistance to those who cannot find employment on their own.

Legal Aid

One generally thinks that legal aid is provided exclusively by attorneys.
However, there are many aspects of legal issues that are related to individual
difficulties and involve the social worker. For example, while an actual
divorce may be handled by attorneys, the events leading up to the divorce
and what takes place afterward represent personal matters of decision and
adjustment. Social workers are effective in assisting with these issues, and
thus they often work in conjunction with attorneys. Social workers can be
employed by legal aid societies, which are private agencies, by public defender
programs usually operated by state government, or by other public or private
agencies that assist persons in finding the legal services that they need to solve
a particular problem.

Migrant Workers

A significant portion of the agricultural industry depends on migrant
workers for its existence. These workers and their families travel from place
to place where the crops must be harvested. They often have no permanent
home of their own, live in quarters provided for them by their employers, and
have few material possessions other than what is required for survival. Their
children often have few or no educational facilities, they lack medical care,
and they are often seen as vagrants by the communities near which they work.

Social workers have recognized for a long time the adversity that migrant workers face. They also recognize that it is difficult to provide services to persons who have no permanent residence and yet lack the resources available to most other citizens. Because of the work that social workers and other human services professionals have done to make these services available to migrant workers, their situation is not as desperate as it once was, although much yet needs to be done. Public welfare agencies, primarily at the state level, church-related agencies, some federal agencies, labor unions, and other private agencies employ social workers who provide many of the services that people require, which we describe in other sections of this chapter. These include medical, educational, housing, drug abuse, delinquency, and services to lessen discrimination.

Military

Military personnel are frequently young persons who are away from their homes and communities for the first time. They are often recently married and in unfamiliar living situations. Military personnel encounter all the problems that most individuals face, but the problems often become aggravated because these people are away from their hometowns where they would know better how to obtain assistance. We therefore include the military setting because this is a special situation in which social workers give assistance to individuals who need their services. There are career opportunities for social workers in all three services, especially the army, either as civilian or as military personnel. Social workers can work on military bases, in military hospitals, or with private agencies such as the Red Cross or United Services Organization, which often have offices on military bases to furnish services to military personnel.

Neighborhood Concerns

Social workers have long known that the problems that individuals face are related to the circumstances in which they live. Therefore, social workers have historically worked in neighborhoods where they assist the residents with the problems of maintaining the physical and social adequacy of the neighborhood. Social workers work with neighborhood social groups, juvenile gangs, neighborhood improvement groups, and educational groups. They also assist with individual problems that residents encounter be they job related, in the family, or related to some other aspect of the neighborhood. Social workers also work with the larger community to enlist support for the solution of the problems of the neighborhood for which they carry responsibility, pointing out that, when one neighborhood deteriorates, all neighborhoods in the community are affected. Social workers work with politicians to convince them that the services to the neighborhood should be maintained at a level consistent with that of other neighborhoods. They may even lobby at the state or federal level when some action may be taken by the government that will be detrimental to the neighborhood (such as tearing down houses to make way for a freeway) or when services needed for the neighborhood are not being furnished (such as special programs in the schools for neighborhood children).

Services to neighborhoods are furnished through neighborhood centers (formerly settlement houses), which are private and sometimes church related, local community action agencies, which are run by the local government and supported through federal funds, and sometimes through the local public recreation department, which furnishes programs to the area.

Psychiatric Problems

Some people are so afflicted with neuroses or psychoses that they are unable to care for themselves. They must have either partial or full-time care to prevent them from harming themselves and others. Social workers who provide services to these persons are part of mental health teams that work in mental hospitals, in public mental health centers, and sometimes in private practice. The social worker can give treatment under the direction of a physician and will often work with the members of the individual's family, try to get the person out into the community if he or she is in a hospital, and try to help the person find a job, a place to live if necessary, and so on. The social worker also spends some time holding seminars and classes for persons in the community to acquaint them with the particulars of psychiatric problems so that they can understand what happens to people afflicted with them and so that members of the community can take steps to avoid these problems themselves. A master's degree is usually required for employment in psychiatric social work services.

Referral

Social work as a profession furnishes perhaps the most comprehensive service of any occupational group. Obviously no one worker or single agency can furnish all the services that the profession makes available. Therefore it is important that social workers know where the various services can be found. Then, if a client needs a service not offered by their organization, workers can send the person to the agency or professional specialist where the service can be made available. Social workers seldom perform referral services as a specialized activity, but, rather make referrals as a part of their responsibilities to the persons they serve. It is mentioned here because it is a special activity that forms part of the help that social workers make available.

Schools

Academic performance of students is related to factors other than what goes on in the classroom itself. Truancy, uncontrollability, low grades, and poor relationships with teachers all point to problems related to the family, the neighborhood, or the students themselves. Social workers are employed by school systems to work with the students, their families, police, churches, and other community resources to improve the performance of the student in school. Social workers also work with the teachers, counselors, and administrators to make the programs of the schools as responsive as possible to the requirements of the students with these problems.

Senior Citizens

Persons at or near retirement are expected to make one of the major adjustments to life required in our society. After working all their adult lives, they are suddenly not working. This requires personal, social, and financial adjustments. Health problems may arise that senior citizens have never experienced before. Long-time friends and loved ones may die. Senior citizens face the prospect of having to move from their home of many years either to a smaller home or to a retirement facility. Those no longer able to take care of themselves frequently enter a nursing home. Time previously spent on the job must now be filled with leisure activities.

Social insurance and pensions cover much of loss of job earnings for most persons. Some, however, do not have enough money for their retirement years and must seek financial assistance. Social workers who are employed in the Social Security Administration make social insurance benefits available to qualified retirees. They also furnish financial assistance to senior citizens who have insufficient insurance and pension benefits through Old Age Assistance and general relief through the public welfare agencies. Social workers in public welfare agencies also assist persons to obtain nursing home and other residential care if they need it and cannot obtain it for themselves. They help the elderly person and the family of the elderly person adapt to these changes.

Sexual Problems

The formal recognition by society of problems that individuals encounter with sexual behavior is a social concern of fairly recent development. For example, rape is only now being defined as more than simply an individual problem of certain women. Rape clinics are being established in hospitals, police departments are developing special services for rape victims, and rapists are being apprehended and punished for their acts. Social workers are important in assisting rape victims to alleviate the suffering that accompanies this experience.

Programs are also being established to aid homosexuals, persons with problems of impotence, couples with problems of sexual relationships, prostitutes, and individuals young and old who are faced with decisions as to how they wish to engage in sexual behavior. Some of these services are provided through specialized centers such as rape clinics; others are provided through regular social agencies such as family service associations, church-related agencies, and public agencies such as public welfare departments and mental health centers. Social workers furnishing these services provide individual treatment, work with families, cooperate with other community resources such as the police and the schools, and furnish public education through speeches, seminars, and contacts with business and political leaders of the community. A master's degree is usually required for employment in this line of service.

Substitute Family

This assistance is often called foster family service. It is usually provided to children who for some reason can no longer live in their family of origin or cannot be cared for by relatives. In special instances substitute families are provided for senior citizens and other adults who need temporary care that a family can provide. In any event, social workers whose job it is to provide substitute families often cannot find enough families in which to place the persons who need this care.

Foster family care services are provided by child welfare divisions of public welfare agencies, private agencies such as children's service societies, church-related agencies, and the many institutions that provide a variety of care for children. This is a highly skilled, demanding service and usually requires a master's degree.

Temporary Assistance

Sometimes people lose their jobs, are ineligible for unemployment insurance, and cannot immediately find another job. Families sometimes move from one location to another hoping to improve their circumstances but do not find the kind of employment they hoped for as soon as they expected. Sometimes people exhaust their resources through accident, illness, or other personal tragedy, including the death of the provider. Offenders released from prison sometimes have no resources on which to draw until they can find work. Sometimes a family loses its home through fire, tornado, or other acts of God. People in these circumstances need assistance for a time until they can get back on their feet. Social workers provide these services through public programs such as general assistance, through private organizations such as the Red Cross and church-related organizations such as Catholic Charities, as well as through federal agencies that provide disaster relief services.

For Further Information

We have described some of the many services that social workers perform for persons who face problems for which they require assistance. It should be kept in mind that these services are often provided in conjunction with other human services professionals and with other social workers as well.

If you wish to find out more information about any of the services discussed, we recommend that you consult the most *recent* edition of the *Encyclopedia of Social Work*. It comes in two volumes, is published in New York by the National Association of Social Workers, and contains articles that discuss most of the services we have outlined here. Following the articles are references to other written sources that provide considerably more information about the service or services in which you are interested.

When you have found what you want to know about the services that interest you, you will then want to know where you can find employment. We recommend the following sources.

For information about opportunities in private agencies, consult the *National Directory of Private Social Agencies* edited by Helga Croner. This directory is updated monthly, so it is as current as is possible. The directory lists some thirty different services and the names and addresses of the private agencies around the country that give these services. The directory is published by Social Service Publication, Queens Village, N.Y.

For information about opportunities in public agencies, consult the most *recent* edition of the *Public Welfare Directory* edited by Michele Moore. This directory, published in Washington, D.C. by the American Public Welfare Association, lists employment sources in public agencies by category of service in all the counties in all the fifty states. It also lists federal sources of employment as well as the sources of employment in Canadian public welfare agencies. Some sources of international employment in public welfare are also given.

Both private and public sources of employent are contained in *Helping Others: A Guide to Selected Social Service Agencies and Occupations* edited by Norma Haines and published in New York by John Day. Check with your librarian to find the latest edition. This guide lists sources and categories of employment for seventy-four *private* agencies—secular, religious, and inter-national. It lists sources of employment for twenty-seven *federal* agencies and programs and for forty-four *state* agencies and programs.

After you have found out the type of service in which you are interested and the kind of agency in which you might like to work, the next step is to visit the local counterpart of that agency. Talk to the professionals who work there. They can tell you what the work is like, what the opportunities are, how to get on the mailing list for job openings, and what you still need to do to qualify for the kind of service you want to give.

Summary

In this Chapter we described a number of problem categories that persons encounter today for which assistance from social workers is available. We listed organizations through which social workers provide the assistance. Finally, we included sources of information about employment opportunities.

In Chapter 13 we return to the theme of the relationship of welfare programs to society. We will discuss some changes in society that may take place (possibly even in your lifetime) which could have an important effect on the problems people face, and the way in which people are assisted to deal with problems.

part /four
Trends

chapter / 13

Possibilities for the Future: Implications for Welfare Programs

Even as there are many goals for welfare programs and a variety of explanations of society and the individual, so there are also many ways of projecting the possibilities that exist for humankind in the future. This is not new. People have been making predictions since the earliest times, and some of these are still being read today. The book of Revelation in the *Bible* and the works of Nostradamus, a sixteenth-century astrologer, are two examples.

Present-day prognosticators include the writers of science fiction as well as the social or physical scientists who with the help of computers make both short- and long-range predictions. A short-range prediction might state that at the present rate of usage the world will exhaust its supply of fossil fuel in one hundred years. A long-range prediction might be that the world will be covered by a great sheet of ice (or will burn up like the sun) in a billion or so years. There is frequent disagreement for as the ancient savant remarked, "Predictions are difficult to make, particularly when they concern the future." Even so, people continue to seek out what the future holds for them so that in some way they may be prepared to cope with it when it comes.

An essentially optimistic outlook toward the future prevailed throughout the period of the Great Depression and World War II. It was generally felt that, if the United States could cope with two problems of such magnitude, it could solve any other problems that might beset it; therefore, the future would continuously be better than the present. This "can do" attitude led to John F. Kennedy's proclamation of the Great Society in the 1960s. The wonder of wonders was that the Great Society would be achieved at the same time as the United States was fighting its longest, most expensive war in Indochina. During the 1960s literature of futurology was almost without exception utopian. One of the most famous books of the period was Charles Reich's *The Greening of America.*[1]

But then the Great Society foundered, and the war in Indochina was lost. Suddenly the future was in doubt. Perhaps poverty could not be eliminated after all. Perhaps America would have to face the prospect of a permanently stratified society. Perhaps there were problems at home and abroad that exceeded the resources and will of the nation. Instead of always getting better, perhaps things might even get worse.

About the time the United States lost the exuberance of the 1960s, the approaches to the discussion of the future changed. In the literature of the 1970s one is more likely to find optimistic certainties replaced by somber probabilities. For instance, the projection of a social class of permanently poor as a likely possibility is part of the report of the 1977 NCSW task force.[2]

Given that short-range or long-range predictions about the course of society are implicit in all welfare planning, it is important for persons who aim to become human services professionals to examine some of the social themes projected in the literature and attempt to understand how these have affected and continue to affect welfare programs. Note that when we speak of predictions we are not speaking of those of a statistical variety, such as birthrate, rate of unemployment, and the like. Rather, we are speaking of social patterns and social values that some say might be modified in the future.

Contemporary Themes in Futurology

The discussion is limited to secular themes, even though theological writings still have much to say about what human beings can expect for the future. In fact, the earliest systematic efforts to comprehend the future were made by the religious scholars, but because theological themes deal with aspects of existence that are beyond the limits of life on earth, they exceed the scope of this book.

The themes to be discussed are listed roughly in order from the most to the least optimistic:

1. Continuing progress in providing a satisfactory life for all
2. Democratization of social institutions with consequent economic and social equality

3. Rapid technological change resulting in noticeable social and cultural lag
4. Continuing trends toward individualism
5. Piecemeal adaptation
6. Stability—the continuation of things as they are
7. Stagnation—the static society
8. Environmental limits to growth
9. Societal and cultural limits to growth
10. Statism, the eventual dominance of the state over social and individual affairs
11. Doomsday, the eventual annihilation of society

Each of these theories or themes about the future has its adherents.

Continuing Progress in Providing a Satisfactory Life for All

The idea that both humans and their society are continually evolving toward a more perfect state is a major theme in American society. When people believe that they are better off than their progenitors and that their children will be better off than they are, they are enjoined to work within their society. This serves to link them to society rather than to alienate them from it. Until recently there has been little in the literature to discourage people from this belief in the value of "progress," and this theme has contributed much to the objectives of welfare programs. Most of the first humanitarian efforts in the United States assumed that the result would be a more abundant and happy life for all.[3] This theme persisted throughout the nineteenth century and still exists in the present, although the specifics change from time to time.

The economist, Robert Theobald, is representative of the theorists who have discussed the American society in terms of its continuing progress toward perfection.[4] Writing in the 1960s, Theobald stated that, because the United States had solved most of its production problems, the single most important problem for the future would be to teach people how to utilize leisure, because work, as people had known it, would shortly become obsolete. Because machines can produce what is needed, humans have the power to provide well for everyone. Energy is available, because, when America runs out of fossil fuels, nuclear energy will be perfected to take over. Americans have the power to create whatever they desire from the raw materials found in nature, and the computer is available to help people find the right answers to any problems that might still exist. Thus society is progressing nicely but some individuals have a tendency to lag behind. Therefore educational facilities must continue to work toward developing persons able to make productive use of the abundance that is there for the taking.

Because there is a possibility of some people's not taking advantage of the benefits opening up to them through the continued progression of control of the material environment, the goal must now be for the development of a new humanism in which each individual has the power over his or her own life to do with it what he or she wills. Persons who do not strive for this new humanism will remain poor, unhappy, and isolated, in other words, left out of participation in the abundant life that is there for the taking. The apples are red, ripe, and succulent, but each person must figure out how to get them off the tree. Those who decline to exercise initiative must do without the apples.

From this point of view, welfare programs should eliminate free "hand-outs" of portions of the available abundance and instead educate the poor and underprivileged to reach out for themselves and take their share.

Politicians like to project the view that progress toward the good life for all is inevitable, particularly during their administration. With regard to welfare programs, they tend to take Theobald's view in that society has already progressed to the point that the abundance is available to all if only the poor could be stimulated in some way to obtain their share.

Presidents Kennedy and Johnson placed the responsibility for overcoming the inertia of the poor on society. Kennedy's message to Congress in 1962 was the first presidential message devoted entirely to public welfare programs. In it he stated,

> The reasons [for poverty] are often more social than economic, more often subtle than simple. Some are in need because they are untrained for work—some because they cannot work, because they are too young or too old, blind or crippled. Some are in need because they are discriminated against for reasons they cannot help. Responding to their ills with scorn or suspicion is inconsistent with our moral precepts and inconsistent with their nearly universal preference to be independent. But merely responding with a relief check to complicated social or personal problems—such as ill health, faulty education, domestic discord, racial discrimination or inadequate skills—is not likely to provide a lasting solution. Such a check must be supplemented, or in some cases made unnecessary, by positive services and solutions, offering the total resources of the community to meet the total needs of the family to help our less fortunate citizens *to help themselves.* (emphasis added)[5]

The Economic Opportunity Act of 1964, passed under President Johnson, has as its findings and declaration of purpose

> Sec. 2. Although the economic well-being and prosperity of the United States have progressed to a level surpassing any achieved in world history, and although these benefits are widely shared throughout the Nation, poverty continues to be the lot of a substantial number of our people. The United States can achieve its full economic and social potential as a nation only if every individual has the opportunity to contribute to the full extent of his capabilities and to participate in the workings of our society. It is, therefore, the policy of the United States to eliminate the paradox of *opportunity* for education and training, the *opportunity* to work, and the *opportunity* to live in decency and dignity. It is the purpose

of this Act to strengthen, supplement, and coordinate efforts in furtherance of that policy. (emphasis added)[6]

President Nixon was more inclined to place the responsibility on the individual. In his message to Congress in 1969, he emphasized that progress would be guaranteed only by motivating the unemployed to work. In this message a plan was proposed "in which it is in the interest of every employable person to do his fair share of work." This plan included a guaranteed income, "For a family of four with less than $1,000 income, this payment would be $1,600 a year; for a family of four with $2,000 income, this payment would supplement that income by $960 a year." The supplement was kept ludicrously low to motivate people to find employment. The message went on to propose the Manpower Training Act, which would assist persons thus motivated to obtain skills so that they might participate in the abundance that America was capable of providing.[7]

President Carter rode the middle ground between Presidents Kennedy and Nixon. In his proposals for welfare reform, he stated that society must create conditions wherein everyone who was able to work should be given the opportunity, but, if even a minimum wage job was there and the individual did not take it, then he or she should be penalized through reduction of benefits.[8]

While other interpretations of the past and predictions for the future have achieved recognition in recent years, it can be seen that many welfare programs depend heavily on the theme that society has been gradually evolving toward perfection in its ability to provide a satisfactory life for all persons and that the role of welfare is to train, educate, cure or rehabilitate, and, in whatever way possible, provide incentives for those who lag behind to keep up.

Democratization of Social Institutions

The political institutions of America have long held out to people the value of democratization. A supreme expression of this is contained in the Declaration of Independence—"We hold these truths to be self-evident, that all men are created equal. . . ."

Most modern writing on the subject of democratization bases the achievement of this goal on the primacy of science and technology in the society. Science requires that knowledge be specialized and that this, in turn, requires a decentralization of knowledge because it is not possible for a small group of people to control the vast array of knowledge that science produces. When all this knowledge becomes disseminated throughout the population and individuals are able to evaluate their circumstances, they will demand that they be allowed to participate in the decisions that affect them.[9]

Furthermore, since science and technology have created an abundance of material goods, individuals no longer need to allocate the lion's share of their efforts to meeting their basic material needs. They can devote their energies to more "humane" matters. This expansion of opportunity makes it impossible for families to continue their authoritarian structure as was the case in the patriarchial family, for individuals have the freedom to escape from the patriarchial tyranny. This forces the decentralization of decisionmaking in the family and the development of families who stay together because of desire rather than because of coercion.[10]

Reich approaches this topic from a slightly different perspective. He states that, because of the wonders of science and technology and the consequent freedom from material concerns, individuals (especially the young) will evolve to a higher level of consciousness where, as individuals, they will demand equality of definition and services from a society that has heretofore functioned in a tyrannical and high-handed fashion toward its members. These demands will be so overwhelming that they will result in the democratization of the institutions of the society.[11] This change will be so fundamental that it will be revolutionary.

Both these approaches to democratization assume that the wonders of science and technology produce a liberating effect on the elements of the society. Bennis says that the effect will be on the institutions themselves; Reich says that the effect will be on the individuals directly. Both assume that, once the influence is felt, it triggers a continuing response that will not cease until the inevitable goal of complete democratization of all institutions is reached. This approach to the future assumes an inherent democratizing characteristic in science and technology that will produce in the elements of society a demand first for economic equality and, following that, social and political equality.

The implications for welfare programs are clear. If institutions and/or individuals move toward economic equality, the need for welfare services as they are known today will diminish, until finally they will either disappear or assume a minor function to assist those individuals who because of personal circumstances cannot participate fully in the fruits of the general democratization. In the process, welfare programs will become democratic also, facilitating the democratization of the family and supporting the increasing power of individuals to define their own expectations and take the steps necessary to realize them. Human services professionals themselves will be able to modify welfare organizations to serve the clients more effectively, and, as the consciousness of the human services workers expands, they will take more responsibility for the operation of the services. This will enhance the power of the recipients of services to take command of their own lives.

Rapid Technological Change

There are those who say that society has changed rapidly in the last fifty to seventy-five years, that more changes can be expected in the future, and that this will produce certain challenges for those who are trying to adapt.

The proponents of the theme of rapid change usually divide the society into two major parts, the material and the nonmaterial. Some divide the nonmaterial further into two subparts, the cultural and the individual. The major thesis of this projection for the future is that the material or technological aspect of the society changes very rapidly and that the nonmaterial or organizational and individual aspects of the society are forced to run to the point of exhaustion merely to keep within hailing distance. In fact, often material changes far outstrip the nonmaterial, resulting in inconveniences, breakdowns, and friction between technology and society. Ogburn calls this phenomenon "cultural lag."[12]

Toffler, one of the most popular, contemporary proponents of cultural lag, says in his book, *Future Shock*,[13] that accelerating technology has wreaked fundamental changes on our culture and institutions. This results in stress on individuals who find themselves required to adapt to ever-changing conditions often to the point where their adaptive mechanisms are strained beyond their capacities. Because social planning does not take into account social provisions that will enable individuals to "keep pace" with accelerating technological change, a complete breakdown of the society is possible. As in the two previous orientations, projections for increasing cultural lag assume that economic and social inequities are minor problems, because technology has created not merely an abundance but rather an overwhelming abundance.

Once again, for those who hold with this theory, the implications for the future of welfare programs are obvious. Because the major problem lies with the individual's ability to adapt to his or her circumstance, social services, therapy, and counseling must be improved and made more available to assure that the nonmaterial aspects of the society keep up with the advances made in the material sector.

Under conditions of rapid change, welfare programs should shift their emphasis from income transfers to the dissemination of social and occupational skills and to the provision of personal services to prevent the breakdown of adaptive processes. For the poor, this means that they must learn to be more mobile, because poverty is no longer caused so much by the lack of opportunity as by the lack of skill and of knowledge of the parts of the country where the jobs can be found. Social services will continue to need to provide occupational skills and to assist the poor to move to wherever there is opportunity for employment. Opportunity will arise in the region of the country where the current technological change is foremost.

Education, one of the primary services designed to overcome cultural lag, will need to diversify, to individualize its offerings, to move away from standard degrees, and to decentralize its authority so that students can shop around for courses of study that are useful to them at a given point in time even as they would choose food (or lightbulbs or toilet paper) in a supermarket.[14] These strategies will enable individuals to develop adaptive skills throughout their lives, which in turn will permit them to "keep up" with the changes taking place about them.

Continuing Trends toward Individualism

We have noted frequently throughout this book that individualism is a strong value in the American culture. This is especially true from the standpoint of economic theory. Because of the strength of this value, many futurists who project an abundant material life also project greater individual freedom. They reason that, as humans are freed from the necessity to work long hours to provide for basic necessities, they are also freed from the employing organizations' total control over their lives. Since they are freed from the specter of poverty, they can give attention to the realization of their potential as individuals.

Riesman, for instance, in *The Lonely Crowd* looks forward to the evolution of the "autonomous" individual who is capable of conforming to the behavioral norms of the society but is also capable of choosing whether or not to conform.[15] Bennis and Toffler both look forward to the individual who can live with ambiguity. This individual will be able to adapt continuously to the temporariness of personal and social circumstances, yet remain in tune with his or her surroundings, but will also be able to choose or reject participation in those particular situations that do not permit the "realization of self." This projection implies a development for the future of society wherein the sum of the parts equals the whole rather than that of the whole being greater than the sum of the parts.[16]

If the material aspects of society are so well in hand that it is now possible for individualism to be fully developed, as is stated by the writers we have cited, then there is a marked lag between the material and nonmaterial aspects of modern life. Because welfare programs formally emphasize the necessity of work and the integrity of the family, the services are contradictory to the development of individualism.

Certain modifications in welfare services are therefore necessary to lessen the dependence of recipients on work for their own personal fulfillment. To put it another way, the value of individualism should be emphasized in welfare services and the value of work should be deemphasized. Occupational skills should still be taught, but at the same time social skills should be imparted. These will enable recipients to work only enough to earn their livelihood while using their leisure time in pursuits that permit the "realization of self." Welfare services should also lessen their emphasis on the integrity of the family, because dependency on the family group can stifle the growth of individuality. This can be especially true if the family demands considerable resources that are furnished by the labor of only one of its members. Individuality can also be stifled if the family is controlled by one or more of its adult members with the rest being subject to their authority. Therefore, welfare services should be oriented toward the democratization of the family. This also holds true for the other organizations with which the individual interacts. Individuals should be taught to have the skills to conform, but they should also be allowed to choose whether or not they wish to do so.

It is important to keep in mind that this theme for the future is based on the projection of continued material abundance and the concept of society as an integrated social system.

Piecemeal Adaptation

Contrary to the concept that society is composed of integrated parts that are systematically dependent on each other with the technological sector in the lead, there is another concept that presents an entirely different view of society. This view states that the society is composed of interrelated parts but that this interrelationship is such that there is *independence* among the parts. Put another way, society is not a closed, perfect social system with a predictable, constant relationship among the parts of that system wherein, for instance, a change in the economic system would have a predictable, specific effect on the family.

LaPiere states that the parts of the society vary in their degree of dependence on each other. Thus change in one part has an imprecise, unpredictable effect on other parts. Adaptation to change is piecemeal, rather than complete.[17] In some cases, change in one part of society would have a significant effect on another part; in other cases, it might have almost none. Proponents of this theme for the future point out that technology is indeed advanced in the American society, yet work is still held to be the highest form of individual activity. Surpluses in many commodity areas are being produced, yet there is a marked inequality of distribution of wealth and power. An advanced technology might indicate that work should be deemphasized; nonetheless, one of the fundamental changes in the family is that currently it is usual for more than one family member to hold a full-time job.

From this point of view, the unevenness of change is the rule rather than the exception, because when change does occur, it is in certain parts of society but not necessarily in others. It can occur in the nonmaterial sectors and not in the material ones, and vice versa. It is difficult, if not impossible, to predict where and when change will occur and even more uncertain as to what the overall effect will be. Those who predict continued piecemeal adaptation also foresee continued unevenness and dislocation.

The welfare system as it presently functions is a prime example of piecemeal adaptation. With regard to the distribution of resources, most of the income transferred is to those who can demonstrate a history of work rather than a history of unemployment. Furthermore, the advances of technology have made it increasingly difficult for the unskilled to obtain employment. Still, the government continues to institute public works programs that provide jobs requiring no skills and then forces the unskilled to take these jobs even though it is well known that there is little future in the marketplace for the unskilled when the public works jobs are withdrawn. Social services are designed to help families improve their functioning, while other segments of the welfare system provide economic incentives for family breakup.

Those who hold this view see little possibility for significant change in the welfare system in the near future.

Stability

The equilibrium or functional explanation of society was discussed in Chapter 2, so it is not necessary to restate the major elements of a stable society here. Keep in mind that the equilibrium theory does not deny the possibility of change; rather it points out that, while some parts of society may change, others do not and any adaptation that takes place serves only to restore the equilibrium. For instance, Parker notes that, even though there has been marked technological advancement in American society, the percentage of distribution of wealth among the classes has remained about the same since the American Revolution. This is a remarkable example of selective social stability.[18]

Even though stability is usually welcomed, reformers and other advocates of change view continuing stability as a negative circumstance. LaPiere describes a model of stability that he calls "static incongruence," which produces frustration, personal breakdown, graft and exploitation simply because there is a marked lack of fit between what individuals expect from the society and what is available for them from the society.[19] On the other hand, LaPiere describes a model of stability in which a positive state of affairs exists, which he calls "static congruence." By this he means a set of circumstances in which the expectations of individuals mesh quite well with what they are able to obtain from the society in which they live.[20]

Welfare programs are very stable in their objectives and processes, even though some of the various forms of programs and organizational characteristics may be modified. We have also stated that this condition will probably obtain for the foreseeable future. This stability can be interpreted either as "static congruence" or "static incongruence," depending upon which perspective one uses. Recipients, some advocates, and critics would tend to see welfare services in a state of static incongruence. Recipients might hope that welfare services would make greater benefits available to them and that the many restrictions that are placed upon benefits might be removed, but, because they realize that they have little power to influence the character of the services, they resign themselves for the most part to the discrepancy between what they desire and what they receive. Advocates might observe welfare services ensuring that most recipients remain in about the same socioeconomic circumstances as they started out and be disappointed with the discrepancy between what exists and what they perceive to be the promise and fulfillment of welfare services. Critics, on the other hand, might be unhappy that welfare services exist at all to "coddle" the poor who they believe would not be poor but for the existence of welfare services, services that they have tried without success to eliminate. Thus, for different reasons, certain special-interest groups decry the stability that is enjoyed by welfare programs and see the stability as a negative social condition.

Supporters and providers, however, generally see the stability of welfare programs as a positive social condition and resist changing it. Supporters perceive that welfare programs reinforce the general social stability by offering enough services to the poor and underprivileged so that they will not attack the general social order that must necessarily be maintained if the dominant groups are to continue to prosper. Providers also desire stability of welfare programs, because this enhances their job security and all the benefits that accompany this predictability. These special interests perceive welfare programs according to LaPiere's model of static congruence, both instrumentally and as a goal. They perceive welfare programs as instrumentally stabilizing in that they can be used to keep the poor and underprivileged from destabilizing the society; they see welfare programs remaining as they are as a goal, because they are a necessary and integral component to the stability of the overall social order.

Stagnation

The general thesis of this view of the future is a well-known one, a determined evolution toward an eventual permanent state of balance. This formed the basis of Marx's thought; it is the foundation of Plato's political philosophy; it is the design of movement of society as set forth in the book of Revelation of the *Bible*. What sets the projection of stagnation apart from others is that it predicts an eventual situation not unlike a lake without an outlet into which a swift-running river flows. The river rushes headlong to a pool of water in which there is no direction, only an eddying about. This point of view is best summarized by Seidenburg in his book, *Post-Historic Man*. Seidenburg predicts that the energy spawned by the same forces that culminated in the industrial society and the growth of the value of the individual will run down, and stagnation or entropy will be the state of society.[21] The energy released by the tension between the individual and society will dissipate as individuals merge into the collective social mass. Social institutions, from being separate and distinct and in contention with one another as they are now, will become indistinct and diffuse, with its being difficult to tell one from another. The ideology of the machine that is organization will dominate everything, and, as organization becomes supreme, every activity will come under organized control. The result will be a state of balance, diffusion, eclipse of individualism, ultimate development of organization, and stagnation; not necessarily from the exhaustion of material energy, but from the exhaustion of nonmaterial, social, and psychological energy.[22]

The human services professionals who staff welfare programs could find something of value in what Seidenburg has to say, even though they might disagree with his projection for the future as a universal end result. Much attention is given today to making welfare services more efficient, that is, to organize them more effectively, to assure the highest return for the money invested, and to institute cost-effective procedures that in some instances reduce welfare activities to assembly-line procedures. System analysts have turned their attention to welfare services and tend to see welfare recipients as raw materials that must be processed by the organization to produce the desired end product. In some instances the character of the end product is not as important as the organization of the process to ensure production. As Seidenburg says, the application of the principle of the machine, which in a sense is the epitome of organization, and the fullest development of objectivity, tends to eliminate the irregular, the caprice, the uncategorized, the unique, and convert everything it deals with to the commonplace of sameness.[23] Human services professionals can take seriously the admonitions of such writers as Seidenburg who project ultimate stagnation through the utilization of the principle of the machine to evaluate their own work; to ascertain if, even while they uphold the principle of the value of the individual, through their organizational affiliation they may eliminate humanism through the refinement of organizational efficiency.

Environmental Limits to Growth

The decade of the 1970s marked the appearance of publications that questioned the ability of the world to sustain the growth made possible by advanced technology. Questions were raised as to whether resource exhaustion, accelerating pollution, and the unbridled birthrate would, if unchecked, lead to the collapse of civilization as it is known today. Some projections are quite pessimistic, stating flatly that technology, if applied as it is currently, would lead to the collapse.[24] Other projections are guardedly optimistic, stating that the industrialized world is moving toward a global attack on the problem of environmental limits and that the probabilities are good that the technological society will persist for some time as it now is, with the emergence of man-made limits on the trends toward overdevelopment.[25] The Ford Foundation report on America's energy future is an example of this guardedly optimistic line.[26]

Whatever line is taken, this projection is a sobering one because it runs contrary to the optimism of the unlimited potential of wealth for the United States. That there should be any limits to material resources that make continued economic growth possible is almost subversive in its connotation. Nonetheless, the message for the future from this projection is clear; failure to curb the present use of technology will result in global calamity in the foreseeable future.

This prospect poses a dilemma for welfare programs. Welfare programs are based on the assumption that a continuing surplus will be produced by American economic institutions and that the major task of human services workers is to ensure that sufficient of that surplus goes to the poor and underprivileged so that they do not feel completely alienated from the economic institution. But, if the surplus diminishes or even disappears, from where will the funds come to sustain the poor? The only place will be from the resources controlled by the middle and upper classes, and history shows that these classes are notoriously resistant to a redistribution of resources.

Therefore, human services workers are faced with at least two fairly negative alternatives: (1) to find the power to take resources from the middle and upper classes and give to the poor and underprivileged through progressive taxation or other means such as an increasing socialization of economic institutions or (2) to rely more heavily on personal services to get the poor and underprivileged to accept a deteriorating economic condition, especially when compared with the other economic categories of the society.

It is entirely possible that the human society will be able to place limits on the use of technology as is envisioned by the Ford Foundation report and by Mesarovic. If that can be done, a slower but sustained rate of growth can be achieved in the foreseeable future. A smaller surplus can then be generated for this period resulting in less of more for everyone, but assuring fairly well that welfare programs as presently constituted will continue even if at a lower level of activity that might be more consonant with the economic activity of the rest of society.

Societal and Cultural Limits to Growth

Most of the foregoing projections see technology as a thing unto itself, the independent variable that causes the other social elements to react. In the projection of societal and cultural growth limits, technology is seen as growing out of the society and therefore as a component of the society. Seeing technology in this fashion does not necessarily lead to a more optimistic view of the future, because other elements may also provide limits for the future.

Projections of this sort have considerable currency in contemporary thinking and can take many forms. Cooper, for instance, states that the family as currently constituted places limits to the adequate functioning of individuals in society.[27] Galbraith says that the limits are provided from the technostructure and from education.[28] Friedman states that the control of government imposes a stifling influence on economic and social affairs.[29] Some spokespersons for religion find the entire society to be venal and damaging to all persons, on the grounds that no one can lead a pure life in an evil world. Thus the diagnosis of social and cultural limits runs the gamut from putting the blame on a single element of society that presumably could be corrected to the condemnation of the entire society and a hope for its replacement either in this world or in the next.

One of the most comprehensive analyses of social and cultural limits for future growth was developed by Fred Hirsch in *Social Limits to Growth*.[30] Hirsch states that the major problem faced by capitalistic industrialism is in having made abundance available to the masses. Up to now individualism has served society well, but currently there is disparity between the individualistic ethos and social return. Hirsch illustrates this by the discussion of "material" and "positional" goods. Material goods are those that are enjoyed for their intrinsic value. Their worth to the owner is not dependent on whether others also own them. An example of a material good might be a television set that is used only to receive programs that the individual enjoys.

A positional good, on the other hand, provides extrinsic satisfaction, because its ownership conveys a sense of superior status to the owner. An example of a positional good might be a house in the suburbs that is bought so that the family can escape the crowding of city residential neighborhoods and enjoy the wide-open vistas of the countryside.

Problems arise, however, when many families share the same goal; if they all move to the country, they merely transfer the crowding to a different locale. The rural vista does not enfold them as it did before, and they end up with only a view of those they had sought to escape. The value of positional goods, Hirsch says, depends on the fact that they are available only to the minority. The satisfaction of their possession is lost when they are attained by all. Hirsch says that the value attached to positional goods and the individual effort expended to attain positional goods is reaching a state of diminishing returns for the effort expended. If this value is not modified, it will constitute a significant limit to the viability of society.

Hirsch describes another important limit inherent in American society, namely, the contradictions that exist among three major social values: the individualistic ethos,[31] political equality,[32] and economic inequality.[33] Uncontrolled individualism leads to negative social returns so that the state must intervene to limit individualism for the common good. Political equality infers economic equality, because it leads to drives toward equal opportunity, equal access, and equal return for efforts expended. This runs counter to the importance attached to the attainment of positional goods, which is dependent upon economic inequality.[34] This results in internal pressures that "undermine the system's drive and equipoise. That is the current crisis of the system."[35]

Hirsch's analysis has important implications for welfare programs. One of the most important is the value that our society places on positional goods; that is, if Hirsch is correct, poverty can never be eliminated. Those at the lower end of the economic scale will always be short of positional goods and therefore feel poor. For society to maintain its present order, welfare costs will continue to increase, both to maintain a semblance of political equality and to prevent the ultimate disillusionment of those with the least amount of positional goods. Welfare costs will also increase because the providers also struggle for their share of positional goods and thereby demand higher wages, proprietary business relationships, and increasing professional status. This then, according to Hirsch's analysis, contributes to moral erosion,[36] and places limits on the effectiveness of welfare programs both for individual and societal benefit.

Statism

Even as some prognosticators chart the inexorable evolution of society toward an abundant life for all, others predict that advanced technology can lead us nowhere but to increasing central state control, and this will be at the expense of individual freedom, as these two conditions are seen as incompatible with each other.[37] George Orwell describes this state of affairs in his political novel, *1984.*[38] Heilbroner, in *Business Civilization in Decline*, states that economic progress is not synonomous with social stability and that the capitalistic system has built into it certain proclivities to disorder that require increasing intervention by the state if the social order is to be maintained.[39] These are (1) generalized disorder such as inflation and depression, (2) localized disorder such as insolvency of cities and breakdown in local transportation facilities, and (3) a constricting environment that will exhaust resources before technology can catch up and provide substitutes. The emphasis upon technology to solve the problems created by technology (homeopathy) will give rise to an ever stronger technical elite that will struggle for power with the entrenched economic elite. This will reinforce the trend toward statism necessitated by the tendencies toward disorder already listed. Therefore in about a century the state will become so powerful and pervasive that individualism as it is known today will no longer exist and society will enforce collective values rather than the individualistic ones that are presently important. This is necessary, even though deplored, Heilbroner says, because the state will be the only institution that can guarantee survival.[40]

Welfare programs already ensure the continuance of the social order. If the trend predicted by the prophets of statism is accurate, then one can anticipate the expansion of welfare services to a larger and larger segment of the population so that the impact of the tendencies toward disorder can be diverted. Furthermore, as welfare programs expand, human services workers as members of the technical elite will be caught up in the struggle with the economic elite for control of the state apparatus that operates welfare programs. The forces in welfare that advocate public responsibility toward the poor and underprivileged will contribute to and reinforce the trend toward the ascendancy of the state over the business civilization. The very institutionalization of welfare programs is an admission that sole reliance on the individualistic ethos produces a negative social return that must be counteracted by public support of individuals who lose through uncontrolled economic competition. If, as the prophets of statism say, the continuance of industrialism as it now exists leads to increasing disorder and a constricting environment, then the value of collective responsibility as represented by public welfare programs will be reinforced and lead to the gradual dismemberment of the "business civilization."

Doomsday

We have described a number of projections that raise the red flag on uncontrolled technological development, but stop short of predicting collapse because of the belief in the ability of human societies to redirect a runaway technology to the accomplishment of constructive goals. However, some scholars predict that the uncontrollability of technological expansion will destroy present civilization. In other words, the very knowledge and techniques that have been hailed as the means of human progress will turn about and become the means of destruction of the way of life based upon it.

Roberto Vacca states this thesis forcefully in his book, *The Coming Dark Age*.[41] He combines in general the thesis of the negative enviromental consequences of technology with that of inherent system disorders as expressed in the section under statism to argue that a runaway technology will produce societal and individual disorder of such magnitude that a "knockout" becomes inevitable. Vacca is unremittingly pessimistic about the trends of the present age. On the other hand, he believes that humans will not destroy themselves entirely and that, after a protracted period not unlike the European dark ages, human progress will commence once again.

The Challenge of the Future

It is almost impossible to comprehend an eventuality like Doomesday, nor is it necessary to do so. Still, it is instructive for human services workers to recognize that human betterment is not *automatically* the outcome of their efforts in welfare organizations. A blind acceptance of "things as they are" may conceivably suffice in the short run, but it is incumbent upon every person who admits to desiring to "serve people" to try to project the long-run effect of his or her efforts.

We have pointed out a number of characteristics of welfare programs that could have negative consequences in the long run for the recipients of welfare services and conceivably for society as a whole. This need not be inevitable. Ellul, who otherwise is quite pessimistic about the long-term effects of the technological society says

> The very fact that man can see, measure, and analyze the determinisms that press on him means that he can face them and by so doing, act as a free man*. . . . By grasping the real nature of the technological phenomenon, and the extent to which it is robbing him of freedom, he confronts the blind mechanism as a conscious being.[42]

We wish to emphasize in this final statement that there is no inherent directionality in the societal structures that humans create for themselves. These directionalitites are infused into the structures by the individuals who work within them. The major problem is that the human tendency is to make the *observed* directionalities the *real* or *absolute* ones, not realizing that there are many possible outcomes of the systematic efforts of human beings. Our hope for human services professionals and the welfare programs that they operate is similar to that expressed by Jacques Ellul. The very fact that human beings can see, measure, and analyze the determinisms that press on them means that they can face them and, by so doing, act as a free people.

---

* Ellul wrote this passage in 1964 when the masculine gender was regularly used to refer to members of both sexes. Although we cannot change the words of another author, we intend that the meaning of this quotation apply equally to all persons concerned with future trends in welfare services.

References

1. Reich, C. *The Greening of America.* New York: Random House, 1970.
2. National Conference on Social Welfare. *The Future for Social Services in the United States. Final Report of the Task Force, 1977.* pp. 71–73.
3. Axinn, J., and Levin, L. *Social Welfare, A History of the American Response to Need.* New York: Dodd, 1975, pp. 33–36.
4. Theobald, R. *An Alternative Future for America II.* Chicago: Swallow Press, 1970, ch. 5.
5. Axinn, J., and Levin, L. Op. cit., pp. 255–256.
6. Ibid, p. 263.
7. Ibid., pp. 292–293.
8. Social Legislation Information Service. *Washington Social Legislation Bulletin* 25 (September 12, 1977): pp. 66–68.
9. Bennis, W., and Slater, P. *The Temporary Society.* New York: Harper Colophon, 1969, ch. 1.
10. Ibid, ch. 2.
11. Reich, C. Op. cit., pp. 385–395.
12. Ogburn, W. F. *Social Change.* Part IV. New York: Dell, 1966, ch. 1.
13. Toffler, A. *Future Shock.* New York: Bantam Books, 1971, pp. 80–81.
14. Ibid., pp. 272–275.
15. Riesman, D. *The Lonely Crowd.* New Haven, Conn.: Yale U. Press, 1966, p. 242.
16. Bennis, W., and Slater, P. Op. cit., ch. 6.
17. LaPiere, R. *Social Change,* New York: McGraw-Hill, 1965, pp. 69, 88–89.
18. Parker, R. *The Myth of the Middle Class.* New York: Liveright, 1972, p. 54.
19. LaPiere, R. Op. cit., pp. 93–96.
20. Ibid., pp. 89–93.
21. Seidenburg, R. *Post-Historic Man: An Inquiry.* New York: Viking Press, 1974, pp. 112–113, 226–238.
22. Crozier, M. *The Stalled Society.* New York: Viking Press, 1973, ch. 5.
23. Seidenburg, R. Op. cit., pp. 84–90.
24. Meadows, D., et al. *The Limits to Growth.* New York: Universe, 1972, p. 142.
25. Mesarovic, M. and Pestel, E. *Mankind at the Turning Point.* New York: Dutton, 1974, p. 141; Ch. 11.
26. Freeman, S. D., et al. *A Time to Choose.* Cambridge, Mass.: Ballinger, 1974, ch. 1, 13.
27. Cooper, D. *The Death of the Family.* New York: Pantheon, 1970.
28. Galbraith, J. K. *The New Industrial State.* New York: New American Library, 1967.
29. Friedman, M. *Capitalism and Freedom.* Chicago: University of Chicago, 1962.
30. Hirsch, F. *Social Limits to Growth.* Cambridge, Mass.: Harvard U. Press, 1976.
31. Ibid., pp. 117–118
32. Ibid, pp. 161–163
33. Ibid., pp. 173–176.
34. Ibid., p. 176.

35. Ibid., p. 177.
36. Ibid., pp. 141–143.
37. Ellul, J. *The Technological Society*. New York: Vintage, 1964, p. 318.
38. Orwell, G. *1984*. New York: Harcourt, 1949.
39. Heilbroner, R. *Business Civilization in Decline*. New York: Norton, 1976.
40. Ibid., p. 117.
41. Vacca, R. *The Coming Dark Age*. New York: Doubleday, 1974, pp. 3, 4 and ch. 6.
42. Ellul, J. Op. cit., p. xxxiii.

Glossary

Some of the terms found in the glossary are discussed in the text. They are included here to provide easy reference for definition or for explanation of an important item. Other items not found in the text have been included because they are terms that social workers and other human services professionals will encounter in their work.

Accountability   Demonstrating that social welfare programs are effective in meeting needs. This usually requires that program objectives be clearly specified.

Accountable Period   The time period over which countable income is measured to determine eligibility and benefit payments.

Adequacy   The effectiveness of a program in meeting the needs of the target population; the people whom the program intends to serve.

Administration   The management of resources and tasks in organizations.

Advocate   Helping clients obtain services, including establishment of new ones.

AFDC   (Aid to Families with Dependent Children) Federal program to aid families in which the mother cannot earn enough to support the family and in which in most cases the father is absent.

AFDC-UF   (Aid to Families with Dependent Children and Unemployed Father) Extends AFDC aid when fathers are present but jobless. Optional. Twenty-five states have this program.

Almshouse Formerly a facility to house those considered needy, furnishing the basic living requirements.

Basic Benefit Level Benefit received when the recipient has no income or, in some programs, no countable income. This is also the maximum benefit and is sometimes called the guarantee.

Benefit Reduction Rate The amount by which benefits are reduced when a recipient's income is increased by one dollar. For example, a 30 per cent benefit reduction rate means that when a recipient's countable income increases by one dollar, benefits are reduced by 30 cents. Thus, the recipients retain 70 cents out of an additional dollar of countable income.

Bound Out Indentured or apprenticed to work for someone for a period of years. This method of providing for needy persons is no longer in use.

Breakeven Level The level of countable income at which the welfare recipient ceases to receive any benefits from the program.

Bureaucracy A formal organization characterized by clearly defined goals, specified rules, division of authority, specification of labor, and recruitment and training procedures, with a recognizable social function to perform.

Cash Out Replacing an in-kind or voucher program with a roughly equivalent amount of cash benefits.

Case work Interventive method that seeks to improve social functioning by concentrating on one person, examining the individual's behavior within that person's social context.

Categorical Programs Transfer programs in which eligibility is defined not only by income but by additional factors, such as demographic characteristics (age, number of parents present, disability).

Children's Allowances Payment of a cash amount to parents of minor children.

Civil Rights Movement The ongoing attempt to achieve equal rights for all minority groups. The term sometimes refers to the attempts to achieve equality for black people in the 1960s.

Client The person being helped.

Community A spatially defined social unit within which there are identifiable patterns of social interdependence.

Community Organization Interventive method that seeks to improve social functioning by using organizations in the local community to solve problems.

Community Planner One who assists community groups to work effectively toward meeting the community's needs.

Confidentiality Ensuring that information obtained from and relating to clients is only used with the clients or with their permission.

Consultant One professional working with other professionals to assist them in becoming more effective in their work.

Countable Income The income measure used to determine program eligibility and benefit level. It is "net income" in that it is income remaining after disregarding certain amounts, excluding certain types of income and deducting allowable expenses.

Deduction In arriving at countable income, certain expenses may be deducted from gross income. Examples of deductions include work expenses, medical expenses and high housing costs.

Diagnosis Interpreting information about a client to understand the client's situation and the problems in it.

Direct Relief Monetary aid as opposed to work relief.

Dole Public assistance.

Eligibility Requirements The criteria used to decide who is eligible to receive services. Such factors as age, income, employment, and number of children may be used to determine eligibility.

Equity The degree to which a program is actually available to the people for whom it is designed to serve.

Evaluation Assessment of needs and resources; development of alternative means to meet needs; reaching a decision among the alternatives.

Extended Family A family comprised of three or more generations.

FAP (Family Assistance Plan). Originally proposed by the Nixon administration to establish a minimum income for families of $2,400 per year for a family of four, providing that employable parents, including mothers with young children, work.

Filing Unit The person or group of persons that makes application to receive benefits.

Food Stamps Vouchers for the purchase of food that are sold to eligible persons at less than their redeemable value.

General Relief Public assistance given by the states or localities usually to people who do not fit federal requirements for aid, generally single people, childless couples, the working poor. The federal government does not subsidize this program.

Group Work An interventive method that seeks to improve social functioning by using the small group as the focal point of service.

Guaranteed Income An amount paid by the government to individuals and families. If the amount earned is below the guaranteed amount, the government makes up the difference.

Helping Interaction between a person seeking assistance and a person giving assistance based on trust, respect, sharing; oriented toward providing assistance.

Horizontal Equity People in similar circumstances receiving similar treatment.

Income Assistance Usually known as *welfare*. Transfers based on the recipient's income. Also referred to as *means-tested* or *income-tested* programs.

Income Disregard Income that is not included in calculating countable income. In the Supplemental Security Income program, for example, the first $20 per month of unearned income and the first $65 of earned income are disregarded in determining countable income.

Indoor Relief Aid given to people through requiring that they live in almshouses or on poor farms.

Indenture Former practice of removing young persons from their homes if the parents sought assistance and placing the young persons in homes of more well-to-do where they received their keep in return for their labor.

Industrial Revolution Changes in production in a society through the substitution of mechanical for human or animal power. The changes began in the seventeenth century and are still going on.

Intact Family A family with both parents present in the home.

In-Kind Benefits Transfer benefits that come directly in the form of a good or service. Includes voucher payments whose use is restricted to the purchase of specific goods or services.

Laissez-Faire Capitalism The conviction that minimal governmental regulation of the economic system promotes healthy competition and maximum efficiency. Formalized by Adam Smith in 1776.

Less Eligibility The practice of giving no more welfare money to recipients than that earned by the lowest paid worker. This is designed to prevent the able bodied from accepting relief over jobs.

Low-Income Population Individuals and families making the least amount of money, stated in percentage of the population. Sometimes stated as the poverty population.

Means Test Investigation of a welfare applicant's financial resources to determine his or her eligibility for assistance. May involve extensive probing into the applicant's personal life, interviews with friends, etc.

Medicaid Federal program of reimbursement of hospitals for the care of welfare recipients and those declared medically indigent.

Negative Income Tax A form of guaranteed income. People without income or with income below the taxable level would file a tax return and receive money from the government.

Need Standard In AFDC, the amount of money recognized by a state as the level required monthly to meet basic needs for a family of a specified size.

Norms Rules for behavior.

NWRO (National Welfare Rights Organization). A coalition of interest groups and welfare recipients organized to protect the rights of recipients and increase welfare benefits.

Nuclear Family A family composed of two generations—parents and their children.

Outdoor Relief Aid given to people in their own homes.

Poverty Income thresholds developed by the Social Security Administration and updated annually below which persons are considered poor. The poverty threshold for a nonfarm family of four was $5,038 in 1974 and $5,820 in 1976.

Primary Group A small group characterized by intensive, face-to-face interaction and personal relationships.

Problem Solving Gathering information, defining problems, assessing resources, formulating a plan of action, and evaluating the process after the plan is placed into action.

Profession Occupational group characterized by use of specialized knowledge and skills in service to the public; close colleagial relationships to monitor competence in training and performance.

Public Service Employment Jobs funded by the government that are created more to provide jobs than to do needed work.

Punishment Attempts to decrease the likelihood of a certain behavior by removing a positive reinforcement and/or presenting a negative stimulus.

Referral Sending a client to another social welfare resource when the agency or person contacted initially is not able to provide the assistance needed.

Rehabilitation Services to solve an already existing problem and to prevent its recurring in the future.

Residence Requirement Welfare benefits contingent on residence in a specified locale for a given period of time.

Residual Welfare Services Services available only when need can be demonstrated. Eligibility is determined by a variety of means tests.

Role Norms associated with a social position.

Rural Community Characterized by small population, low density, homogeneousness, and relative isolation from other communities.

Secondary Group A group in which interaction is focused on the performance of specified tasks.

Settlement House A neighborhood facility that helps residents meet their social, recreational, educational, and collective action needs.

Social Darwinism The application of Darwin's theory of the "survival of the fittest" to economic affairs.

Social Insurance Transfers based in part on minimum employment, payment by employee and/or payroll taxes, and the occurrence of a risk-covered event, such as unemployment compensation and social security.

Social History Background information about a client that provides a basis for analysis and problem solution.

Social Institution A cluster of positions, roles, and norms organized to meet a social goal.

Social Service A noneconomic welfare provision such as therapy or training supported either by public or private funds or by a combination thereof.

Social Stratification Social differentiation wherein classifications of people are ranked vertically.

Social System An organized interrelated group of activities that are internally cohesive but are affecting each other in their operation.

Social Work A profession that seeks to help people singly and in groups to meet their financial and social needs.

Supplemental Assistance State or local aid given to families whose workers' wages are too low to support them.

Survivors' Benefits A social security benefit that a worker's widow or minor children can receive when the worker dies. The creation of this benefit removed many widows from the AFDC rolls.

Target Efficiency The extent to which benefits go to those who "need" them. Need is generally defined in terms of income. For instance, the proportion of benefits of a particular program that goes to families with income below the poverty line is a measure of target efficiency.

Title XX Amendments to the Social Security Act authorizing the provision of certain social services by public welfare agencies.

Transfers Benefits received from the government that are not in payment for goods or services and that are financed out of taxes.

Unworthy Poor The supposedly lazy, profligate, or sinful persons who do not work and therefore are undeserving of welfare assistance.

Urban Community Characterized by large population, high density, heterogeneity, and extensive ties with other communities.

Vertical Equity Those in greater need should receive larger benefits. Those who earn more should have larger disposable incomes.

Voucher A form of noncash benefits. Instead of receiving the goods or service directly, a voucher is issued that limits purchasing power to a particular category of goods or service, such as food stamps.

Warning Out Former practice of ordering new arrivals out of town who officials thought might be poor and require public assistance.

Welfare Transfers in which the benefits are based on the recipient's income. Welfare programs are sometimes referred to as "means-tested" or "income-tested" programs.

WIN (Work Incentive Program) Established by Congress in 1967, it required states to register welfare recipients for jobs and training.

Work Ethic The value that work improves one's character and that people should work for what they receive.

Workhouse A facility formerly used to house those considered shiftless, in which basic survival requirements were furnished in return for forced work.

WPA (Work Progress Administration) The major work relief program of the Depression years. At its peak, it employed a fourth of the unemployed in the nation.

Work Relief Government-financed jobs for the unemployed who need assistance. The jobs may not pay standard wages. Some states use work relief to force recipients to work off what they have received from welfare.

Work Requirement A rule by which eligibility for welfare benefits depends on job search, training, rehabilitation, or other measures intended to return the individual to employement.

Worthy Poor The people who work hard but still cannot make ends meet. Also sometimes called the deserving poor. The terms "worthy" and "unworthy" poor are less in use presently than they were at the turn of the century. The concepts, however, are still frequently expressed.

Index

Davis, Kingsley, 15
Day care services, definition of, 197
Day services program, definition of, 197
De Lone, R., 200, 229
Defense Department, 121*t.*, 127
Delinquency, role of social worker in, 255
Democratization, of social institutions, 273–74
Department of Agriculture, 119
Department of Health and Human Services (DHHS), 119
Dependency and indemnity compensation (DIC), 135
Deutsch, F., 32
Development, stages of human, 32
Diagnosis, definition of, 198
Disabilities. *See also* Handicaps developmental, services to deal with, 159
Discrimination, in applying theory of programmed individual, 31
role of social workers in combatting, 255–56
Dix, Dorothea, 67, 68
Domhoff, G., 54
Donations to needy, 52
Douglass, J., 37, 81, 109
Drugs, role of social workers in dealing with, 256
Durant, W., 98
Durkheim, Emile, 12, 15
Dyer, W., 28

Economic maintenance programs, 109–48
contemporary, 118–30
classification of, 120–22
eligibility for, 123–30
development of, 114–116
documents on services for, 132–48
by income transfers, 116–118
proposals for modification of, 130–31
Economic Opportunity Act of 1964, 17, 209, 210, 272–73
Economic organization, changes in, 45–47
Economic and social differences, programs to mitigate, 201–15

by modification of external group relationships, 203
by modification of internal group characteristics, 202–203
by geographic dispersal, 204
strategy for provision of services in, 211–15
Educational services, definition of, 198
Eligibility criteria, for income transfers, 123, 124*t.*, 125*t.*, 126
Elkind, D., 32
Ellul, J., 284
Emotional problems, role of social worker in dealing with, 256
Employees, in private welfare agency, 230–31
Encyclopedia of Social Work, 264–65
English Poor Laws, 58–60, 73
Erikson, E., 30, 32, 33
Ethic. *See also* Values
altruistic, 53, 97–99
work, 53
Etzioni, A., 44–45, 248
Evaluation, definition of, 198
Evolutionary individual, 32–33
Evolutionary theory, 11–14

Fabian Society, 13–14
Family(ies), antifamily impact of welfare on, 245–47
community setting of, 221–22
definition of, 178
financial management by, role of social worker in, 257
foster, role of social worker in, 264
functional theory on, 17
structure in, 220–21
substitute, role of social worker in, 264
Family planning, definition of, 198
role of social worker in, 257
services in, 160
Family service agency, goals of, 232–34
rules of, 236-38
worker stratification in, 229-31
Fanshel, D., 229
Farming. *See* Agriculture
Feagin, J., 102
Feder, B., 38

Parker, R., 102, 112, 278
Pavlov, I., 31
Peale, N., 28
Peer groups, 81, 85–86
Peirce, F., 245
Personal care services, definition of, 199
Personal characteristics, services to deal
    with, 159-61
Personal improvement, 150-99
    case study involving services for, 163-
        66
    categories of individuals receiving
        services for, 156-61
    documents on programs for, 167-99
    origin and growth of services for, 152-
        54
    planning of, by state, 172-74
    present services for, 154-56, 155*t*.
    programs for, 150-99
    reporting, evaluation, and
        administrative requirements in,
        169-72
    techniques in provision of services for,
        161-63
Personnel. *See also* Human services,
        professional: Social worker
    in public and private welfare agencies,
        6-7, 227-31
    recruitment of, 239-42
Pestel, E., 280
Piaget, Jean, 32
Pierce, Franklin, 67-68
Pincus, A., 34
Piven, F., 21, 48, 116
Placement and supervision, definition of,
    199
Pluralism, normative, 37-39
Poor. *See also* Poverty
    geographical dispersal of, 204
    "worthy" and "unworthy," 70, 153
Poor farms, 63, 66, 115
Poor Laws, English, 58-60, 73
Poverty. *See also* Poor
    attitudes toward, 58, 60, 62, 68-75,
        103, 160
    autonomy theory related to, 28-29
    causes of, 111-14
        opportunity theory, 113-14
        stability theory, 112
        subcultural theory, 112-13

definitions of, 109-11
    relativism in, 51-52
    functional theory on, 16
    programs to mitigate, 201-15
Poverty line, grants for families below,
    29
    statistics on, 51
Power, centralization of, 47-49, 70
    of special-interest groups, 104
Pregnancy. *See* Family planning;
        Illegitimacy
Presthus, R., 227
Prisons, early, in United States, 66-67
Private vendors, 160-61
Private welfare agencies. *See* Charities;
        Welfare agencies
Problematic situations, learning to
        anticipate, 95-97
Problems, social, differentiated from
        problematic situations, 94-95
Progress, necessary sequence of, 14
    in society, theory of, 271
Proprietary agency, 223*n*.
Prostitution, compromise law rleative to,
    90
Protective payment services, definition
        of, 199
Psychiatric problems, role of social
        worker in, 262
Psychological handicaps, services to deal
        with, 159-61
Public assistance, Carter on reform of,
        145-47
    early attitudes toward, 68
    personal services eligibility and, 154
Public review process, 183-87
Public welfare agencies. *See* Charities;
        Welfare organizations
Public Welfare Directory, 265
Public Works Administration, 116
Purchase-of-service arrangements, 156,
    160

Quakers, as humanitarians, 66

Railroad Retirement, Disability and
        Survivors Insurance, document
        on, 137
Railroad retirement board, 121*t*.

Vatter, H., 48
Vendors, private, 160-61
Veterans, economic assistance to, 121*t*.,
   122
Veterans compensation programs,
   document on, 135–36
Vocational rehabilitation program, 159

Wald, Lillian, 70
Warner, L., 37
Watson, John, 31
Webb, Beatrice, 14, 59
Webb, Sidney, 14, 59
Weber, M., 128
Welfare, definitions of, 4-5
Welfare organizations, 222-49
   community and, 247-49
   face-to-face groups and, 83-86
   formal and informal, 222-23
   indoctrination of new members of,
      243
   informal structure in, 244-47
   as institution, 222-47
   internal characteristics of, 222-23
   as intraorganizational, 222-23
   private, 223-27
      stratification of workers in,
         document on, 229-31
   public, 223, 226-28
      objectives of, 234
      rank and office in, 228-29
   recruitment by, 239-42
   role division in 227-31
   rules in, 235-38
      enforcement of, 243
   stability of, 248-49

Welfare programs. *See also* Economic
   maintenance, as antifamily, 245-47
Carter on modification of, 29, 142-48
definition of, 6
emergence of formal, 43-55
history of, 57-76
limits to growth of, 280-82
stability and stagnation in, 278-80
staffing of, 6-7. *See also* Personnel
theories of society that determine, 8-23
trends in recent, 269-84
Whiting, B., 38
Wilensky, Harold, 12-13
Will, R., 48, 55
Wilson, G., 98
*Wisconsin Welfare Reform Study Report
   and Recommendations,* 132
Wolpe, J., 32
Work ethic, 53, 245-46
Work groups, in local community, 80, 84
Work Incentive Program (WIN), 115, 128
Work relief, in cyclic theory, 21-22. *See
   also* Relief
Work setting, organization of, 219-50
   structure in society and, 220-22
   welfare as institution and, 222-47
   welfare organizations and community,
      247-49
Work test, for income transfers, 123,
   124*t*., 126-27
   for social security benefits, 126
Workhouses, 62
Workmen's Compensation, document
   on, 134

Yinger, M., 5, 98, 157*n.*